T0233245

Lecture Notes in Computer Science 8941

Commenced Publication in 1973
Founding and Former Series Editors:
Gerhard Goos, Juris Hartmanis, and Jan van Leeuwen

More information about this series at http://www.springer.com/series/7408

Christiano Braga · Narciso Martí-Oliet (Eds.)

Formal Methods: Foundations and Applications

17th Brazilian Symposium, SBMF 2014
Maceió, AL, Brazil,
September 29 – October 1, 2014
Proceedings

 Springer

Editors
Christiano Braga
Universidade Federal Fluminense
Niterói
Brazil

Narciso Martí-Oliet
Universidad Complutense de Madrid
Madrid
Spain

ISSN 0302-9743
Lecture Notes in Computer Science
ISBN 978-3-319-15074-1
DOI 10.1007/978-3-319-15075-8

ISSN 1611-3349 (electronic)

ISBN 978-3-319-15075-8 (eBook)

Library of Congress Control Number: 2014960283

LNCS Sublibrary: SL2 – Programming and Software Engineering

Printed on acid-free paper

Springer International Publishing AG Switzerland is part of Springer Science+Business Media
(www.springer.com)

Preface

This volume contains the papers presented at the 17th Brazilian Symposium on Formal Methods (SBMF 2014). The conference was held in Maceió, Brazil, from September 29 to October 1, 2014, as a part of CBSoft 2014, the Fifth Brazilian Conference on Software: Theory and Practice.

The Brazilian Symposium on Formal Methods (SBMF) is an event devoted to the dissemination of the development and use of formal methods for the construction of high-quality computational systems, aiming to promote opportunities for researchers with interests in formal methods to discuss the recent advances in this area. SBMF is a consolidated scientific-technical event in the software area. Its first edition took place in 1998, reaching the 17th edition in 2014. The proceedings of the last editions were published in Springer's Lecture Notes in Computer Science as volumes 5902 (2009), 6527 (2010), 7021 (2011), 7498 (2012), and 8195 (2013).

The conference program of SBMF 2014 included two invited talks, given by David Deharbe (Universidade Federal do Rio Grande do Norte, Natal, Brazil) and Narciso Martí-Oliet (Universidad Complutense de Madrid, Madrid, Spain), who also taught at CBSoft respective tutorials on Rigorous development of imperative software components and Specifying, programming, and verifying in Maude.

A total of 13 research papers were presented at the conference: 9 full papers and 4 short papers. The first were included in these proceedings, together with the invited talks, while the latter were included only in the preproceedings available at the conference.

These contributions were selected from 34 submissions that came from 18 different countries: Brazil, Canada, Colombia, Denmark, France, Germany, India, Israel, Italy, Pakistan, Portugal, South Africa, Switzerland, Tunisia, Turkey, Ukraine, UK, and Uruguay.

The processes of submission by the authors, paper reviews, and deliberations of the Program Committee were all assisted by EasyChair.

We would like to begin our acknowledgments by thanking all the authors who submitted papers and showed interest in the subject, and next all the Program Committee members and the referees for their hard work in evaluating submissions and suggesting improvements. We are also very grateful to the local organizers of CBSoft 2014, who were coordinated by Marcio Ribeiro, Baldoino Santos Neto, and Leandro Dias da Silva, all from the Universidade Federal de Alagoas, who did an excellent job and managed to run the conference smoothly. And we cannot forget thanking our respective families, for their patience while we were devoting time to SBMF instead of being with them.

SBMF 2014 was organized by the Universidade Federal de Alagoas (UFAL), promoted by the Brazilian Computer Society (SBC), and sponsored by the following organizations, who we thank for their generous support:

- Brazilian National Institute of Science and Technology for Software Engineering (INES),
- CAPES, the Brazilian Higher Education Funding Council,
- CNPq, the Brazilian Scientific and Technological Research Council,
- Google Inc., and
- Universidade Federal de Alagoas.

We hope you enjoy reading these proceedings as much as we enjoyed preparing them.

December 2014   Christiano Braga
                                                               Narciso Martí-Oliet

Organization

Program Committee

Aline Andrade	UFBA, Brazil
Wilkerson L. Andrade	UFCG, Brazil
Luis Barbosa	Universidade do Minho, Portugal
Christiano Braga	UFF, Brazil
Michael Butler	University of Southampton, UK
Ana Cavalcanti	University of York, UK
Márcio Cornélio	UFPE, Brazil
Andrea Corradini	Università di Pisa, Italy
Jim Davies	University of Oxford, UK
David Deharbe	UFRN, Brazil
Ewen Denney	SGT/NASA Ames, USA
Clare Dixon	University of Liverpool, UK
Jorge Figueiredo	UFCG, Brazil
Marcelo Frias	Instituto Tecnológico de Buenos Aires, Argentina
Rohit Gheyi	UFCG, Brazil
Juliano Iyoda	UFPE, Brazil
Zhiming Liu	Birmingham City University, UK
Patricia Machado	UFCG, Brazil
Anamaria Martins Moreira	UFRN, Brazil
Narciso Martí-Oliet	Universidad Complutense de Madrid, Spain
Tiago Massoni	UFCG, Brazil
Ana Melo	USP, Brazil
Alvaro Moreira	UFRGS, Brazil
Carroll Morgan	University of New South Wales, Australia
Alexandre Mota	UFPE, Brazil
Arnaldo Moura	UNICAMP, Brazil
Leonardo Moura	Microsoft Research, USA
David Naumann	Stevens Institute of Technology, USA
Jose Oliveira	Universidade do Minho, Portugal
Marcel Vinicius Medeiros Oliveira	UFRN, Brazil
Peter Olveczky	University of Oslo, Norway
Alberto Pardo	Universidad de la República, Uruguay
Alexandre Petrenko	CRIM, Canada

Leila Ribeiro	UFRGS, Brazil
Augusto Sampaio	UFPE, Brazil
Leila Silva	UFS, Brazil
Adenilso Simao	ICMC/USP, Brazil
Heike Wehrheim	University of Paderborn, Germany
Jim Woodcock	University of York, UK

Local Organizers

Marcio Ribeiro	UFAL, Brazil
Baldoino Santos Neto	UFAL, Brazil
Leandro Dias da Silva	UFAL, Brazil

Program Chairs

Christiano Braga	UFF, Brazil
Narciso Martí-Oliet	Universidad Complutense de Madrid, Spain

Steering Committee

Adenilso Simão	ICMC/USP, Brazil
Carroll Morgan	University of New South Wales, UK
Rohit Gheyi	UFCG, Brazil
David Naumann	Stevens Institute of Technology, USA
Juliano Iyoda	UFPE, Brazil
Leonardo de Moura	Microsoft Research, USA
Christiano Braga	UFF, Brazil
Narciso Martí-Oliet	Universidad Complutense de Madrid, Spain
Márcio Cornélio	UFPE, Brazil

Additional Reviewers

Dury, Arnaud	Nguena Timo, Omer Landry
Fridlender, Daniel	Pang, Jun
Hanazumi, Simone	Salehi Fathabadi, Asieh
Hermann Haeusler, Edward	Salem, Paulo
Loos, Sarah	Santiago, Regivan
Moraes, Alan	Savicks, Vitaly
Motz, Regina	Vandin, Andrea

Contents

LLVM-Based Code Generation for B 1
  Richard Bonichon, David Déharbe, Thierry Lecomte, and Valério Medeiros Jr.

Equational Abstractions in Rewriting Logic and Maude 17
  Narciso Martí-Oliet, Francisco Durán, and Alberto Verdejo

Formalization of Zsyntax to Reason About Molecular Pathways in HOL4 . . . 32
  Sohaib Ahmad, Osman Hasan, Umair Siddique, and Sofiéne Tahar

Towards a Family of Test Selection Criteria for Symbolic Models
of Real-Time Systems 48
  *Diego R. Almeida, Alan Moraes, Wilkerson L. Andrade,
  and Patrícia D.L. Machado*

Model-Driven Engineering in the Heterogeneous Tool Set 64
  Daniel Calegari, Till Mossakowski, and Nora Szasz

A Coinductive Animation of Turing Machines 80
  Alberto Ciaffaglione

Towards Completeness in Bounded Model Checking Through Automatic
Recursion Depth Detection 96
  Grigory Fedyukovich and Natasha Sharygina

A Probabilistic Model Checking Analysis of a Realistic Vehicular Networks
Mobility Model 113
  Bruno Ferreira, Fernando A.F. Braz, and Sérgio V.A. Campos

A Dynamic Logic for Every Season 130
  Alexandre Madeira, Renato Neves, Manuel A. Martins, and Luís S. Barbosa

Completeness and Decidability Results for Hybrid(ised) Logics 146
  Renato Neves, Manuel A. Martins, and Luís S. Barbosa

Parameterisation of Three-Valued Abstractions 162
  Nils Timm and Stefan Gruner

Author Index 179

LLVM-Based Code Generation for B

Richard Bonichon[1], David Déharbe[1(✉)], Thierry Lecomte[2],
and Valério Medeiros Jr.[1]

[1] UFRN, Natal, Brazil
david@dimap.ufrn.br
[2] Clearsy, Aix-en-Provence, France

Abstract. We present b2llvm, a multi-platform code generator for the
B-method. The b2llvm code generator currently handles the following
elements of the B language: simple data types, imperative instructions
and component compositions. In particular, this paper describes a translation for essential implementation constructs of the B language into
LLVM source code, implemented into the b2llvm compiler. We use an
example-based approach for this description.

1 Introduction

The B-method is a refinement-based software design method [1]. Its language has
both abstract constructs, suitable for declarative-like specifications, and imperative constructs, commonly found in programming languages. B development
typically starts with a specification, in a so-called *machine*, followed by incremental refinements to an *implementation*, where only imperative-like constructs
may be employed [6]. Such an implementation is then translated [5] to source
code in a programming language, say C or Ada. The steps in the B-method are
verified using certified theorem proving technologies. However the translation
to a programming language, and its subsequent compilation to the target platform, do not benefit from the same mathematical rigor. In practice, *redundancy*
in the tool chains and execution platforms is employed to increase the level of
confidence to the desired levels.

The goal of this work is to contribute a redundancy element, by creating a
new open-source machine-code generation tool chain. To achieve this, we base
our work on the LLVM compilation framework [8]. LLVM is an active open-
source compiler infrastructure used by many compiling toolchains. It provides
an intermediate assembly language suitable to the applications of many compiler
techniques such as optimization, static analysis, code generation, debugging. We
defined a translation from B0 (the subset of the B language that is used to
describe imperative programs) to the LLVM intermediate representation, which
is implemented in the b2llvm tool[1].

V. Medeiros Jr.—The research presented in this paper was partially supported by
CNPq projects 308008/2012-0 and 573964/2008-4 (National Institute of Science and
Technology for Software Engineer - INES).

[1] The b2llvm project is hosted at https://www.b2llvm.org/b2llvm.

C. Braga and N. Martí-Oliet (Eds.): SBMF 2014, LNCS 8941, pp. 1–16, 2015.
DOI: 10.1007/978-3-319-15075-8_1

The rest of the paper is organized as follows. Section 2 presents selected aspects of the LLVM intermediate representation language. Next, in section 3, we review some important concepts of the B-method regarding the structure of projects. A user perspective of the code generator is then presented in section 4. In section 5 we present some details of the code generation process through illustrative examples. Also, section 6 discusses verification and validation aspects. We conclude and consider future work in section 7.

2   Target LLVM Subset

The LLVM project defines an intermediate representation language (LLVM IR), as a means to implement different compiler components. Front-ends translate source programming languages to LLVM IR, optimizers and other static analysis tasks may be applied to the IR, and back-ends translate from LLVM IR to target platform assembly languages. LLVM IR is a single-static assignment (SSA) language, i.e., a variable may only be assigned in a single instruction. Figure 1 exemplifies LLVM IR syntax with a simple program together with its equivalent C program.

```
define void @inc(i32* %pi) {
entry:
    %0 = load i32* %pi
    %1 = add i32 %0, 1
    store i32 %1, i32* %pi
    ret void
}
```

```
void inc(int * pi)
{
    *pi += 1;
}
```

Fig. 1. Simple example of a C function and its corresponding LLVM IR function. The first line contains the signature: return type **void**, the name **@inc** and one parameter named **%pi** and typed **i32***. Next is the body with a single block, labeled **entry**, and temporary variables **%0** and **%1**, created in the conversion to SSA. The block has four instructions: **load**, **add**, **store** and **ret**. For instance, **%1 = add i32 %0, 1** performs an addition (**add**), has result type **i32** and assigns to **%1** the sum of variable **%0** and integer literal **1**.

Figure 2 presents the subset of LLVM IR targeted by the b2llvm code generator. LLVM IR programs are organized into modules, one per translation unit. A module may contain declarations of external entities (functions and constants) and definitions of internal items (functions, variables and constants). Data must be typed and the name and type of external entities must be declared. All names, e.g. non-reserved identifiers, must start with @, when they are global, or %, when they are local. For instance, **@max = external constant i32** declares **@max** as a 32-bit integer constant and **declare void @inc(i32*)** declares **@inc** as a function with one parameter, namely a pointer to an integer, and a **void** return type.

$$
\begin{aligned}
module &::= item^+ \\
item &::= const\_decl \mid function\_decl \mid \\
&\quad type\_def \mid const\_def \mid var\_def \mid function\_def \\
const\_decl &::= name \texttt{ = external constant } type \\
type\_def &::= name \texttt{ = type } type \\
type &::= \texttt{void} \mid itype \mid \texttt{\{ } type^+ \texttt{ \} } \mid type\texttt{*} \\
const\_def &::= name \texttt{ = constant } type\ iliteral \\
var\_def &::= name \texttt{ = common global } type \texttt{ zeroinitializer} \\
function\_decl &::= \texttt{declare } type\ name\ \texttt{(} type^+ \texttt{)} \\
function\_def &::= \texttt{define } type\ name\ \texttt{(} param^+ \texttt{) \{ } block^+ \texttt{ \}} \\
param &::= type\ name \\
block &::= lbl\ \texttt{: } inst^+ \\
inst &::= name \texttt{ = alloca } type \\
&\mid name \texttt{ = } \langle\ \texttt{add} \mid \texttt{sub} \mid \texttt{mul} \mid \texttt{sdiv} \mid \texttt{srem} \ \rangle itype\ exp\ \texttt{, } exp \\
&\mid name \texttt{ = icmp } \langle\ \texttt{eq} \mid \texttt{ne} \mid \texttt{sgt} \mid \texttt{sge} \mid \texttt{slt} \mid \texttt{sle} \ \rangle\ \texttt{i1 } exp\ \texttt{, } exp \\
&\mid name \texttt{ = call } type\ \texttt{(} arg^+ \texttt{)} \\
&\mid name \texttt{ = getelementptr } type\ \texttt{* } exp\texttt{, } index\texttt{, } index \\
&\mid name \texttt{ = load } type\ exp \\
&\mid \texttt{store } type\ exp\texttt{, } type\ \texttt{* } exp \\
&\mid \texttt{br i1 } exp\ \texttt{, label } lbl\ \texttt{, label } lbl \\
&\mid \texttt{br label } lbl \\
&\mid \texttt{ret } \langle\ type\ exp \mid \texttt{void} \ \rangle \\
exp &::= name \mid iliteral \mid \texttt{getelementptr (} type\ exp\ \texttt{, } index\ \texttt{, } index\ \texttt{)} \\
index &::= itype\ iliteral \\
branch &::= iliteral\ iliteral\ lbl \\
arg &::= type\ exp
\end{aligned}
$$

Fig. 2. Grammar of the target LLVM IR subset: *itype*, *iliteral*, *lbl* and *name* correspond respectively to integer types, integer literals, labels and names. Choices are separated by | and optionally delimited by $\langle$ and $\rangle$. The $^+$ superscript denotes a comma-separated list of elements of the annotated entity.

The type system contains the empty type void, a (countable) infinite, number of integer types, one for each possible bit width (e.g., i8 is the type for 8-bit integers), and type constructors pointer (declared with monadic operator · *) and structure (declared with polyadic operator {··· }). For instance { i8*, i8, i8 } is the type for structures with three fields, the first having as type pointer to i8. Grammar rule *type_def* states how types are named, e.g., %T1 = type {i32, i32} and %T2 = type {%T1*, %T1*}. In LLVM IR, pointer values are integers.

Local entities are constants, variables or functions. An example of constant definition is @secret = constant i32 42 and is composed of a name, type and value. A variable definition has a name, a type and code generation attributes, e.g @count = common global i32 zeroinitializer. Attributes provide information for target code generation, e.g., linkage type, scope, initialization. For each such definition, a memory block is allocated statically and stores the variable value. Function definitions are composed of the signature and body. The signature contains the return type, name, parameters, and attributes for target code generation. The body is a sequence of blocks of instructions in single-static assignment form.

Grammar rule *inst* describes the different kinds of instructions. All instructions producing a value assign it to a fresh variable (since it is a SSA language). Instruction `alloca` allocates a memory block, with the size of the given type, on the stack segment. This memory is automatically freed when the current frame is popped from the stack. Arithmetic operations are binary and comparisons return a 1-bit integer value. Instruction `call` invokes the given function with the given arguments, assigning the result to a fresh variable. In general, `getelementptr` gets the address of an element in an aggregate object through indexing. This instruction assumes that a sequence with several aggregate values may be stored starting from the given position. It therefore gets two indices: the first identifies which value is selected in the sequence, and the second selects the element of interest in the aggregate. In the LLVM IR code produced by b2llvm, such sequences are composed of a single structure value. Hence, the first index has value 0 (and type `i32`) to select the first structure at the given location *exp*, and the second index selects a field in that structure. Instruction `load` assigns to a fresh variable *name* the contents of a memory address of type *type* specified by *exp* (e.g. in figure 1). Instruction `store` writes a value to memory address (e.g., see figure 1). Instruction `br` is either conditional, and directs the execution to one of two blocks, or unconditional and the execution jumps to the given block. Instruction `switch` directs the control flow to one of several blocks, according to the value of the given expression. Finally, instruction `ret` ends the current function call, optionally returning a value. The expression language is thus limited to names (local and global), integer literals and selection of an element in a structure.

We make no assumption on the existence of a library to obtain resources managed by the operating system, such as dynamic memory allocation. Consequently, all data must be allocated either statically, or on the current stack frame (using the `alloca` instruction).

3 On the Structure of B Developments

Industrial applications of the B-method are large-scale developments that use constructs for modular design. The b2llvm code generator supports these constructs. We discuss them in this section.

A B *project* consists in specifying a system at an abstract level and in deriving a consistent software system. This is essentially done by decomposing the specification into *modules* and by producing computer-executable artifacts from such modules. In a B development, software is organized in libraries of *modules* which may be composed to build new modules and realize projects.

A module has a specification, called a *machine*, and is developed formally by a series of modules called *refinements*. Such modules may be used to specify additional requirements, to define how abstract data may be encoded using concrete data types, or to define how operations may be implemented algorithmically. From a formal point of view, each module is simulated by the subsequent refinement modules. A refinement is called an *implementation* when its data is scalar and behavior is described in a procedural style. Implementations may be translated into an imperative programming language such as C.

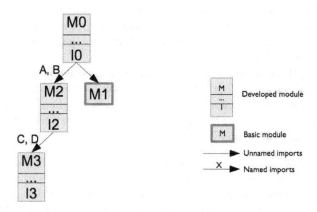

Fig. 3. Structure of the imports relation in a B project

Machines, refinements and implementations are called the *components* of a module. When a module is implemented with the B-method, it is called a *developed* module. It is also possible that a module is only specified, but not implemented, in B. It is then called a *base* module. b2llvm handles projects with both kinds of modules.

Among the modularity constructs in the B notation, handling the *import* relation requires the application of separate compilation techniques. At the implementation level, one module may import several instances of a module (base or developed) to form its internal data structures. The implementation of an imported developed module may in turn import other instances, and there is no pre-established limit to such chain of imports. The import relation between module instances forms a tree, where the root is an implementation and the descendants of a node are the instances imported from the module in that node. Figure 3 shows the structure of a B project with an implementation I0 of a specification M0. I0 imports one unnamed instance of base module M1 and two instances named A and B of developed module M2. Its implementation I2 in turn imports two instances C and D of a developed module M3, implemented as I3 (which has no imports itself).

4   General Design of the Code Generator

The input to b2llvm is a large subset of the B implementation language, also known as B0: simple data types INT and BOOL, enumerations, concrete variables, concrete constants, *sees* clause, importation (i.e., instantiation) of modules, and all instructions, including operation calls. Support for arrays and record types is also underway and will be integrated to the code generator. This input is given as XML-formatted files produced by Atelier-B version 4.2. In addition to producing LLVM IR from B implementations, b2llvm is designed to satisfy the following two requirements:

static memory allocation Many safety-critical systems preclude the use of dynamic memory allocation. Therefore, all memory has to be allocated statically, save for the function call frame stack. As a side effect, no dynamic memory allocation library is required.

separate compilation An internal change in a module should only require generating new IR code for that module, and not for the modules that depend on it. This condition is important for large projects, where the development may be distributed. Nevertheless, a change in an interface still requires the recompilation of all dependent modules.

We will use the example of the B project structure from figure 3 to explain decisions taken in the design of the code generator. This project consists of four modules and the corresponding final binary must include one instance of module M0, one instance of M1, two instances of M2 and four instances of M3.

M1 is a base module, and the corresponding instance is produced by another tool chain. Nevertheless, M0 may use all the symbols defined in the interface of M1 and we have to include corresponding declarations in the LLVM IR file for M0. Similarly, M0 accesses the interface of M2, and M2 accesses that of M3. The first design decision is that, given a module M, we need a procedure producing the LLVM IR declarations for all the elements in the interface of M. The code thus produced is called the *interface section* of (the translation of) M.

Next, modules may have a data space and the code generator needs to allocate memory to store the representation of the corresponding data. Dynamic memory allocation is excluded, and the sole solution is static memory allocation, that is using global variables. Also, when the code generator processes a B module, the number of its instances at run time is unknown, and we would not want to have to regenerate code each time the module is used in a project to suit the number of instances. So, the second design decision is to distinguish between code generation of a module and code generation of its instances. To cope with it, the b2llvm code generator has two operation modes:

- *COMP*, for module compilation, consists in producing an LLVM IR implementation of the data, i.e., a type encoding the state space, and of the behavior, i.e., functions implementing initialization and operations.
- *PROJ*, for module instances, is applied whenever we need to instantiate modules, that is, when we want to produce code for a full project. Then, given the root module of the project, all transitively imported components are identified and instantiated, by generating LLVM IR global variables having the type associated with the corresponding module. Note that the definitions of such module types are generated in COMP mode.

The code generated for a module with a data space needs to address individually the variables and the imported module instances composing such a space. To do so, these are aggregated within a structure-like data type. Hence, when a module has a data space, b2llvm produces the definition of a LLVM IR structure type, named %M$state$. This definition is called the *typedef section* of (the translation of) M.

To support separate compilation, the representation of the imported module instances cannot be part of the structure itself. Instead, the instances of the imported modules are represented as references to the corresponding encoding structures (i.e., as pointers). We call `%M$ref$` the type pointer to `%M$state$`.

---

typedef: If the module has data space, a LLVM IR structure type is defined:
```
%M$state$ = type { type+ }
```

interface: If the module has a data space, an LLVM IR type M_ref, pointer to M_data and an initialization function are defined:
```
%M$ref$ = type %M$state$*
declare void @M$init$(%M$ref$, type+)
```
One function is declared for each operation in the module:
```
declare void @M$op(%M$ref$, type+)
```

implementation: For developed modules, defines the functions declared in the interface:
```
define void @M$op(%M$ref$ %self$, param+) {
    block+
    exit: ret void
}
```

Fig. 4. Summary of the different sections and the pattern of LLVM IR code composing them

To encode the behavior of a module, for each operation op, a function named `@M$op` encoding its behavior is generated. The parameter list of such functions contains one item for each input and output of the corresponding operation. There is also one parameter of type `%M$ref$`, which is a reference to the structure encoding the instance associated with that operation. Also, b2llvm produces a function `@M$init$` responsible for executing the initialization of M. The parameters of this function are the addresses of the instances found in the import tree of the module (including the module itself). These parameters are necessary to call the corresponding initialization functions in the correct dependency order and to bind the references to the imported modules to elements of the structure of the initialized module. These LLVM IR function definitions and the definition of the type `@M$ref$` form the so-called *implementation section* of (the translation of) M. Figure 4 summarizes the three sections defined in our approach for the code generation and figures 5 and 6 present the overall structure for the code generated in *COMP* mode and *PROJ*, respectively.

5 Details of the Code Generator

We have specified the code generation process with a comprehensive set of formal rules. Due to space constraints, we cannot thoroughly present this specification[2]. Instead, we give an informal description of the code generation process, based

---

[2] This specification is available online at http://www.b2llvm.org/b2llvm/downloads.

```
for each transitively imported stateful module Q, generate
    %Q$state$ = type opaque    (declares type for Q state space)
    %Q$ref$ = type %Q$state$*    (and corresponding pointer type)
for each imported module Q, generate
    include the interface section of Q
if M is stateful
    include the typedef section of M
    %M$ref$ = type %M$state$*
include the implementation section of M
```

Fig. 5. Code template for the *COMP* mode

```
for each transitively imported stateful module Q
    include the typedef section of Q
    %Q$ref$ = type %Q$state$*
for each stateful instance Q, imported transitively through path
    declare a variable of type %Q$state$:
    @Q[path] = common global %M$state$ zeroinitializer
include the interface section of M
define a function %$init$ with a call to the
    initialization function of M with the proper bindings
    define void @$init$(void) {
        call void @M$init$(@M, { instances⁺ }) {
        exit: ret void
    }
```

Fig. 6. Code template for the *COMP* mode

on two examples: first, a counter with no external dependencies and, second, part of a watchdog timer that includes one instance of the same counter. We complete this section by describing an example of code generation for a project.

5.1   The Standalone Module **counter**

The implementation counter_i of the module counter is presented in figure 7.

```
1    IMPLEMENTATION counter_i
2    REFINES counter
3    CONCRETE_VARIABLES value, error
4    INVARIANT value: INT & error : BOOL & /* omitted gluing invariant */
5    INITIALISATION  value := 0; error := FALSE
6    OPERATIONS
7        inc = IF value < MAXINT THEN value := value + 1
8             ELSE error := TRUE END;
9        res <-- get = res := value
10   END
```

Fig. 7. Example B implementation

Here, the code generator needs to access neither the corresponding B machine, nor the gluing invariant of the implementation. This module is stateful as it has two state variables value and error (respectively an integer and a Boolean) and two operations inc and get. Figure 8 contains its corresponding typedef section: LLVM IR aggregate type %counter$state$ has two elements, a i32 at position 0 represents value and a i1 at position 1 represents error.

```
1    %counter$state$ = type {i32, i1}
```

Fig. 8. Corresponding LLVM IR typedef section

Figure 9 contains the corresponding interface section, comprised of the declarations of all the entities defined in the module that may be used by third-party components (this is illustrated in section 5.2): a pointer type %counterref to reference an aggregate storing the state of the component, the initialization function %counter$init$, and the functions %counter$inc and %counter$get, each responsible for implementing one module operation. Each such function takes as first parameter the address of the representation of the module state. The last function also takes as parameter the address of a i32, where the value of the operation value is stored.

```
1    %counter$ref$ = type %counter$state$*
2    declare void @counter$init$(%counter$ref$)
3    declare void @counter$inc(%counter$ref$)
4    declare void @counter$get(%counter$ref$, i32*)
```

Fig. 9. Corresponding LLVM IR interface section

Figure 10 contains the implementation section. It consists of the definition of all the functions implementing the module behavior. All function bodies contain an entry and an exit statement block. In addition, a block for each conditional branch is created; e.g., blocks starting line 18 and 25 respectively correspond to the IF branches from line 7 and 8 in the inc operation.

This example illustrates the encoding for different kinds of expressions and instructions. First, let us consider expressions: the example given in figure 7 includes operation parameters, integer and Boolean literals, implementation (state) variables, an addition and a comparison.

Operation parameters are encoded as function arguments, which have identifiers in LLVM IR. So the b2llvm code generator simply maintains a symbol table mapping each B operation parameter to the identifier of the corresponding LLVM IR function parameter. For instance, operation get has output res (l. 9, fig. 7), which is represented by %res of function @counter$get (l. 31, fig. 10). Integer and Boolean literals are encoded directly as 32-bit and 1-bit LLVM integer values; for instance MAXINT and TRUE are encoded respectively as 2147483647 and 1 (l. 15 and l. 26, fig. 10). Implementation variables are encoded as elements of the aggregate %self$, which is a parameter in each function. Their address is

```
1    define void @counter$init$(%counter$ref$ %self$) {
2    entry:
3      %0 = getelementptr %counter$ref$ %self$, i32 0, i32 0
4      store i32 0, i32* %0
5      %1 = getelementptr %counter$ref$ %self$, i32 0, i32 1
6      store i1 0, i1* %1
7      br label %exit
8    exit:
9      ret void
10   }
11   define void @counter$inc(%counter$ref$ %self$) {
12   entry:
13     %0 = getelementptr %counter$ref$ %self$, i32 0, i32 0
14     %1 = load i32* %0
15     %2 = icmp slt i32 %1, 2147483647
16     br i1 %2, label %label0, label %label1
17   label0:
18     %3 = getelementptr %counter$ref$ %self$, i32 0, i32 0
19     %4 = load i32* %3
20     %5 = add i32 %4, 1
21     %6 = getelementptr %counter$ref$ %self$, i32 0, i32 0
22     store i32 %5, i32* %6
23     br label %exit
24   label1:
25     %7 = getelementptr %counter$ref$ %self$, i32 0, i32 1
26     store i1 1, i1* %7
27     br label %exit
28   exit:
29     ret void
30   }
31   define void @counter$get(%counter$ref$ %self$, i32* %res) {
32   entry:
33     %0 = getelementptr %counter$ref$ %self$, i32 0, i32 0
34     %1 = load i32* %0
35     store i32 %1, i32* %res
36     br label %exit
37   exit:
38     ret void
39   }
```

Fig. 10. LLVM implementation section for counter_i

obtained with the `getelementptr` instruction, giving the position of the variable representation in this aggregate: 0 for variable value and 1 for variable error.

We now provide detailed explanation for the translation of the assignment value := value + 1 (l. 7, fig. 7) to LLVM IR instructions (l. 18-22, fig. 10):

l. 18-20 First, the right-hand side of the assignment is evaluated, and the result is stored in temporary %5, as follows:

    l. 18 A `getelementptr` instruction gets the address of the representation of variable value in the structure encoding the state of the module, and the result is stored into temporary %3.

    l. 19 A `load` instruction fetches the data in this location into temporary %4.

    l. 20 An `add` instruction sums this value with one (1) and the result is stored into temporary %5.

l. 21 Second, the left-hand side of the assignment is evaluated, the result being stored in temporary %6. Since this is again the variable value, it is essentially the same operation as in l. 18 and %6 is redundant with %3 (but we do not deal with optimization at this stage).

l. 22 Finally, the assignment effectively take place with the value in %5 begin stored at the evaluated address %6 (that of the representation of variable value).

For an IF instruction (e.g., lines 7-8, fig. 7), b2llvm generates code to evaluate the condition (e.g., lines 13-15, fig. 10), a conditional branch (l. 16, fig. 10), and one block with the encoding of each branch (l. 17-23 and 24-27, fig. 10). Note that each such block must end with an unconditional branch to the instruction following the conditional. b2llvm handles the creation of all the required block labels.

Of course, the code thus generated is not optimal: e.g., the exit block in the initialisation is useless. Indeed, code generation is designed to be as simple as possible. No optimizations are implemented into b2llvm. A positive consequence of choosing LLVM as target architecture is the possibility of applying many off-the-shelf optimizers developped for LLVM to the output of b2llvm.

5.2   The Composed Module **wd**

Our second example is the wd module detailed in figure 11. It contains module

```
IMPLEMENTATION wd_i
REFINES wd
VALUES timeout=50
IMPORTS counter
INVARIANT overflow = FALSE & timeout - value = ticker
INITIALISATION
    VAR count IN
        count := 0;
        WHILE count < timeout DO
            inc; count := count+1
        INVARIANT value = count
        VARIANT timeout - count
        END
    END
OPERATIONS
    tick =
    VAR elapsed, diff IN
        elapsed <-- get;
        diff := timeout - elapsed;
        IF diff > 0 THEN inc END
END;
```

Fig. 11. Implementation of B module **wd** (excerpts)

instantiation, operation calls, and a loop instruction. The state of this module is exactly the state of the unique instance of its counter component, and is encoded as an aggregate with a unique element, of type pointer to the state representation of the corresponding module (see typedef section in figure 12).

```
1    %wd$state$ = type {%counter$ref$}
```

Fig. 12. Typedef section for module WD

Functions @wd$init$ and @wd$tick are defined in the implementation section, presented in figure 13. We first discuss the latter.

```
1    define void @wd$init$(%wd$ref$ %self$, %counter$ref$ %arg0$) {
2    entry:
3      %count = alloca i32
4      %0 = getelementptr %wd$ref$ %self$, i32 0, i32 0
5      store %counter$ref$ %arg0$, %counter$ref$* %0
6      call void @counter$init$(%counter$ref$ %arg0$)
7      store i32 0, i32* %count
8      br label %label1
9    label1:
10     %1 = load i32* %count
11     %2 = icmp slt i32 %1, 50
12     br i1 %2, label %label2, label %label0
13   label2:
14     %3 = getelementptr %wd$ref$ %self$, i32 0, i32 0
15     %4 = load %counter$ref$* %3
16     call void @counter$inc(%counter$ref$ %4)
17     %5 = load i32* %count
18     %6 = add i32 %5, 1
19     store i32 %6, i32* %count
20     br label %label1
21   label0:
22     br label %exit
23   exit:
24     ret void
25   }
26   define void @wd$tick(%wd$ref$ %self$) {
27   entry:
28     %elapsed = alloca i32
29     %diff = alloca i32
30     %0 = getelementptr %wd$ref$ %self$, i32 0, i32 0
31     %1 = load %counter$ref$* %0
32     call void @counter$get(%counter$ref$ %1, i32* %elapsed)
33     %2 = load i32* %elapsed
34     %3 = sub i32 50, %2
35     store i32 %3, i32* %diff
36     %4 = load i32* %diff
37     %5 = icmp sgt i32 %4, 0
38     br i1 %5, label %label1, label %label0
39   label1:
40     %6 = getelementptr %wd$ref$ %self$, i32 0, i32 0
41     %7 = load %counter$ref$* %6
42     call void @counter$inc(%counter$ref$ %7)
43     br label %label0
44   label0:
45     br label %exit
46   exit:
47     ret void
48   }
```

Fig. 13. Implementation section for module WD

Function @wd$tick$ implements operation tick. It has no input and no output. Its sole argument is the address of the representation of a wd instance. It has two local variables, elapsed and diff, and both are integers. Operation variables are represented in stack memory, which is reserved with the alloca instruction (e.g., lines 28-29). LLVM requires that such allocations appear first in function bodies. The procedure in b2llvm responsible for encoding B operation declarations has a dedicated preliminary pass that collects all local variables and issues the corresponding allocations. The encoding of operation calls is illustrated lines 30-32. First, the address of the called operation module is computed (lines 30-31), possibly followed by the computation of other parameters. Then a

LLVM function call is issued (e.g., 1 .32). Notice that the output of the operation is stored on the stack at the location given by parameter %elapsed. Another example of operation call is given in lines 40-42. The remaining code in the function body uses previously described techniques.

Function @wd$init$ implements the initialization of a wd instance, the address of which is given in parameter %self$. It also gets the address of one module instance for each component. In this example, there is one instantiation of module counter and its representation is given through parameter %arg0$. Following an allocation for the representation of variable count, the components are bound and initialized: each component representation is bound to an element of the aggregate representing the current instance (e.g., lines 4-5). Also, each component representation is initialized by calling the corresponding LLVM function (e.g., line 6). The order of these initializations complies to the dependency order. This example illustrates code generation for loops. First the loop condition is evaluated (lines 10-11 in the example), and a conditional branch jumps either to the code implementing the loop body, or to the first instruction after the loop encoding (e.g., line 12). Also, the loop body ends with an unconditional branch to the block evaluating the loop condition (e.g., line 20).

5.3   Generating a System Instance

To conclude this section, we demonstrate and discuss the result of the code generation in PROJ mode. For this, we take the wd module as example and consider the resulting code in figure 14. It follows the template given in figure 6 and is composed of the following: lines 1-2 are the type definitions of the imported component and line 3 is the global variable corresponding to its sole instance, then lines 4-8 correspond to the interface section of the root component (comprised of the declarations of types and functions), and concluded by the definition a system initialization function called @$init$ (lines 9-13). The role of this function is to call the initialization function of the top-level module passing it the state-representation variables as parameters.

6   Verification and Validation

Considering the verification of the proposed translation, several approaches are possible: inspection, testing and proof. Only the first is currently available, and work is underway to provide a framework based on the second approach.

A first approach is based on human inspection of the generated code. Currently, b2llvm provides two options to assist such inspections. The first option provides additional functions to output the values of state variables of the system: they can be called to visualize the evolution between operation calls. The first option consists in annotating the code generated with information on the intent of the code and references to the original B implementation. Figure 15 contains an excerpt of such annotated LLVM IR.

```
1    %counter$state$ = type {i32, i1}
2    %counter$ref$ = type %counter$state$*
3    %wd$state$ = type {%counter$ref$}
4    %wd$ref$ = type %wd$state$*
5    @$wd = common global %wd$state$ zeroinitializer
6    @$counter = common global %counter$state$ zeroinitializer
7    declare void @wd$init$(%wd$ref$, %counter$ref$)
8    declare void @wd$tick$(%wd$ref$)
9    define void @$init$() {
10   entry:
11       call void @wd$init$(%wd$ref$ @$wd, %counter$ref$ @$counter)
12       ret void
13   }
```

Fig. 14. Code generation in *PROJ* mode

```
1    ;;1 The type for the state of "counter" is defined in "counter_i",
2    ;; it is an aggregate such that:
3    ;;1.1 Position "0" represents variable "value".
4    ;;1.2 Position "1" represents variable "error".
5    %counter$state$ = type {i32, i1}
6    ;;2 The type for references to state encodings of "counter" is:
7    %counter$ref$ = type %counter$state$*
8    ;;3 The function implementing initialisation for "counter" is
9    ;;    named "@counter£init£" and has the following parameters:
10   ;;3.1 "%self£": address of LLVM aggregate storing state of "counter";
11   define void @counter$init$(%counter$ref$ %self$) {
```

Fig. 15. Excerpt of annotated LLVM code generated by b2llvm

A second approach is runtime verification, by application of simulation, test and assertions. For instance, we can use existing approaches to generate tests [2,11] from the B development artifacts. Such tests can then be converted to LLVM IR to produce and run test harnesses. A typical scenario for such a test would consist in setting the state variables to some given values, call the function implementing the operation being verified, and then inspect these same variables to check if they have the expected values. Work in this direction, based on [11] is currently underway.

It would also be possible to perform dual animation: B model with Pro-B [10] together with the generated code with the LLVM interpreter. In addition, B artifacts contain several kinds of assertions: state invariants, loop invariants, preconditions, as well as *ad hoc* assertions. If the conditions found in those assertions are expressed in the B0 language, b2llvm can also translate them to LLVM IR. Using them to monitor the generated code at run-time would additionally require to provide an LLVM implementation of the assertion semantics (e.g., the assert command found in the standard C library) and link the generated code to this implementation.

Finally, to formally verify the correctness of the translation, the semantics of B and LLVM IR need to be specified in a suitable framework. Vellvm [12] is a Coq formalization of the LLVM IR semantics that uses CompCert's memory model [9]. This could be a starting point for a proof of the correctness of the translation rules. It would still require to formalize the semantics of B and of the translation rules in that same setting. This is left as future work.

7   Conclusion

This paper presents an approach to generate executable code from a large subset of the B implementation language using LLVM, a modern compiler design infrastructure. This is a work in progress, yet the definition is self-contained and has a large enough scope to be applied to B implementations where the data belongs to basic types. Its implementation, called b2llvm, is already publicly available and will eventually be distributed as an extension to Atelier-B under an open-source license.

Our current work is to extend the scope to the full B implementation language. This entails the inclusion into the translation of rules to handle aggregate data types as well as some syntactic sugar. We are also planning for producing a LLVM IR output with debugging information. Such output would be indeed very helpful to provide feedback to the user when applying testing to validate the produced code.

To prove the correctness of the translation, we would have to define the semantics of B and LLVM IR in a unified framework. Possible starting points are Vellvm [12], a framework to reason about the correctness of LLVM programs and transformations, and the existing formalizations of the B method (e.g., [3,4,7]). We would have to extend such a framework to encompass both B and LLVM IR. Another possible approach would be to translate verification conditions from the B development artifacts as assertions in the generated LLVM IR. The compiled program would include checks that such assertions hold while executing.

References

1. Abrial, J.-R.: The B-book: assigning programs to meanings. University Press, Cambridge (1996)
2. Ambert, F., Bouquet, F., Legeard, B., Peureux, F., et al.: BZ-Testing-Tools (2002)
3. Bodeveix, J.-P., Filali, M., Muñoz, C.: A formalization of the B-method in Coq and PVS. In: Electronic Proc. B-User Group Meeting FM 99, pp. 33–49 (1999)
4. Chartier, P.: Formalisation of B in Isabelle/HOL. In: Bert, D. (ed.) B 1998. LNCS, vol. 1393, pp. 66–82. Springer, Heidelberg (1998)
5. ClearSy. ComenC, B0 implementation translation into C language (2008). http://www.comenc.eu
6. ClearSy. Atelier B User Manual Version 4.0. Clearsy System Engineering (2009)
7. Jaeger, É., Dubois, C.: Why would you trust B? In: Dershowitz, N., Voronkov, A. (eds.) LPAR 2007. LNCS (LNAI), vol. 4790, pp. 288–302. Springer, Heidelberg (2007)
8. Lattner, C., Adve, V.S.: LLVM: a compilation framework for lifelong program analysis & transformation. In: 2nd IEEE/ACM International Symposium on Code Generation and Optimization, pp. 75–88 (2004)

9. Leroy, X.: Formal verification of a realistic compiler. Communications of the ACM **52**(7), 107–115 (2009)
10. Leuschel, M., Butler, M.: ProB: An automated analysis toolset for the B method. Software Tools for Technology Transfer (STTT) **10**(2), 185–203 (2008)
11. de Matos, E.C.B., Moreira, A.M.: Beta: A B based testing approach. In: Gheyi, R., Naumann, D. (eds.) SBMF 2012. LNCS, vol. 7498, pp. 51–66. Springer, Heidelberg (2012)
12. Zhao, J., Nagarakatte, S., Martin, M.M.K., Zdancewic, S.: Formalizing the LLVM intermediate representation for verified program transformations. In: POPL, pp. 427–440 (2012)

Equational Abstractions in Rewriting Logic and Maude

Narciso Martí-Oliet[1]([⊠]), Francisco Durán[2], and Alberto Verdejo[1]

[1] Facultad de Informática, Universidad Complutense de Madrid, Madrid, Spain
narciso@ucm.es
[2] E.T.S.I. Informática, Universidad de Málaga, Málaga, Spain

Abstract. Maude is a high-level language and high-performance system supporting both equational and rewriting computation for a wide range of applications. Maude also provides a model checker for linear temporal logic. The model-checking procedure can be used to prove properties when the set of states reachable from an initial state in a system is finite; when this is not the case, it may be possible to use an equational abstraction technique for reducing the size of the state space. Abstraction reduces the problem of whether an infinite state system satisfies a temporal logic property to model checking that property on a finite state abstract version of the original infinite system. The most common abstractions are quotients of the original system. We present a simple method for defining quotient abstractions by means of equations identifying states. Our method yields the minimal quotient system together with a set of proof obligations that guarantee its executability, which can be discharged with tools such as those available in the Maude formal environment. The proposed method will be illustrated by means of detailed examples.

Keywords: Maude · Rewriting logic · Model checking · Abstraction · Formal environment

1 Introduction

Given a concurrent system, we want to check whether certain properties hold in it or not. If the number of reachable states is *finite*, one can use model checking; however, if the number of such states is *infinite* (or just too large), model checking does not work. For these systems, we can calculate an *abstract* version of the infinite-state transition system, with a finite set of states, to which model checking can be applied. A simple method for defining an abstraction is by means of a *quotient* that collapses the set of states [5].

In the rewriting logic framework implemented in Maude [1], a concurrent system is specified by a rewrite theory $\mathcal{R} = (\Sigma, E, R)$, where Σ is a signature

Research supported by MINECO Spanish projects StrongSoft (TIN2012–39391–C04–04) and TIN2011–23795, and Comunidad de Madrid program N-GREENS Software (S2013/ICE-2731).

C. Braga and N. Martí-Oliet (Eds.): SBMF 2014, LNCS 8941, pp. 17–31, 2015.
DOI: 10.1007/978-3-319-15075-8_2

declaring types and operations, E is a set of equations, and R is a set of rules. The quotient abstraction is specified by a set of equations E, added to $\mathcal{R}$, resulting in a rewrite theory $\mathcal{R} = (\Sigma, E \cup E, R)$. However, such a quotient will only be useful, for model-checking purposes, if $\mathcal{R}$ is executable, as detailed later, and the state predicates are preserved by equations [5]. These *proof obligations* (executability and state predicate preservation) can be discharged using tools in the Maude Formal Environment [3].

This paper has the three following goals:

1. To introduce Maude as a framework for modeling systems and model checking their properties.
2. To present a simple method of defining quotient abstractions by means of equations collapsing the set of states.
3. To show how the Maude Formal Environment tools can help in discharging the associated proof obligations.

All of this is going to be done by means of examples. The theoretical basis for the work summarized here has already been described in previous papers, where the reader can find all the missing details [2, 3, 5].

The following section introduces two examples; in the first, the set of reachable states is finite and model checking will be applied to get the desired results, while in the second this will not be possible because the set of reachable states is infinite. Section 3 first summarizes the concepts necessary and then introduces the equational abstraction method and the associated proof obligations. In Section 4 we apply in detail the method to the second example and manage to get an abstract version satisfying all the requirements, so that we can model check on it the desired property.

2   Maude by Example

In order to model a system in rewriting logic, that is, to specify such a system in Maude, we distinguish between its static part (state structure) and its dynamics (state transitions). The static part is specified as an equational theory, while the dynamics are specified by means of rules. Computation in a transition system is then precisely captured by the term rewriting relation using those rules, where terms represent states of the given system. Moreover, rules need only specify the part of the system that actually changes, so that the frame problem is avoided.

This distinction is reflected in Maude by the difference between functional and system modules [1]. Functional modules in Maude correspond to equational theories (Σ, E) which are assumed to be Church-Rosser (confluent and sort decreasing) and terminating; their operational semantics is equational simplification, that is, rewriting of terms until a canonical form is obtained. Equations are used to define functions over static data as well as properties of states. Usually the equations E are divided into a set A of structural axioms (such as associativity, commutativity, or identity), also known as equational attributes, for which matching algorithms exist in Maude, and a set E' of equations that are Church-Rosser and terminating modulo A.

System modules in Maude correspond to rewrite theories $(\Sigma, A \cup E', R)$; rewriting with R is performed modulo the equations $A \cup E'$. Furthermore, the rules R must be coherent with the equations E' modulo A [2], allowing us to intermix rewriting with rules and rewriting with equations without losing rewrite computations by failing to perform a rewrite that would have been possible before an equational deduction step was taken. By assuming coherence, Maude always reduces to canonical form using E before applying any rule in R.

Next we illustrate the application of these general ideas to two different examples.

2.1 Crossing the River

In our first example, we consider a famous puzzle where a shepherd needs to transport to the other side of a river a wild dog, a lamb, and a cabbage. He has only a boat with room for the shepherd himself and another item. The problem is that in the absence of the shepherd the wild dog would eat the lamb, and the lamb would eat the cabbage.

We represent the shepherd and his belongings as objects[1] with only an attribute indicating its river side location. The group is put together by means of an associative and commutative juxtaposition operation. Constants left and right represent the two sides of the river. Operation ch(ange) is used to modify the corresponding attributes. Finally, the rules represent the ways of crossing the river that are allowed by the small capacity of the boat. For instance, the rule labeled wdog, for wild dog, specifies that when the shepherd and the wild dog are on the same side of the river they can cross together.

```
mod RIVER-CROSSING is
  sorts Side Group .
  ops left right : -> Side [ctor] .
  op ch : Side -> Side .
  eq ch(left) = right .
  eq ch(right) = left .
  ops s w l c : Side -> Group [ctor] .
  op __ : Group Group -> Group [ctor assoc comm] .
  var S : Side .
  rl [shepherd] : s(S) => s(ch(S)) .
  rl [wdog] : s(S) w(S) => s(ch(S)) w(ch(S)) .
  rl [lamb] : s(S) l(S) => s(ch(S)) l(ch(S)) .
  rl [cabbage] : s(S) c(S) => s(ch(S)) c(ch(S)) .
endm
```

In Section 2.4 we will see how to solve the puzzle, that is, how to find a way of crossing the river satisfying all the constraints and without having the possibility of losing any item in the process, by means of the Maude model checker.

---

[1] Although Maude has a specific notation for objects, we do not make use of it in this example.

2.2   An Unordered Communication Channel

For our second example, consider a communication channel in which messages can get out of order. There is a sender and a receiver. The sender is sending a sequence of data items, for example numbers. The receiver is supposed to obtain the data items in the same order they were sent. To achieve this in-order communication in spite of the unordered nature of the channel, the sender sends each data item in a message together with a sequence number. The receiver sends back an acknowledgement indicating that the item has been received.

Sequences are specified as lists, while the contents of the unordered channel are modeled as a multiset of messages of sort Conf(iguration) using the appropriate equational attributes. The entire system state is a 5-tuple of sort State, built by means of the operator {_,_|_|_,_} in the module below, where the components are: a buffer with the items to be sent, a counter for the acknowledged items, the contents of the unordered channel, a buffer with the items received, and a counter for the items received.[2]

```
fmod UNORDERED-CHANNEL-EQ is
  sorts Nats List Msg Conf State .
  op 0 : -> Nats [ctor] .
  op s : Nats -> Nats [ctor] .
  op nil : -> List [ctor] .
  op _;_ : Nats List -> List [ctor] .   *** list cons
  op _@_ : List List -> List .          *** list append
  op [_,_] : Nats Nats -> Msg [ctor] .
  op ack : Nats -> Msg [ctor] .
  subsort Msg < Conf .
  op null : -> Conf [ctor] .
  op __ : Conf Conf -> Conf [ctor assoc comm id: null] .
  op {_,_|_|_,_} : List Nats Conf List Nats -> State [ctor] .
  vars N : Nats .         vars L P : List .
  eq nil @ L = L .
  eq (N ; L) @ P = N ; (L @ P) .
endfm
```

Having defined all the necessary infrastructure in the previous funcional module, the following system module adds the rules modeling the transitions sending and receiving messages. For instance, the rule labeled rec specifies that a message [N, J] in the channel is read by the receiver, which adds the data N at the end of its sequence, increments its counter to s(J), and puts the corresponding acknowledgement ack(J) in the channel.

```
mod UNORDERED-CHANNEL is
  including UNORDERED-CHANNEL-EQ .
  vars N M J : Nats .     vars L P : List .     var  C : Conf .
```

---

[2] Maude provides predefined modules for natural numbers, lists, and many other datatypes, but they cannot be used in this specification because they are not compatible with most tools in the Maude Formal Environment.

```
rl [snd]: { N ; L, M | C | P, J } => { N ; L, M | [N, M] C | P, J } .
rl [rec]: { L, M | [N, J] C | P, J }
       => { L, M | ack(J) C | P @ (N ; nil), s(J) } .
rl [rec-ack]: { N ; L, J | ack(J) C | P, M } => { L, s(J) | C | P, M } .
endm
```

At the end of Section 4 we will manage to model check that the intended property is indeed satisfied by going through an appropriate quotient specified by a set of equations.

2.3   The Maude Formal Environment

The Maude Formal Environment [3] provides several tools for proving essential properties of Maude modules:

- Maude Termination Tool (MTT) to prove termination of equations and of rules in modules by connecting to external termination tools (we use the APRoVe tool [4] below).
- Church-Rosser Checker (CRC) to check the Church-Rosser property of equational specifications.
- Sufficient Completeness Checker (SCC) to check that defined functions have been fully defined in terms of constructors.
- Coherence Checker (ChC) to check the coherence between rules and equations in system modules.
- Inductive Theorem Prover (ITP) to verify inductive properties of functional modules (we will not make use of this tool in our examples).

To show how these tools are used, we apply them to the system module UNORDERED-CHANNEL introduced above. First, we check termination of the equational part.

```
Maude> (select tool MTT .)
The MTT has been set as current tool.

Maude> (select external tool aprove .)
aprove is now the current external tool.

Maude> (ct UNORDERED-CHANNEL .)
Success: The module UNORDERED-CHANNEL is terminating.
```

Second, we check that the equational part is also Church-Rosser, which depends on its termination (if the specification has no unjoinable critical pairs, then it is locally confluent; if it is in addition terminating, then it is confluent [2]). The submit command, which submits all pending proof obligations to the corresponding tools, makes the connection between the proofs.

```
Maude> (select tool CRC .)
The CRC has been set as current tool.
```

```
Maude> (ccr UNORDERED-CHANNEL .)
Church-Rosser check for UNORDERED-CHANNEL
All critical pairs have been joined.
The specification is locally-confluent.
The module is sort-decreasing.

Maude> (submit .)
The termination goal for the functional part of UNORDERED-CHANNEL has
    been submitted to MTT.
The functional part of module UNORDERED-CHANNEL has been checked
    terminating.
Success: The module is therefore Church-Rosser.
Success: The module UNORDERED-CHANNEL is Church-Rosser.
```

Third, we check that the equational part is sufficiently complete, which depends on it being also terminating and Church-Rosser.

```
Maude> (select tool SCC .)
The SCC has been set as current tool.

Maude> (scc UNORDERED-CHANNEL .)
Sufficient completeness check for UNORDERED-CHANNEL
Completeness counter-examples: none were found
Freeness counter-examples: none were found
Analysis: it is complete and it is sound
Ground weak termination: not proved
Ground sort-decreasingness: not proved

Maude> (submit .)
The sort-decreasingness goal for UNORDERED-CHANNEL has been submitted
    to CRC.
The termination goal for the functional part of UNORDERED-CHANNEL has
    been submitted to MTT.
Church-Rosser check for UNORDERED-CHANNEL
    The module is sort-decreasing.
Success: The functional module UNORDERED-CHANNEL is sufficiently
    complete and has free constructors.
```

Finally, we check that the rules are coherent with respect to the equations, and this depends on all the previous checks.

```
Maude> (select tool ChC .)
The ChC has been set as current tool.

Maude> (cch UNORDERED-CHANNEL .)
Coherence checking of UNORDERED-CHANNEL
All critical pairs have been rewritten and no rewrite with rules can
happen at non-overlapping positions of equations left-hand sides.
The sufficient-completeness, termination and Church-Rosser properties
must still be checked.
```

```
Maude> (submit .)
The Church-Rosser goal for UNORDERED-CHANNEL has been submitted to CRC.
The Sufficient-Completeness goal for UNORDERED-CHANNEL has been
    submitted to SCC.
The termination goal for the functional part of UNORDERED-CHANNEL has
    been submitted to MTT.
Sufficient completeness check for UNORDERED-CHANNEL    [...]
Church-Rosser check for UNORDERED-CHANNEL    [...]
The functional part of module UNORDERED-CHANNEL has been checked
    terminating.
The module UNORDERED-CHANNEL has been checked Church-Rosser.
Success: The module UNORDERED-CHANNEL is coherent.
```

2.4   Model Checking

Temporal logic allows the specification of properties such as safety properties (ensuring that something bad never happens) and liveness properties (ensuring that something good eventually happens), related to the possibly infinite global behavior of a system. Maude includes a model checker to prove properties expressed in linear temporal logic (LTL) [1].

The semantics of temporal logic is defined on Kripke structures, which are triples $\mathcal{A} = (A, \to_{\mathcal{A}}, L)$ such that A is a set of states, $\to_{\mathcal{A}}$ is a total binary relation on A representing the state transitions, and $L : A \longrightarrow \mathcal{P}(AP)$ is a labeling function associating to each state $a \in A$ the set $L(a)$ of those atomic propositions in AP that hold in a.

Given a system module M specifying a rewrite theory $\mathcal{R} = (\Sigma, E, R)$, one chooses a type k in M as the type of states (this is done in the module below by means of a subsort declaration) and extends the module by declaring some state properties Π (of type Prop) and defining their meaning by means of additional equations using the basic "satisfaction operator"

```
op _|=_ : State Prop -> Bool .
```

Section 3 below details how then a Kripke structure $\mathcal{K}(\mathcal{R}, k)_{\Pi} = (T_{\Sigma/E,k}, (\to_{\mathcal{R}}^1)^{\bullet}, L_{\Pi})$ is obtained. The relation $\mathcal{K}(\mathcal{R}, k)_{\Pi}, t \models \varphi$, where φ is a linear temporal formula and t is the initial state, can be model checked under a few assumptions about the module M and its extension with the properties, including the one stating that the set of states reachable from t is finite.

In the crossing-the-river example, the state type is Group and we define the following two basic properties:

– success characterizes the (good) state in which the shepherd and his belongings have all crossed the river; if we assume that in the initial state all of them are on the left side, in the final state all of them are on the right side.
– disaster characterizes the (bad) states in which some eating takes place, because the shepherd is on the other side.

```
mod RIVER-CROSSING-PROP is
  protecting RIVER-CROSSING .
  including MODEL-CHECKER .
  subsort Group < State .
  op initial : -> Group .
  eq initial = s(left) w(left) l(left) c(left) .
  ops disaster success : -> Prop [ctor] .
  vars S S' S'' : Side .
  ceq (w(S) l(S) s(S') c(S'') |= disaster) = true if S =/= S' .
  ceq (w(S'') l(S) s(S') c(S) |= disaster) = true if S =/= S' .
  eq (s(right) w(right) l(right) c(right) |= success) = true .
  eq G:Group |= P:Prop = false [owise] .
endm
```

Since the model checker only returns either **true** or paths that are counterexamples of properties, in order to find a solution to the puzzle, that is, to find a safe path in the river crossing example, we need a formula that expresses the negation of the property we want: a counterexample will then witness a safe path for the shepherd. If no safe path exists, then it is true that whenever **success** is reached, a disastrous state has been traversed before. The following LTL formula specifies this implication:

```
<> success -> ((~ success) U disaster)
```

A counterexample to this temporal logic formula (or any other equivalent formula) is a safe path, completed so as to have a cycle.

```
Maude> red modelCheck(initial, <> success -> ((~ success) U disaster)) .
result ModelCheckResult: counterexample(
    {s(left) w(left) l(left) c(left),'lamb}
    {s(right) w(left) l(right) c(left),'shepherd}
    {s(left) w(left) l(right) c(left),'wdog}
    {s(right) w(right) l(right) c(left),'lamb}
    {s(left) w(right) l(left) c(left),'cabbage}
    {s(right) w(right) l(left) c(right),'shepherd}
    {s(left) w(right) l(left) c(right),'lamb}
    {s(right) w(right) l(right) c(right),'lamb}
    {s(left) w(right) l(left) c(right),'shepherd}
    {s(right) w(right) l(left) c(right),'wdog}
    {s(left) w(left) l(left) c(right),'lamb}
    {s(right) w(left) l(right) c(right),'cabbage}
    {s(left) w(left) l(right) c(left),'wdog},
    {s(right) w(right) l(right) c(left),'lamb}
    {s(left) w(right) l(left) c(left),'lamb})
```

The path described by the first eight lines in this answer to our model checking request provides the solution that we wanted for the crossing-the-river puzzle.

3   Equational Abstractions

The unordered channel example cannot be model checked directly because the space of reachable states is infinite, since the first rule may be repeatedly applied, sending multiple copies of each message into the channel. It requires thus the application of the abstraction technique in order to be model checked. We summarize here the basic concepts necessary to understand our equational abstraction method [5].

An AP-simulation $H : \mathcal{A} \longrightarrow \mathcal{B}$ between Kripke structures $\mathcal{A}$ and $\mathcal{B}$ over the same set AP of atomic propositions is a total relation $H \subseteq A \times B$ such that, when $a \to_{\mathcal{A}} a'$ and aHb, then there is $b' \in B$ with $a'Hb'$ and $b \to_{\mathcal{B}} b'$, and, furthermore, if aHb then $L_{\mathcal{B}}(b) \subseteq L_{\mathcal{A}}(a)$. The simulation H is strict when the previous inclusion is indeed an equality.

A simulation $H : \mathcal{A} \longrightarrow \mathcal{B}$ reflects the satisfaction of a formula φ if $\mathcal{B}, b \models \varphi$ and aHb implies $\mathcal{A}, a \models \varphi$.

Theorem 1. *[5] AP-simulations reflect satisfaction of $LTL^-(AP)$ formulas (where $LTL^-(AP)$ is the negation-free fragment of LTL).*
Strict simulations reflect satisfaction of $LTL(AP)$ formulas.

Often we only have a Kripke structure $\mathcal{M}$ and a surjective function to a set of abstract states $h : M \longrightarrow A$. The minimal system $\mathcal{M}^h_{\min}$ (over A) corresponding to $\mathcal{M}$ and h is defined by $(A, \to_{\mathcal{M}^h_{\min}}, L_{\mathcal{M}^h_{\min}})$, where:

- $x \to_{\mathcal{M}^h_{\min}} y \iff \exists a. \exists b. (h(a) = x \wedge h(b) = y \wedge a \to_{\mathcal{M}} b)$
- $L_{\mathcal{M}^h_{\min}}(a) = \bigcap_{x \in h^{-1}(a)} L_{\mathcal{M}}(x)$.

Theorem 2. *[5] $h : \mathcal{M} \longrightarrow \mathcal{M}^h_{\min}$ is indeed a simulation.*

Minimal systems can also be seen as quotients. For a Kripke structure $\mathcal{A}$ and $\sim$ an equivalence relation on A, define $\mathcal{A}/\sim \ = (A/\sim, \to_{\mathcal{A}/\sim}, L_{\mathcal{A}/\sim})$, where:

- $[a_1] \to_{\mathcal{A}/\sim} [a_2] \iff \exists a'_1 \in [a_1]. \exists a'_2 \in [a_2]. a'_1 \to_{\mathcal{A}} a'_2$
- $L_{\mathcal{A}/\sim}([a]) = \bigcap_{x \in [a]} L_{\mathcal{A}}(x)$.

Theorem 3. *[5] Given $\mathcal{M}$ and h surjective, the Kripke structures $\mathcal{M}^h_{\min}$ and $\mathcal{M}/\sim_h$ are isomorphic, where $x \sim_h y$ iff $h(x) = h(y)$.*

The adjective minimal is appropriate since $\mathcal{M}^h_{\min}$ is the most accurate approximation to $\mathcal{M}$ consistent with h, but it is not always possible to have a computable description of $\mathcal{M}^h_{\min}$ because the transition relation:

$$x \to_{\mathcal{M}^h_{\min}} y \iff \exists a. \exists b. (h(a) = x \wedge h(b) = y \wedge a \to_{\mathcal{M}} b)$$

is not recursive in general. Here we present methods that, when successful, yield a computable description of $\mathcal{M}^h_{\min}$. As explained before, a concurrent system is specified by a rewrite theory $\mathcal{R} = (\Sigma, E, R)$ which determines, for each type k, a transition system $(T_{\Sigma/E,k}, (\to^1_{\mathcal{R}})^\bullet)$ where

- $T_{\Sigma/E,k}$ is the set of equivalence classes $[t]$ of terms of type k, modulo the equations E;
- $(\rightarrow^1_{\mathcal{R}})^\bullet$ completes the one-step rewrite relation $\rightarrow^1_{\mathcal{R}}$ with an identity pair $([t],[t])$ for each deadlock state $[t]$, to get a total relation.

LTL properties are associated to $\mathcal{R}$ and a type k by specifying the basic state predicates Π in an equational theory $(\Sigma', E\cup D)$ extending (Σ, E) conservatively. State properties are constructed with operators $p : s_1 \ldots s_n \rightarrow Prop$ and their semantics is defined by means of equations D using the basic "satisfaction operator" $\_\models\_ : k\ Prop \rightarrow Bool$. A state property $p(u_1, \ldots, u_n)$ holds in a state $[t]$ iff

$$E \cup D \vdash\ t \models p(u_1, \ldots, u_n) = true.$$

The Kripke structure associated to $\mathcal{R}$, k, and Π, with atomic propositions

$$AP_\Pi = \{p(u_1, \ldots, u_n)\ \text{ground} \mid p \in \Pi\}$$

is then defined as $\mathcal{K}(\mathcal{R}, k)_\Pi = (T_{\Sigma/E,k}, (\rightarrow^1_{\mathcal{R}})^\bullet, L_\Pi)$ where

$$L_\Pi([t]) = \{p(u_1, \ldots, u_n) \mid p(u_1, \ldots, u_n)\ \text{holds in}\ [t]\}.$$

Assuming that the equations $E \cup D$ are Church-Rosser and terminating, and that the rewrite theory $\mathcal{R}$ is executable, the resulting Kripke structure is indeed computable.

We can define an abstraction for $\mathcal{K}(\mathcal{R}, k)_\Pi$ by specifying an equational theory extension $(\Sigma, E) \subseteq (\Sigma, E \cup E')$ which gives rise to an equivalence relation $\equiv_{E'}$ on $T_{\Sigma/E}$

$$[t]_E \equiv_{E'} [t']_E \iff E \cup E' \vdash t = t' \iff [t]_{E\cup E'} = [t']_{E\cup E'}$$

and therefore a quotient abstraction $\mathcal{K}(\mathcal{R}, k)_\Pi/\equiv_{E'}$. We then need to answer the following question: Is $\mathcal{K}(\mathcal{R}, k)_\Pi/\equiv_{E'}$ the Kripke structure associated to another rewrite theory?

We focus on those rewrite theories $\mathcal{R}$ satisfying the following requirements:

- $\mathcal{R}$ is k-deadlock free, that is $(\rightarrow^1_{\mathcal{R}})^\bullet = \rightarrow^1_{\mathcal{R}}$ on $T_{\Sigma/E,k}$,
- $\mathcal{R}$ is k-topmost, so k only appears as the coarity of a certain operator $f : k_1 \ldots k_n \longrightarrow k$, and
- no terms of type k appear in the conditions.

A rewrite theory $\mathcal{R}$ can often be transformed into an equivalent one satisfying these requirements [5]. In particular, the unordered channel example satisfies these requirements.

Let us take a closer look at the quotient:

$$\mathcal{K}(\mathcal{R}, k)_\Pi/\equiv_{E'} = (T_{\Sigma/E,k}/\equiv_{E'}, (\rightarrow^1_{\mathcal{R}})^\bullet/\equiv_{E'}, L_{\Pi/\equiv_{E'}}).$$

First, $T_{\Sigma/E}/\equiv_{E'} \cong T_{\Sigma,E\cup E'}$. Then, under the above assumptions, $\mathcal{R}/E' = (\Sigma, E \cup E', R)$ is k-deadlock free and

$$(\rightarrow^1_{\mathcal{R}/E'})^\bullet = \rightarrow^1_{\mathcal{R}/E'} = (\rightarrow^1_{\mathcal{R}})^\bullet/\equiv_{E'}.$$

Therefore, at a purely mathematical level, $\mathcal{R}/E'$ seems appropriate. Now, executability requires that the equations $E \cup E'$ are Church-Rosser and terminating, and that the rules R are coherent with respect to $E \cup E'$. To check or enforce these conditions, one can use the tools available in the Maude Formal Environment, as shown in Section 2.3.

Concerning the state properties in the quotient system, given its definition

$$L_{\Pi/\equiv_{E'}}([t]_{E \cup E'}) = \bigcap_{[x]_E \subseteq [t]_{E \cup E'}} L_{\Pi}([x]_E).$$

it may not be easy to come up with equations D' defining $L_{\Pi/\equiv_{E'}}$. But it becomes easy if the properties are preserved by E' in the following sense:

$$[x]_{E \cup E'} = [y]_{E \cup E'} \implies L_{\Pi}([x]_E) = L_{\Pi}([y]_E).$$

In this case we do not need to change the equations D and therefore we have

$$\mathcal{K}(\mathcal{R}, k)_{\Pi}/\equiv_{E'} \cong \mathcal{K}(\mathcal{R}/E', k)_{\Pi}.$$

Property preservation can be proved inductively or, instead, one can use tools in the Maude Formal Environment to mechanically discharge the corresponding proof obligations.

Once E, E', and R satisfy all these executability requirements, by construction, the quotient simulation $\mathcal{K}(\mathcal{R}, k)_{\Pi} \longrightarrow \mathcal{K}(\mathcal{R}, E)_{\Pi}/\equiv_{E'} \cong \mathcal{K}(\mathcal{R}/E', k)_{\Pi}$ is strict, so it reflects satisfaction of arbitrary LTL formulas. Moreover, since $\mathcal{R}/E'$ is executable, for an initial state t having a finite set of reachable states we can use the Maude model checker to check if a property holds. In this way, we model check on the abstract version the properties we are interested in checking for the original system.

4   Equational Abstraction on the Unordered-Channel Example

Let us go back to the unordered-channel example in Section 2.2. The rule

```
rl [snd]: { N ; L, M | C | P, J } => { N ; L, M | [N, M] C | P, J } .
```

allows sending several times the same message, but then the reachable state space is infinite. To identify repeated copies of sent messages, we add the following equation:

```
mod UNORDERED-CHANNEL-ABSTRACTION is
  including UNORDERED-CHANNEL .
  vars M N P K : Nats .      vars L L' : List .      var C : Conf .
  eq [A1]: { L, M | [N, P] [N, P] C | L', K }
         = { L, M | [N, P] C | L', K } .
endm
```

Verification of Executability Requirements. We can then check using the tools[3] in the Maude Formal Environment that the proposed abstraction is terminating, Church-Rosser, and sufficiently complete (although in the last case we get a warning due to the fact that the added equation is not linear, and therefore cannot be handled by the SCC tool).

```
Maude> (ct UNORDERED-CHANNEL-ABSTRACTION .)
Success: The module UNORDERED-CHANNEL-ABSTRACTION is terminating.

Maude> (ccr UNORDERED-CHANNEL-ABSTRACTION .)
Maude> (submit .)
Success: The module UNORDERED-CHANNEL-ABSTRACTION is Church-Rosser.

Maude> (scc UNORDERED-CHANNEL-ABSTRACTION .)
Warning: The functional module UNORDERED-CHANNEL-ABSTRACTION is
    sufficiently complete and has free constructors. However',
    module UNORDERED-CHANNEL-ABSTRACTION may still not be
    sufficiently complete or not have free constructors.
```

However, the coherence check fails because the ChC tool returns a critical pair:

```
Maude> (select tool ChC .)
The ChC has been set as current tool.

Maude> (cch UNORDERED-CHANNEL-ABSTRACTION .)
Coherence checking of UNORDERED-CHANNEL-ABSTRACTION
The following critical pairs cannot be rewritten:
  cp UNORDERED-CHANNEL-ABSTRACTION2 for A1 and rec
    { L:List,M:Nats | #3:Conf[N:Nats,J:Nats]| P:List,J:Nats }
    => { L:List,M:Nats | #3:Conf ack(J:Nats)[N:Nats,J:Nats]|
    P:List @ N:Nats ; nil,s(J:Nats) }.
  The sufficient-completeness, termination and Church-Rosser
  properties must still be checked.
```

In this particular example, the critical pair indicates that one can lose possible rewrites by applying first the equation and that this can be solved by adding the rule which provides the corresponding rewrite steps. Therefore, to recover coherence, we add the appropriate rule, which is just a simple renaming of the returned critical pair.

Since, after the equational abstraction, multiplicity of messages in the channel no longer matters, the new rule allows to receive a message without deleting it from the channel; thus, in the channel of the righthand side of the rule, we can see that the [N, K] message is kept in the channel together with the corresponding acknowledgement ack(K).

---

[3] In the code shown in this section we omit some intermediate commands and show part of the output, to emphasize thus the final result.

```
mod UNORDERED-CHANNEL-ABSTRACTION-2 is
  including UNORDERED-CHANNEL-ABSTRACTION .
  vars M N K : Nats .     vars L L' : List .    var C : Conf .
  rl [snd2]: { L, M | [N, K] C | L', K }
             => { L, M | [N, K] ack(K) C | L' @ N ; nil, s(K) } .
endm
```

Now we can check that all the executability conditions are indeed satisfied; for instance, in checking coherence we get no critical pair this time.

```
Maude> (select tool ChC .)
The ChC has been set as current tool.
```

```
Maude> (cch UNORDERED-CHANNEL-ABSTRACTION-2 .)
Coherence checking of UNORDERED-CHANNEL-ABSTRACTION-2
    All critical pairs have been rewritten and no rewrite with rules can
    happen at non-overlapping positions of equations left-hand sides.
    The sufficient-completeness, termination and Church-Rosser properties
    must still be checked.
Maude> (submit .)
Success: The module UNORDERED-CHANNEL-ABSTRACTION-2 is coherent.
```

Verification of Property Preservation. We can now move to the specification of the properties. Here the essential property we are looking for is that the protocol achieves in-order communication in spite of the unordered channel. This property may be defined by means of a prefix property on lists, as done in the following module which imports a module BOOLEAN (not shown here) providing Boolean values and standard operations on them.

```
mod UNORDERED-CHANNEL-PROP is
  protecting BOOLEAN .
  protecting UNORDERED-CHANNEL .
  sort Prop .
  op _~_ : Nats Nats -> Bool .    *** equality predicate
  op _|=_ : State Prop -> Bool [frozen] .  *** satisfaction
  vars M N K P : Nats .     vars L L' L'' : List .    var  C : Conf .
  eq 0 ~ 0 = true .
  eq 0 ~ s(N) = false .
  eq s(N) ~ 0 = false .
  eq s(N) ~ s(M) = N ~ M .
  op prefix : List -> Prop [ctor] .
  eq [I1]: { L', N | C | K ; L'', P } |= prefix(M ; L) =
     (M ~ K) and { L', N | C | L'', P } |= prefix(L) .
  eq [I3]: { L', N | C | nil, K } |= prefix(L) = true .
  eq [I4]: {L', N | C | M ; L'', K } |= prefix(nil) = false .
endm
```

We assume that all initial states are of the form

```
{n1 ; ... ; nk ; nil , 0 | null | nil , 0}
```

where the sender's buffer contains a list of numbers n1 ; ... ; nk ; nil and
has its counter set to 0, the communication channel is empty, the receiver's
buffer is also empty, and the receiver's counter is initially set to 0. The following
module puts everything together and declares a concrete initial state.

```
mod UNORDERED-CHANNEL-ABSTRACTION-CHECK is
   extending UNORDERED-CHANNEL-ABSTRACTION-2 .
   including UNORDERED-CHANNEL-PROP .
   op init : -> State .
   eq init = {0 ; s(0) ; s(s(0)) ; nil , 0 | null | nil , 0} .
endm
```

It is easy to see that the set of abstract states is finite and that the module
UNORDERED-CHANNEL is deadlock free. Moreover, to show property preservation,
we can check that the equations in both modules UNORDERED-CHANNEL-PROP and
UNORDERED-CHANNEL-ABSTRACTION-CHECK are terminating, Church-Rosser, and
sufficiently complete, and rules are still coherent.

```
Maude> (ct UNORDERED-CHANNEL-ABSTRACTION-CHECK .)
Success: The module UNORDERED-CHANNEL-ABSTRACTION-CHECK is terminating.

Maude> (ccr UNORDERED-CHANNEL-ABSTRACTION-CHECK .)
Maude> (submit .)
Success: The module UNORDERED-CHANNEL-ABSTRACTION-CHECK is Church-Rosser.

Maude> (scc UNORDERED-CHANNEL-ABSTRACTION-CHECK .)
Maude> (submit .)
Warning: The functional module UNORDERED-CHANNEL-ABSTRACTION-CHECK
   is sufficiently complete and has free constructors. However [...]

Maude> (cch UNORDERED-CHANNEL-ABSTRACTION-CHECK .)
Maude> (submit .)
Success: The module UNORDERED-CHANNEL-ABSTRACTION-CHECK is coherent.
```

Model Checking the Property. Finally, we can model check the desired property
on the abstract version of the unordered communication channel, as follows:

```
mod UNORDERED-CHANNEL-ABSTRACTION-MODEL-CHECK is
   including UNORDERED-CHANNEL-ABSTRACTION-CHECK .
   including LTL-SIMPLIFIER .   *** optional
   including MODEL-CHECKER .
endm
```

```
Maude> reduce in UNORDERED-CHANNEL-ABSTRACTION-MODEL-CHECK :
   modelCheck(init, []prefix(0 ; s(0) ; s(s(0)) ; nil)) .
rewrites: 361 in 41ms cpu (42ms real) (8780 rewrites/second)
result Bool: true
```

The property then holds also in the original system, as justified in Section 3.

5   Concluding Remarks

The equational abstraction technique introduced in [5] and summarized here is fairly simple and takes advantage of the expressiveness of rewriting logic and its Maude implementation [1], as well as of the tools available in the Maude Formal Environment [3]. Other examples are available in the references, but they do not use the Maude Formal Environment in its current integrated form, as we have done with the main example in this paper.

Related work includes the generalization of the equational theory extension $(\Sigma, E) \subseteq (\Sigma, E \cup E')$ to theory interpretations $(\Sigma, E) \longrightarrow (\Sigma', E'')$ and also to (stuttering) simulations, studied in detail in [6].

Future work will be dedicated to improving the interface of the Maude Formal Environment to make it more user-friendly. Also, the Inductive Theorem Prover (ITP) needs more and better integration with the other tools.

Acknowledgments. We are very grateful to our colleagues José Meseguer and Miguel Palomino, whose work on equational abstraction is summarized in this paper; the organizers of *CBSoft* and *SBMF 2014* for their invitation to present this work in such a nice environment; and Christiano Braga for all his enthusiastic help.

References

1. Clavel, M., Durán, F., Eker, S., Lincoln, P., Martí-Oliet, N., Meseguer, J., Talcott, C.: All About Maude - A High-Performance Logical Framework. LNCS, vol. 4350. Springer, Heidelberg (2007)
2. Durán, F., Meseguer, J.: On the Church-Rosser and coherence properties of conditional order-sorted rewrite theories. Journal of Logic and Algebraic Programming **81**(7–8), 816–850 (2012)
3. Durán, F., Rocha, C., Álvarez, J.M.: Towards a Maude Formal Environment. In: Agha, G., Danvy, O., Meseguer, J. (eds.) Formal Modeling: Actors, Open Systems, Biological Systems. LNCS, vol. 7000, pp. 329–351. Springer, Heidelberg (2011)
4. Giesl, J., et al.: Proving termination of programs automatically with AProVE. In: Demri, S., Kapur, D., Weidenbach, C. (eds.) IJCAR 2014. LNCS, vol. 8562, pp. 184–191. Springer, Heidelberg (2014)
5. Meseguer, J., Palomino, M., Martí-Oliet, N.: Equational abstractions. Theoretical Computer Science **403**(2–3), 239–264 (2008)
6. Meseguer, J., Palomino, M., Martí-Oliet, N.: Algebraic simulations. Journal of Logic and Algebraic Programming **79**(2), 103–143 (2010)

Formalization of Zsyntax to Reason About Molecular Pathways in HOL4

Sohaib Ahmad[1], Osman Hasan[1], Umair Siddique[1 (✉)], and Sofiéne Tahar[2]

[1] School of Electrical Engineering and Computer Science (SEECS),
National University of Sciences and Technology (NUST), Islamabad, Pakistan
{11mseesahmad,osman.hasan,umair.siddique}@seecs.nust.edu.pk
[2] Department of Electrical and Computer Engineering, Concordia University,
Montreal, Quebec, Canada
tahar@ece.concordia.ca

Abstract. The behavioral characterization of biological organisms is a fundamental requirement for both the understanding of the physiological properties and potential drug designs. One of the most widely used approaches in this domain is molecular pathways, which offers a systematic way to represent and analyze complex biological systems. Traditionally, such pathways are analyzed using paper-and-pencil based proofs and simulations. However, these methods cannot ascertain accurate analysis, which is a serious drawback for safety-critical applications (e.g., analysis of cancer cells and cerebral malarial network). In order to overcome these limitations, we recently proposed to formally reason about molecular pathways within the sound core of a theorem prover. As a first step towards this direction, we formally expressed three logical operators and four inference rules of Zsyntax , which is a deduction language for molecular pathways. In the current paper, we extend this formalization by verifying a couple of behavioral properties of Zsyntax based deduction using the HOL4 theorem prover. This verification not only ensures the correctness of our formalization of Zsyntax but also facilitates its usage for the formal reasoning about molecular pathways. For illustration purposes, we formally analyze a molecular reaction of the glycolytic pathway leading from D-Glucose to Fructose-1,6-bisphosphate.

1 Introduction

Molecular biology is extensively used to construct models of biological processes in the form of networks or pathways, such as protein-protein interaction networks and signaling pathways. The analysis of these biological networks, usually referred to as biological regulatory networks (BRNs) or gene regulatory networks (GRNs) [10], is based on the principles of molecular biology to understand the dynamics of complex living organisms. Moreover, the analysis of molecular pathways plays a vital role in investigating the treatment of various human infectious diseases and future drug design targets. For example, the analysis of BRNs has been recently used to predict treatment decisions for sepsis patients [15].

© Springer International Publishing Switzerland 2015
C. Braga and N. Martí-Oliet (Eds.): SBMF 2014, LNCS 8941, pp. 32–47, 2015.
DOI: 10.1007/978-3-319-15075-8_3

Traditionally, the molecular biology based analysis is carried out by biologists in the form of wet-lab experiments (e.g. [7,13]). These experiments, despite being very slow and expensive, do not ensure accurate results due to the inability to accurately characterize the complex biological processes in an experimental setting. Other alternatives for deducing molecular reactions include paper-and-pencil proof methods (e.g. using Boolean modeling [28] or kinetic logic [29]) or computer-based techniques (e.g. [30]) for analyzing molecular biology problems. The manual proofs become quite tedious for large systems, where the calculation of unknown parameters takes several hundred proof steps, and are thus prone to human errors. The computer-based methods consist of graph theoretic techniques [21], Petri nets [11] and model checking [3]. These approaches have shown very promising results in many applications of molecular biology (e.g. [8,14]). However, these methods are not generic and hence have been used to describe some specific areas of molecular biology [4]. Moreover, the inherent state-space explosion problem of model checking [20] limits the scope of this success only to systems where the biological entities can acquire a small set of possible levels.

Theorem proving [12], i.e., a widely used formal methods technique, does not suffer from the state-space explosion problem of model checking, and has also been advocated for conducting molecular biology based analysis [31]. The main idea behind theorem proving is to construct a computer-based mathematical model of the given system and then verify the properties of interest using deductive reasoning. The foremost requirement for conducting the theorem proving based analysis of any system is to formalize the mathematical or logical foundations required to model and analyze that system in an appropriate logic. There have been several attempts to formalize the foundations of molecular biology. For example, the earliest axiomatization even dates back to 1937 [32] and other efforts related to the formalization of biology are presented in [25,33]. Recent formalizations, based on K-Calculus [6] and π-Calculus [22–24], also include some formal reasoning support for biological systems. Another interesting approach is to model signal transduction pathways using pathway logic [27] which is based on rewriting logic. But the understanding and utilization of these techniques is very cumbersome for a working biologist as highlighted by Fontana in [9].

In order to develop a biologist friendly formal deduction framework for reasoning about molecular reactions, we propose to formalize the Zsyntax [4] language in higher-order logic. Zsyntax is a formal language that supports modeling and logical deductions about any biological process. The main strength of Zsyntax is its biologist-centered nature as its operators and inference rules have been designed in such a way that they are understandable by the biologists. Traditionally, logical deductions about biological processes, expressed in Zsyntax , were done manually based on the paper-and-pencil based approach. This limits the usage of Zsyntax to smaller problems and also makes the deduction process error-prone due to the human involvement. As a first step towards overcoming this limitation, we formalized the logical operators and inference rules of Zsyntax in higher-order logic [2]. In the current paper, we build upon these formal definitions to verify a couple of key behavioral properties of Zsyntax based molecular pathways using the HOL4 theorem prover. The formal verification of these properties raises the confidence level in our definitions of Zsyntax operators and inference rules, which have complex interrelationships. Moreover, these formally verified properties can be used to facilitate the formal reasoning about chemical reactions at the molecular level. In order to illustrate the usefulness and effectiveness of our formalization for analyzing real-world problems in molecular biology, we present the formal analysis of a molecular reaction of the glycolytic pathway leading from D-Glucose to Fructose-1,6-bisphosphate [4].

Our current framework handles static reactions but it can be further extended to study the reaction kinetics [4] due to the flexibility of Zsyntax . The main motivation behind using higher-order-logic theorem proving in our work is to be able to leverage upon the high expressiveness of higher-order logic and thus reason about differential equations and probabilistic properties, which form an integral part of reaction kinetics. However, the scope of the current paper is on the formalization of Zsyntax based deduction calculus for molecular pathways but this formalization can later be extended to support reaction kinetics as well because it is done in a higher-order-logic theorem prover.

The rest of the paper is organized as follows: Section 2 provides an introduction to Zsyntax and the HOL4 theorem prover. The higher-order-logic formalization of Zsyntax operators and inference rules using HOL4 is described in Section 3. This is followed by the descriptions of the behavioral properties of Zsyntax along with their formal proof sketches in Section 4. The illustrative case study on the glycolytic pathway is presented in Section 4. We conclude the paper in Section 5 while highlighting some interesting potential applications of our work.

2   Preliminaries

2.1   Zsyntax

Zsyntax [4] exploits the analogy between biological processes and logical deduction. Some of the key features of Zsyntax are: 1) the ability to express molecular reactions in a mathematical way; 2) heuristic nature, i.e., if the conclusion of a reaction is known, then one can deduce the missing data from the initialization data; 3) computer implementable semantics. Zsyntax consists of the following three operators:

Z-Interaction: The interaction of two molecules is expressed by the Z-Interaction (*) operator. In biological reactions, Z-interaction is not associative.

Z-Conjunction: The aggregate of same or different molecules (not necessarily interacting with each other) is formed using the Z-Conjunction (&) operator. Z-Conjunction is fully associative.

Z-Conditional: A path from A to B under the condition C is expressed using the Z-Conditional ($\rightarrow$) operator as: $A \rightarrow B$ if there is a C that allows it.

Zsyntax supports four inference rules, given in Table 1, that play a vital role in deducing the outcomes of biological reactions:

Besides the regular formulas that can be derived based on the above mentioned operators and inference rule, Zsyntax also makes use of *Empirically Valid*

Table 1. Zsyntax Inference Rules

Inference Rules	Definition
Elimination of Z-conditional($\rightarrow$E)	if $C \vdash (A \rightarrow B)$ and $(D \vdash A)$ then $(C \& D \vdash B)$
Introduction of Z-conditional($\rightarrow$I)	$C \& A \vdash B$ then $C \vdash (A \rightarrow B)$
Elimination of Z-conjunction(&E)	$C \vdash (A \& B)$ then $(C \vdash A)$ and $(C \vdash B)$
Introduction of Z-conjunction(&I)	$(C \vdash A)$ and $(D \vdash B)$ then $(C \& D) \vdash (A \& B)$

Formulae (EVF). These EVFs basically represent the non-logical axioms of molecular biology and are assumed to be validated empirically in the lab.

It has been shown that any biological reaction can be mapped and their final outcomes can be derived using the above mentioned three operators and four inference rules [4]. For example, consider a scenario in which three molecules A, B and C react with each other to yield another molecule Z. This can be represented as a Zsyntax theorem as follows:

$$A \& B \& C \vdash Z$$

The Z-Conjunction operator & is used to represent the given aggregate of molecules and then the inference rules from Table 1 are applied on these molecules along with some EVFs (chemical reactions verified in laboratories) to obtain the final product Z. For the above example, these EVFs could be:

$$A * B \rightarrow X \text{ and } X * C \rightarrow Z$$

meaning that A will react with B to yield X and X in return will react with C to yield the final product Z.

The main contribution of our paper is the formal verification of the Zsyntax based deduction method based on the higher-order-logic formalization of the above-mentioned operators and inference rules using the HOL4 theorem prover. This work will in turn facilitate the derivation of biological reactions within the sound core of HOL4.

2.2 HOL4 Theorem Prover

HOL4 is an interactive theorem prover developed at the University of Cambridge, UK, for conducting proofs in higher-order logic. It utilizes the simple type theory of Church [5] along with Hindley-Milner polymorphism [17] to implement higher-order logic. HOL4 has been successfully used as a verification framework for both software and hardware as well as a platform for the formalization of pure mathematics.

In order to ensure secure theorem proving, the logic in the HOL4 system is represented in the strongly-typed functional programming language ML [19]. An ML abstract data type is used to represent higher-order logic theorems and the only way to interact with the theorem prover is by executing ML procedures that operate on values of these data types. The HOL4 core consists of only 5 basic axioms and 8 primitive inference rules, which are implemented as ML functions. Soundness is assured as every new theorem must be verified by applying these basic axioms and primitive inference rules or any other previously verified theorems/inference rules.

A HOL4 theory is a collection of valid HOL4 types, constants, axioms and theorems, and is usually stored as a file in computers. Users can reload a HOL4 theory in the HOL4 system and utilize the corresponding definitions and theorems right away. Various mathematical concepts have been formalized and saved as HOL4 theories by the HOL4 users. We utilize the HOL4 theories of Booleans, arithmetics and lists extensively in our work. Table 2 provides the mathematical interpretations of some HOL4 symbols and functions frequently used in this paper.

Table 2. HOL4 Symbols and Functions

HOL Symbol	Standard Symbol	Meaning
$\wedge$	*and*	Logical *and*
$\vee$	*or*	Logical *or*
$\neg$	*not*	Logical *negation*
::	*cons*	Adds a new element to a list
++	*append*	Joins two lists together
HD L	*head*	Head element of list L
TL L	*tail*	Tail of list L
EL n L	*element*	n^{th} element of list L
MEM a L	*member*	True if a is a member of list L
LENGTH L	*length*	Length of list L
FST	fst (a, b) = a	First component of a pair
SND	snd (a, b) = b	Second component of a pair
SUC n	$n + 1$	Successor of a *num*

3   Formalization of Zsyntax

We modeled the molecules as variables of arbitrary data types (α) in our formalization of Zsyntax [2]. A list of molecules (α *list*) represents the Z-Interaction or a molecular reaction among the elements of the list. The Z-Conjunction operator forms a collection of non-reacting molecules and can now be formalized as a list of list of molecules (α *list list*). This data type allows us to apply the Z-Conjunction operator between individual molecules (a list with a single element) or multiple interacting molecules (a list with multiple elements). The Z-Conditional operator is used to update the status of molecules, i.e., generate a new set of molecules based on the available EVFs (wet-lab verified reactions). Each EVF is modeled in our formalization as a pair (α *list # α list list*) where the first element is a list of molecules (α *list*) indicating the reacting molecules and the second element is a list of list of molecules (α *list list*) indicating the resulting set of molecules after the reaction between the molecules of the first element of the pair has taken place. A collection of EVFs is represented as a list of EVFs ((α *list # α list list)list*) in our formalization.

The elimination of Z-Conditional rule is the same as the elimination of implication rule (Modus Ponens) in propositional logic and thus it can be directly handled by the HOL4 simplification and rewriting rules. Similarly, the introduction of Z-Conditional rule can also be inferred from the rules of propositional logic and can be handled by the HOL4 system without the introduction of a new inference rule. The elimination of the Z-Conjunction rule allows us to infer the presence of a single molecule from an aggregate of inferred molecules. This rule is usually applied at the end of the reaction to check if the desired molecule has been obtained. Based on our data types, described above, this rule can be formalized in HOL4 by returning a particular molecule from a list of molecules:

Definition 1. Elimination of Z-Conjunction Rule
⊢ ∀ L m. z_conj_elim L m = if MEM m L then [m] else L

The function z_conj_elim has the data type (α $list$ → α → α $list$). The above function returns the given element as a single element in a list if it is a member of the given list. Otherwise, it returns the argument list as it is.

The introduction of Z-Conjunction rule along with Z-Interaction allows us to perform a reaction between any of the available molecules during the experiment. Based on our data types, this rule is equivalent to the append operation of lists.

Definition 2. Introduction of Z-Conjunction and Z-Interaction
⊢ ∀ L m n. z_conj_int L m n = FLAT [EL m L; EL n L]::L

The above definition has the data type (α $list$ $list$ → num → num → α $list$ $list$). The HOL4 functions FLAT and EL are used to flatten a list of list to a single list and return a particular element of a list, respectively. Thus, the function z_conj_int takes a list L and appends the list of two of its elements m and n on its head.

Based on the laws of stoichiometry [4], the reacting molecules using the Z-Conjunction operator have to be deleted from the aggregate of molecules. The following function represents this behavior in our formalization:

Definition 3. Reactants Deletion
⊢ ∀ L m n. z_del L m n = if m > n
                   then del (del L m) n
                   else del (del L n) m

Here the function del L m deletes the element at index m of the list L and returns the updated list as follows:

Definition 4. Element Deletion
⊢ ∀ L. del L 0 = TL L ∧
  ∀ L n. del L (n + 1) = HD L::del (TL L) n

Thus, the function z_del L m n deletes the mth and n^{th} elements of the given list L. We delete the higher indexed element before the lower one in order to make sure that the first element deletion does not effect the index of the second element that is required to be deleted. The above data types and definitions can be used to

formalize any molecular pathway (which is expressible using Zsyntax) and reason
about its correctness within the sound core of the HOL4 theorem prover.

Our main objective is to develop a framework that accepts a list of initial
molecules and possible EVFs and allows the user to formally deduce the final
outcomes of the corresponding biological experiment. In this regard, we first
develop a function that compares a particular combination of molecules with all
the EVFs and upon finding a match introduces the newly formed molecule in
the initial list and deletes the consumed instances.

Definition 5. EVF Matching
```
⊢ ∀ L E m n.
z_EVF L E 0 m n =
    if FST (EL 0 E) = HD L
        then (T,z_del (TL L ++ SND (EL 0 E)) m n
        else (F,TL L) ∧
  ∀ L E p m n.
z_EVF L E (p + 1) m n =
    if FST (EL (p + 1) E) = HD L
        then (T,z_del (TL ++ SND (EL (p + 1) E)) m n
        else z_EVF L E p m n
```

The data type of the function z_EVF is: (α list list $\rightarrow$ (α list#α list list) list
$\rightarrow$ num $\rightarrow$ num $\rightarrow$ num $\rightarrow$ bool # α list list). The function LENGTH
returns the length of a list. The function z_EVF takes a list of molecules L and
recursively checks its head, or the top most element, against all elements of
the EVF list E. If there is no match, then the function returns a pair with its
first element being false (F), indicating that no match occurred, and the second
element equals the tail of the input list L. Otherwise, if a match is found then
the function replaces the head of list L with the second element of the EVF pair
and deletes the matched elements from the initial list as these elements have
already been consumed. This modified list is then returned along with a true (T)
value, which acts as a flag to indicate an element replacement.

Next, in order to deduce the final outcome of the experiment, we have to call
the function z_EVF recursively by placing all the possible combinations of the
given molecules at the head of list L one by one.

Definition 6. Recursive Function for calling z_EVF
```
⊢ ∀ L E m n. z_deduction_recur L E m n 0 = (T,L) ∧
  ∀ L E m n q. z_deduction_recur L E m n (q + 1) =
    if FST (z_recur2 L E m n) ⇔ T
      then z_deduction_recur (SND (z_recur2 L E m n)) E
                            (LENGTH (SND (z_recur2 L E m n)) - 1)
                            (LENGTH (SND (z_recur2 L E m n)) - 1) q
      else (T,SND (z_recur2 L E (LENGTH L - 1) (LENGTH L - 1)))
```

The data type of function z_deduction_recur is (α list list $\rightarrow$ (α list #α
list list) list $\rightarrow$ num $\rightarrow$ num $\rightarrow$ num $\rightarrow$ bool # α list list). It accepts
the list of molecules L and the list of EVFs E along with their corresponding

indices m and n, respectively, and a recursion variable q. It returns a pair with the first element being a Boolean flag, which becomes true when there are no more remaining reactions, and the second element being the list of molecules representing the post-reaction state. The function z_decuction_recur recursively calls the function z_EVF for all possible molecule combinations using the function z_recur2, which in turn uses the function z_recur1 for this purpose. The arguments m and n of functions z_recur1 and z_recur2 are initialized with LENGTH L and the sole purpose of these functions is to exhaust all possible combinations of the variables m and n for the function z_conj_int, given in Definition 5. The formalization of the above mentioned functions and more details about their behavior can be obtained from [1, 2].

In order to model a complete experiment for a given list of molecules, the variable of recursion in the function z_deduction_recur should be assigned a value that is greater than the total number of EVFs so that the application of none of the EVF is missed. Similarly, the variables m and n of the function z_deduction_recur should be assigned the values of (LENGTH L - 1) to ensure that all combinations of the list L are checked against the elements of the list of EVFs. Thus, the final deduction function for Zsyntax can be expressed in HOL4 as follows:

Definition 7. Final Deduction Function for Zsyntax
⊢ ∀ L E. z_deduction L E =
     SND (z_deduction_recur L E (LENGTH L - 1) (LENGTH L - 1) LENGTH E)

The data type of function z_deduction is (α list list → (α list # α list list) list → α list list). It accepts the initial list of molecules and the list of valid EVFs and returns a list of final outcomes of the experiment under the given conditions, by calling the function z_decuction_recur.

The formal definitions, presented in this section, allow us to recursively check all the possible combinations of the initial molecules against the first elements of given EVFs. In case of a match, the corresponding EVF is applied by replacing the reacting molecules with their outcome in the molecule list and the process restarts again to find other possible matches from the new list of molecules. This process terminates when no more molecules are found to be reacting with each other and at this point we will have the list of post-reaction molecules. The desired result can then be obtained from these molecules using the elimination of Z-Conjunction rule, given in Definition 1. The main benefit of the development, presented in this section, is that it facilitates automated reasoning about the molecular biological experiments within the sound core of a theorem prover.

4   Formal Verification of Zsyntax Properties

In order to ensure the correctness and soundness of our definitions, we use them to verify a couple of properties representing the most important characteristics of molecular reactions. The first property deals with the case when there is no combination of reacting molecules in the list of molecules and in this case we verify that after the Zsyntax based experiment execution both the pre and post-experiment lists of molecules are the same. The second property captures the behavior of the scenario when the given list of molecules contains only one set of reacting molecules and in this case we verify that after the Zsyntax based experiment execution the post-experiment list of molecules contains the product of the reacting molecules minus its reactants along with the remaining molecules provided initially. We represent these scenarios as formally specified properties in higher-order logic using our formal definitions, given in the previous section. These properties are then formally verified in HOL4.

4.1   Scenario 1: No Reaction

We verify the following theorem for the first scenario:

Theorem 1
⊢ ∀ E L.
       ∼(NULL E) ∧ ∼(NULL L) ∧
       (∀ a m n. MEM a E ∧ m < LENGTH L ∧ n < LENGTH L
             ⇒ ∼MEM (FST a) [HD (z_conj_int L m n)])
       ⇒ z_deduction L E = L

The variables E and L represent the lists of EVFs and molecules, respectively. The first two assumptions ensure that both of these lists have to be non-empty, which are the pre-conditions for a molecular reaction to take place. The next conjunct in the assumption list of Theorem 1 represents the formalization of the no-reaction-possibility condition as according to this condition no first element of any pair in the list of EVFs E is a member of the head of the list formed by the function z_conj_int, which picks the elements corresponding to the two given indices (that range over the complete length of the list of molecules L) and appends them as a flattened single element on the given list L. This constraint is quantified for all variables a, m and n and thus ensures that no combination of molecules in the list L matches any one of the first elements of the EVF list E. Thus, under this constraint, no reaction can take place for the given lists L and E. The conclusion of Theorem 1 represents the scenario that the output of our formalization of Zsyntax based reaction would not make any change in the given molecule list L and thus verifies that under the no-reaction-possibility condition our formalization also did not update the molecule list.

The verification of this theorem is interactively done by ensuring the no-update scenario for all molecule manipulation functions, i.e., z_EVF, z_recur1, z_recur2 and z_deduction_recur, under the no-reaction-possibility condition [1]. For example, the corresponding theorem for z_EVF function is as follows:

Theorem 2
⊢ ∀ E L m n P.
       ∼(NULL E) ∧ ∼(NULL L) ∧ m < LENGTH L ∧ n < LENGTH L ∧
       P < LENGTH E ∧ (∀ a. MEM a E ⇒ ∼MEM (FST a) [HD L])
       ⇒ z_EVF L E P m n = (F,TL L)

The assumptions of above theorem ensure that both lists L and E are not empty and the arguments of the function z_EVF are bounded by the LENGTH of L and E. The last conjunct in the assumption list models the no-reaction-possibility condition in the context of the function z_EVF. The conclusion of the theorem states that no update takes place under the given conditions by ensuring that the function z_EVF returns a pair with the first element being F (False), representing no match, and the second element being equal to TL L, which is actually equal to the original list L since an element was appended on head of L by the parent function.

4.2   Scenario 2: Single Reaction

The second scenario complements the first scenario and caters for the case when a reaction is possible and we verify that the molecules list is indeed updated based on the outcomes of that reaction. In order to be able to track the reaction and the corresponding update, we limit ourselves to only one reaction in this scenario but since we verify a generic theorem (universally quantified) for all possibilities our result can be extended to cater for multiple reactions as well. The theorem corresponding to this scenario 2 is as follows:

Theorem 3
⊢ ∀ E L z m' n'.
      ~NULL E ∧ ~NULL (SND (EL z E)) ∧ 1 < LENGTH L ∧
      m' ≠ n' ∧ m' < LENGTH L ∧ n' < LENGTH L ∧ z < LENGTH E ∧
      ALL_DISTINCT (L ++ SND (EL z E)) ∧
      (∀ a b. a ≠ b ⇒ FST (EL a E) ≠ FST (EL b E)) ∧
      (∀ K m n. m < LENGTH K ∧ n < LENGTH K ∧
      (∀ j. MEM j K ⇒ MEM j L ∨ ∃ q. MEM q E ∧ MEM j (SND q)) ⇒
          if (EL m K = EL m' L) ∧ (EL n K = EL n' L)
            then HD (z_conj_int K m n) = FST (EL z E)
            else ∀ a. MEM a E ⇒ FST a ≠ HD (z_conj_int K m n))
      ⇒ z_deduction L E = z_del (L ++ SND (EL z E)) m' n'

The first two assumptions ensure that neither the list E, i.e., the list of EVFs, nor the second element of the pair at index z of the list E is empty. Similarly, the third assumption ensures that the list L, i.e., the list of initial molecules, contains at least two elements. These constraints ensure that we can have at least one reaction with the resultant being available at index z of the EVF list. The next four assumptions ensure that the indices m' and n' are distinct and these along with the index z fall within the range of elements of their respective lists of molecules L or EVFs E. According to the next assumption, i.e., ALL DISTINCT (L ++ SND (EL z E)), all elements of the list L and the resulting molecules of the EVF at index z are distinct, i.e., no molecule can be found two or more times in the initial list L or the post-reaction list E. The next assumption, i.e., (∀ a b. a ≠ b ⇒ FST (EL a E) ≠ FST (EL b E)), guarantees that all first elements of the pairs in list E are also distinct. Note that this is different from the previous condition since the list E contains pairs as elements and the uniqueness of the pairs does not ensure the uniqueness of its first elements. The final condition models the presence of only one pair of reactants scenario. According to the assumptions of this implication condition, the variable K is used to represent a list that only has elements from list L or the second elements of the pairs in list E. Thus, it models the molecules list in a live experiment. Moreover, the variables m and n represent the indices of the list K and thus they must have a value less than the total elements in the list K (since the first element is indexed 0 in the HOL4 formalization of lists). Now, if the indices m and n become equal to m' and n', respectively, then the head element of the z_conj_int K m n would be equal to FST of EL z E. Otherwise, for all other values of indices m and n, no combination of molecules obtained by HD(Z_conj_int K m n) would be equal to the first element of any pair of the list E. Thus, the if case ensures that the variables m' and n' point to the reacting molecules in the list of molecules L and the variable z points to their corresponding resultant molecule in the EVF list. Moreover, the else case ensures that there is only one set of reacting molecules in the list L. The conclusion of the theorem formally describes the scenario when the resulting element, available at the location z of the EVF list, is appended to the list of molecules while the elements available at the indices m' and n' of L are removed during the execution of the function z_deduction on the given lists L and E.

The proof of Theorem 3 is again based on verifying sub-goals corresponding to this scenario for all the sub-functions, i.e., z_EVF, z_recur1, z_recur2 and z_deduction_recur. The formal reasoning for all of these proofs involved various properties of the del function for a list element and some of the key theorems developed for this purpose in our development are given in Table 3 and more details can be found in [1].

The formalization described in this section consumed about 500 man hours and approximately 2000 lines of HOL4 code, mainly due to the undecidable nature of higher-order logic. However, this effort raises the confidence level on the correctness of our formalization of Zsyntax . This fact distinguishes our work from all the other formal methods based techniques used in the context of BRNs, where the deduction rules are applied without being formally checked. Moreover, our formally verified theorems can also be used in the formal analysis of molecular pathways. The assumptions of these theorems provide very useful insights about the constraints under which a reaction or no reaction would take place. To the best of our knowledge, this is the first time that properties, like Theorems 1 and 3, about a molecular pathway experiment have been formally verified. Thus, the identification of these properties and their formal verification both constitute contributions of this paper.

5   Case Study: Pathway Leading to Fructose-1, 6-Bisphosphate

Formation of Fructose-1,6-bisphosphate (F1,6P) is an intermediate step in glycolysis, i.e., a sequence of enzyme catalyzed reaction that breaks down glucose

Table 3. Formally Verified Properties of the `del` Function

Signature	Theorem
del_ASSOC_THM	⊢ ∀ L E m. m < LENGTH L ⇒ del (L ++ E) m = del L m ++ E
del_LENGTH_THM	⊢ ∀ L E m. m < LENGTH L ⇒ LENGTH (del L m) = LENGTH L − 1
del_EL_THM	⊢ ∀ L m n. m < n ∧ n < LENGTH L ∧ 1 < LENGTH L ⇒ EL m L = EL m (del L n)
del_DISTINCT_THM	⊢ ∀ L n. n < LENGTH L ∧ ALL_DISTINCT L ⇒ ALL_DISTINCT (del L n)
del_MEM_THM	⊢ ∀ L a m. m < LENGTH L ∧ MEM a (del L m) ⇒ MEM a L
del_NOT_MEM_THM	⊢ ∀ L m. ALL_DISTINCT L ∧ m < LENGTH L ⇒∼ MEM (EL m L) (del L m)

and forms pyruvate, which is then used to supply energy to living cells through the citric acid cycle [18]. In this section, we show how this pathway involving F1,6P can be formally verified in HOL4 using our formalization of Zsyntax .

The theorem representing the reaction of the glycolytic pathway leading from D-Glucose to F1,6P [4] can be described in classical Zsyntax format as follows:

$$\text{Glc \& HK \& GPI \& PFK \& ATP \& ATP} \vdash \text{F1,6P}$$

Using our formalization, this theorem can be defined in HOL4 as follows:

```
⊢ DISTINCT [Glc; HK; GPI; PFK; ATP; ADP; G6P; F6P; F16P] ⟹
(z_conj_elim (z_deduction [[Glc];[HK];[GPI];[PFK];[ATP];[ATP]]
              [(([Glc;HK],[[HK];Glc]]);
               ([HK;Glc;ATP],[[HK];[G6P];[ADP]]);
               ([G6P;GPI],[[F6P];[GPI]]);
               ([F6P;PFK],[[PFK;F6P]]);
               ([PFK;F6P;ATP],[[PFK];[F16P];[ADP]])] ) [F16P]
= [[F16P]]
```

The first list argument of the function `z_deduction` is the initial aggregate (IA) of molecules that are available for reaction and the second list argument of the function `z_deduction` represents the valid EVFs for this reaction. The EVFs mentioned in the form of pairs and involving the molecules (G6P, F6P, etc.) are obtained from wet lab experiments, as reported in [4]. The `DISTINCT` function used above makes sure that all molecule variables (from initial aggregate and EVFs) used in this theorem represent distinct molecules. Thus, the function `z_deduction` would deduce the final list of molecules under these particular conditions. The function `z_conj_elim` will return the molecule `F1,6P` if it is present in the post-reaction list of molecules, as previously described.

Figure 1 shows the pathway leading to F1,6P in a step-wise manner. The gray-coloured circles show the chemical interactions and black colour represents the desired product in the pathway, whereas each rectangle shows total number of molecules in the reaction at a given time. It is obvious from the figure that

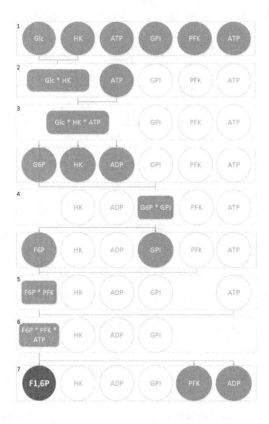

Fig. 1. Reaction Representing the Formulation of F1,6P

whenever a reaction yields a product, the reactants get consumed (no longer remain in the list) hence satisfying the stoichiometry of a reaction.

As part of this work, we also developed a simplifier Z_SYNTAX_SIMP [1] that simplifies the proof with a single iteration of the function z_deduction_recur and works very efficiently with the proofs involving our functions. The proof steps can be completely automated and the proof can be done in one step as well. However, we have kept the reasoning process manual purposefully as this way users can observe the status of the reaction at every iteration, which is a very useful feature to get an insight of what is happening inside a reaction. Each application of Z_SYNTAX_SIMP on the reaction, depicted in Figure 1, would result in moving from a state n to $n + 1$.

The verification time required for each iteration step is given in Table 4. HOL4 was running on a linux based machine (Intel Core i5, 4GB RAM). The iteration time depends on the total number of molecules (elements of list) present at a given iteration. Low number of molecules translate to less number of possible combinations, which in turn leads to less time required to move to the next iteration.

Table 4. Runtime per Iteration

Iteration	Duration (Seconds)
$1 \to 2$	11.996
$2 \to 3$	7.376
$3 \to 4$	12.964
$4 \to 5$	12.756
$5 \to 6$	9.240
$6 \to 7$	0.048

Our HOL4 proof script is available for download [1], and thus can be used for further developments and analysis of different molecular pathways. It is important to note that formalizing Zsyntax and then verifying its properties was a very tedious effort. However, it took only 10 lines of code to define and verify the theorem related to the above case study in HOL4, which clearly illustrates the usefulness of our foundational work.

We have shown that our formalization is capable of modeling molecular reactions using Zsyntax inference rules, i.e., given a set of possible EVFs, our formalism can derive a final aggregate **B** from an initial aggregate **A** automatically. In case of a failure to deduce **B**, the proposed method still provides the biologist with all the intermediate steps so that one can examine the reaction in detail and figure out the possible cause of failure.

The evident benefit of our reasoning approach is its automatic nature as the user does not need to think about the proof steps and which EVFs to apply where. However, the most useful benefit of the proposed approach is its accuracy as the theorems are being verified in a formal way using a sound theorem prover. Thus, there is no risk of human error or wrong application of EVFs. Finally, due to the computer-based analysis, the proposed approach is much more scalable than the paper-and-pencil based analysis presented in [4].

6   Conclusion

Most of the existing formal verification research related to molecular biology has been focussed on using model checking. As a complementary approach, the primary focus of the current paper is on using a theorem prover for reasoning about molecular pathways. The main strength of this approach, compared to existing model checking related work, is that the underlying methods and deduction rules can also be formally verified besides the verification of a particular molecular pathway case. Leveraging upon this strength, we formally verified two key behavioral properties of molecular pathways based on the Zsyntax language, which presents a deduction style formalism for molecular biology in the most biologist-centered way. Besides ensuring the correctness of our formalization of the Zsyntax operators and inference rules, the formally verified properties also play a vital role in reasoning about molecular pathways in the sound core of a theorem prover. The practical utilization and effectiveness of the proposed development has been shown by presenting the automatic analysis of Glycolytic pathway leading to Fructose-1,6-bisphosphate.

The proposed work opens the doors to many new directions of research. Firstly, we are developing a GUI to add more biologist friendly features in it. Moreover, we are also targeting some larger case studies, such as Dysregulation of the cell cycle pathway during tumor progression [16] and Fanconi Anemia/Breast Cancer (FA/BRCA) pathway [26]. Another interesting future direction is to leverage the high expressiveness of higher-order-logic and utilize calculus and differential theoretic reasoning to add reaction kinetics support in our formalism.

References

1. Ahmad, S.: Formal Reasoning about Molecular Pathways using HOL4 (2014). http://save.seecs.nust.edu.pk/projects/holsyntax/holzsyntax.html
2. Ahmad, S., Hasan, O., Siddique, U.: Towards formal reasoning about molecular pathways in HOL. In: International Conference on Enabling Technologies: Infrastructure for Collaborative Enterprises, pp. 378–383. IEEE (2014)
3. Baier, C., Katoen, J.: Principles of Model Checking. MIT Press (2008)
4. Boniolo, G., D'Agostino, M., Di Fiore., P.: Zsyntax: a Formal Language for Molecular Biology with Projected Applications in Text Mining and Biological Prediction. PloS ONE **5**(3), e9511-1–e9511-12 (2010.)
5. Church, A.: A Formulation of the Simple Theory of Types. Journal of Symbolic Logic **5**, 56–68 (1940)
6. Danos, V., Laneve, C.: Formal Molecular Biology. Theoretical Computer Science **325**(1), 69–110 (2004)
7. Hunt, N.H., et al.: Immunopathogenesis of Cerebral Malaria. International Journal for Parasitology **36**(5), 569–582 (2006)
8. Trilling, L., Fab, C., Fanchon, E.: Applications of a Formal Approach to Decipher Discrete Genetic Networks. BMC Bioinformatics **11**(1), 385 (2010)
9. Fontana, W.: Systems Biology, Models, and Concurrency. SIGPLAN Notices **43**(1), 1–2 (2008)
10. Cassez, F., Bernot, G., et al.: Semantics of Biological Regulatory Networks. Electronic Notes Theoretical Computer Science **180**(3), 3–14 (2007)
11. Peter, J.E.G., Peccoud, J.: Quantitative Modeling of Stochastic Systems in Molecular Biology by using Stochastic Petri Nets. Proceedings of the National Academy of Sciences **95**(12), 6750–6755 (1998)
12. Harrison, J.: Handbook of Practical Logic and Automated Reasoning. Cambridge University Press (2009)
13. Hirayama, K.: Genetic Factors Associated with Development of Cerebral Malaria and Fibrotic Schistosomiasis. Korean J. Parasitol. **40**(4), 165–172 (2002)
14. Magnin, M., Paulevé, L., Roux, O.: Abstract Interpretation of Dynamics of Biological Regulatory Networks. Electronic Notes Theoretical Computer Science **272**, 43–56 (2011)
15. Langmead, C.J.: Generalized queries and bayesian statistical model checking in dynamic bayesian networks: application to personalized medicine. In: Proc. International Conference on Computational Systems Bioinformatics, pp. 201–212 (2009)
16. Maglietta, R., Liuzzi, V., Cattaneo, E., Laczko, E., Piepoli, A., Panza, A., Carella, M., Palumbo, O., Staiano, T., Buffoli, F., Andriulli, A., Marra, G., Ancona, N.: Molecular Pathways Undergoing Dramatic Transcriptomic Changes During Tumor Development in the Human Colon. BMC Cancer **12**(1), 608 (2012)

17. Milner, R.: A Theory of Type Polymorphism in Programming. Journal of Computer and System Sciences **17**(3), 348–375 (1977)
18. Nelson, D.: Lehninger Principles of Biochemistry. W.H. Freeman, New York (2008)
19. Paulson, L.C.: ML for the Working Programmer. Cambridge University Press (1996)
20. Pelánek, R.: Fighting state space explosion: review and evaluation. In: Cofer, D., Fantechi, A. (eds.) FMICS 2008. LNCS, vol. 5596, pp. 37–52. Springer, Heidelberg (2009)
21. Posíchal, J., Kvasnička, V.: Reaction Graphs and a Construction of Reaction Networks. Theoretica Chimica Acta **76**(6), 423–435 (1990)
22. Regev, A., Shapiro, E.: Cells as Computation. Nature **419**, 343 (2002)
23. Regev, A., Shapiro, E.: The π-calculus as an abstraction for biomolecular systems. In: Modelling in Molecular Biology. Natural Computing Series, pp. 219–266. Springer (2004)
24. Regev, A., Silverman, W., Shapiro, E.Y.: Representation and simulation of biochemical processes using the pi-calculus process algebra. In: Pacific Symposium on Biocomputing, pp. 459–470 (2001)
25. Rizzotti, M., Zanardo, A.: Axiomatization of Genetics. 1. Biological Meaning. Journal of Theoretical Biology **118**(1), 61–71 (1986)
26. Rodríguez, A., Sosa, D., Torres, L., Molina, B., Frías, S., Mendoza, L.: A Boolean Network Model of the FA/BRCA Pathway. Bioinformatics **28**(6), 858–866 (2012)
27. Talcott, C.: Symbolic modeling of signal transduction in pathway logic. In: Conference on Winter Simulation, WSC 2006, pp. 1656–1665 (2006)
28. Thomas, L., d' Ari, R.: Biological Feedback. CRC Press, USA (1990)
29. Thomas, R.: Kinetic Logic: A Boolean Approach to the Analysis of Complex Regulatory Systems. Lecture Notes in Biomathematics, vol. 29. Springer-Verlag (1979)
30. Tyson, J.J., Nagy, C.A., Novak, B.: The Dynamics of Cell Cycle Regulation. Bioessays **24**(12), 1095–1109 (2002)
31. Wolkenhauer, O., Shibata, D., Mesarovic, M.D.: The Role of Theorem Proving in Systems Biology. Journal of Theoretical Biology **300**, 57–61 (2012)
32. Woodger, J.H., Tarski, A., Floyd, W.F.: The Axiomatic Method in Biology. The University Press (1937)
33. Zanardo, A., Rizzotti, M.: Axiomatization of Genetics 2. Formal Development. Journal of Theoretical Biology **118**(2), 145–152 (1986)

Towards a Family of Test Selection Criteria for Symbolic Models of Real-Time Systems

Diego R. Almeida[1], Alan Moraes[2,3]([⊠]), Wilkerson L. Andrade[3],
and Patrícia D.L. Machado[3]

[1] IFPE, Afogados da Ingazeira, PE, Brazil
diego.rodrigues@afogados.ifpe.edu.br
[2] Informatics Center, UFPB, João Pessoa, PB, Brazil
alan@ci.ufpb.br
[3] Software Practices Laboratory (SPLab), UFCG, Campina Grande, PB, Brazil
{wilkerson,patricia}@computacao.ufcg.edu.br

Abstract. In model-based testing, test cases are generated from a specification model. To avoid an exhaustive search for all possible test cases that can be obtained, usually an expensive and infeasible activity, test case generation may be guided by a test selection criterion. The objective of a test selection criterion is to produce a minimal test suite and yet effective to reveal faults. However, the choice of a criterion is not straightforward specially for real-time systems, because most criteria presented in the literature are general-purpose. Moreover, the relationship between general-purpose and specific criteria for real-time systems is not clear. In this paper, we investigate the criteria that can be applied for test case generation in the scope of model-based testing of real-time systems, specifically of Timed Input-Output Symbolic Transition Systems (TIOSTS) models. We formalize a family of 19 test selection criteria ordered by strict inclusion relation for TIOSTS models. The family combines general-purpose data-flow-oriented and transition-based criteria with specific reactive and real-time systems criteria. We also perform an empirical study to compare the effectiveness of selected criteria. Results of the empirical study indicate that failure detection capability of the generated test suite may vary, but differences are not significant for time failures. We conclude that more effective criteria for the model-based testing of real-time systems are still needed.

1 Introduction

Model-Based Testing is a testing approach that relies on the design of abstract models of an application to generate, execute and evaluate tests [10,22,27]. It has been applied with success in industry, with special emphasis in the avionic, railway and automotive domains [21].

Test case generation algorithms are based on test selection criteria that guide how to search for test cases and when to stop the test case generation process. Different test suites can be generated depending on the chosen test selection criterion [29]. They may vary in size, behavior coverage and failure detection

© Springer International Publishing Switzerland 2015
C. Braga and N. Martí-Oliet (Eds.): SBMF 2014, LNCS 8941, pp. 48–63, 2015.
DOI: 10.1007/978-3-319-15075-8_4

capability. Therefore, test selection criteria need to establish how to guarantee the generation of test suites that are ultimately cost-effective.

Real-time systems are reactive systems whose behavior is constrained by time [18]. So, the testing of these systems should uncover time-related faults that may require specific test cases to be exercised. Most test selection criteria for real-time systems at model level are based on structural elements of a model behavior and its data usage [14]. Some specific test selection criteria for real-time systems have been proposed, such as covering all clock resets and all guard bounds [12]. However, the choice of a criterion is not straightforward, because the relationship between general-purpose and specific criteria for real-time systems is not clear [2].

In this paper, we investigate test selection criteria for real-time systems in the context of model-based testing. We focus on criteria that can be applied to transition systems, because they are usually the basis for conformance testing of real-time systems [17,28]. We use Timed Input-Output Symbolic Transition Systems (TIOSTS) models [5,6], where system behavior is modeled as a transition system with data and time symbolically defined.

Here we make two contributions. First, we formalize a family of 19 test selection criteria partially ordered by strict inclusion relation for TIOSTS models. The family combines TRANSITION-BASED CRITERIA, DATA-FLOW-ORIENTED CRITERIA, REACTIVE SYSTEMS CRITERIA and REAL-TIME SYSTEMS CRITERIA. We prove inclusion or incompatibility whenever our family diverges from the known relationship in other models, because some relation between criteria change when applied to TIOSTS models.

Second, we conduct a controlled experiment to compare the effectiveness of selected criteria. The empirical study measures the size, the failure detection capability and the rate of failures detected by the size of the test suite of different criteria. In order to conduct the empirical study, we implemented a selection of criteria from the family using a depth-first search-based algorithm. Statistical analyses show that the criteria present different failure detection capability, although, significant differences cannot be observed for time-related failures. Furthermore, current specific criteria for real-time systems lack precision, i.e. they miss important failures, pointing to the need for further research in this area.

The paper is structured as follows. Section 2 introduces the TIOSTS model and test selection criteria for model-based testing of real-time systems. Section 3 formalizes a family criteria for TIOSTS. Section 4 presents an empirical study to compare selected criteria. Section 5 discusses related work. Finally, Section 6 presents concluding remarks along with pointers for further research.

2   Background

This section presents the symbolic model on which this work is based and introduces the concept of test selection criterion in the context of model-based testing.

2.1   Timed Input-Output Symbolic Transition System Model

Timed Input-Output Symbolic Transition System (TIOSTS) [5,6] is a symbolic model for real-time systems that handles both data and time. The TIOSTS model was defined as an extension of two existing models: Timed Automata [3] and Input-Output Symbolic Transition Systems [15,24]. Basically, a TIOSTS is an automaton with a finite set of locations where system data and time evolution are respectively represented by variables and a finite set of clocks. The transitions of the model are composed of a guard on variables and clocks, an action with parameters, an assignment of variables, and a set of clocks to reset.

Figure 1 shows an example of TIOSTS that models a machine for refilling a card for using the subway. Initially, the system is in the `Idle` location where it expects the `Credit` input carrying the desired `value` to refill, then this value is saved into the `refillValue` variable[1] and `balance` is initialized to zero.

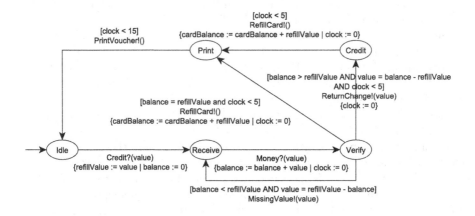

Fig. 1. TIOSTS model of a refilling machine

From the `Receive` location to `Verify` the client informs the amount to be credited to the card. This value is accumulated in the `balance` variable and the `clock` is set to zero. If the current balance is less than the desired value to refill, then the `Receive` location is reached again and the `MissingValue` output is emitted for informing the remaining value (the condition `value = refillValue − balance` contained in the guard means "choose a value for the value parameter that, with the values of `refillValue` and `balance` variables, satisfies the guard").

From the `Verify` location, if the `balance` is greater than `refillValue` some value must be returned to the client in less than 5 time units. After that, the `clock`

---

[1] Action parameters have local scope, thus their values must be stored in variables for future references.

is reset to zero again. Then, the `RefillCard` output action must be performed in less than 5 time units and the `cardBalance` is increased by `refillValue`. Otherwise, from `Verify`, if `balance` is exactly equals to `refillValue`, then the card must be refilled in less than 5 time units. Finally, from the `Print` location, the voucher must be printed in less than 15 time units and `Idle` location is reached again. A formal definition of TIOSTS models is presented in Definition 1 [5].

Definition 1 (TIOSTS). *A TIOSTS is a tuple $W = \langle V, P, \Theta, L, l^0, \Sigma, C, T \rangle$, where:*

- *V is a finite set of typed variables;*
- *P is a finite set of parameters. For $x \in V \cup P$, $type(x)$ denotes the type of x;*
- *Θ is the initial condition, a predicate with variables in V;*
- *L is a finite, non-empty set of locations and $l^0 \in L$ is the initial location;*
- *$\Sigma = \Sigma^? \cup \Sigma^!$ is a non-empty, finite alphabet, which is the disjoint union of a set $\Sigma^?$ of input actions and a set $\Sigma^!$ of output actions. For each action $a \in \Sigma$, its signature $sig(a) = \langle p_1, ..., p_n \rangle$ is a tuple of distinct parameters, where each $p_i \in P$ ($i = 1, ..., n$);*
- *C is a finite set of clocks with values in the set of non-negative real numbers, denoted by $\mathbb{R}^{\geq 0}$;*
- *T is a finite set of transitions. Each transition $t \in T$ is a tuple $\langle l, a, G, A, y, l' \rangle$, where:*
  - *$l \in L$ is the origin location of the transition,*
  - *$a \in \Sigma$ is the action,*
  - *$G = G^D \wedge G^C$ is the guard, where G^D is a predicate over variables in $V \cup set(sig(a))$ [2,3] and G^C is a clock constraint over C defined as a conjunction of constraints of the form $\alpha \# c$, where $\alpha \in C$, $\# \in \{<, \leq, =, \geq, >\}$, and $c \in \mathbb{N}$,*
  - *$A = (A^D, A^C)$ is the assignment of the transition. For each variable $x \in V$ there is exactly one assignment in A^D, of the form $x := A^{D^x}$, where A^{D^x} is an expression on $V \cup set(sig(a))$. $A^C \subseteq C$ is the set of clocks to be reset,*
  - *$y \in \{lazy, delayable, eager\}$ is the deadline of the transition,*
  - *$l' \in L$ is the destination location of the transition.* ◇

The semantics of a TIOSTS is described by Andrade and Machado [5]. Next we define the concepts of **state**, **path** and **test case**.

Definition 2 (State of TIOSTS). *In TIOSTS model, a state is a tuple $\langle l, v_1, ..., v_n, c_1, ..., c_m \rangle$, which consists of a location $l \in L$, a specific valuation for all variables $v_i \in V$, and a valuation for all clocks $c_i \in C$.* ◇

Definition 3 (Path). *A path is a finite sequence of transitions $(t_1, ..., t_k)$, $k \geq 1$, such that the destination location of transition t_i is equal to the origin location of the transition t_{i+1} for $i = 1, 2, ..., k - 1$.* ◇

---

[2] G^D is assumed to be expressed in a theory in which satisfiability is decidable.

[3] Let $set(j)$ be the function that converts the tuple j in a set.

Definition 4 (Test Case). *A test case is a deterministic TIOSTS* $TC = \langle V_{TC}, P_{TC}, \Theta_{TC}, L_{TC}, l^0_{TC}, \Sigma_{TC}, C_{TC}, \mathcal{T}_{TC} \rangle$, *where* $\Sigma^?_{TC} = \Sigma^!_S$ *and* $\Sigma^!_{TC} = \Sigma^?_S$ *(actions are mirrored w.r.t. specification), equipped with three disjoint sets of verdict locations* Pass, Fail, *and* Inconclusive. *Furthermore, each sequence from the initial location* l^0_{TC} *to some verdict location is a path.*   ⋄

According to Definition 4, the execution of a test case can emit one of three possible verdicts: *Pass, Fail,* and *Inconclusive. Pass* means that some targeted behavior of the system under test has been reached, *Fail* means rejection of the SUT, and *Inconclusive* means that targeted behavior cannot be reached anymore.

Figure 2 is a test case for the TIOSTS model of the refilling machine. The test case aims to exercise the scenario where the system emits the `RefillCard` output when the amount to be credited to the card (`value_2`) is equal to desired value to refill (`value_1`). In this case, the verdict is *Pass.* If the amount to be credited to the card (`value_2`) is less than the desired value to refill (`value_1`), and the system emits the `MissingValue` output with parameter equals to `value_1` − `value_2`, then the verdict is *Inconclusive.* It is *Inconclusive* because this behavior is specified in the model, but it is not the scenario the tester would like to observe in the test case execution. The same applies to `ReturnChange` output action of the test case. All other cases lead to the implicit *Fail* verdict.

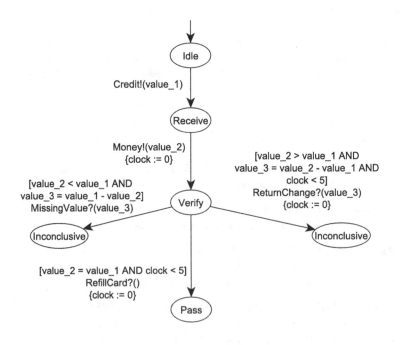

Fig. 2. A test case for the refilling machine

2.2   Test Selection Criteria for Real-Time Systems

In model-based testing, test cases are derived from a model which specifies the expected behavior of a system under test. A *Test Selection Criterion* defines which parts of the system are going to be tested, how often and under what circumstances they will be tested [29]. Test selection criteria are used for two main purposes: to measure the adequacy of the test suite with respect to the level of quality required by the context, and to stop the test generation process after the criterion is reached [29].

We conducted a systematic literature review to identify studies that address test selection criteria for real-time systems at model level [2]. We considered studies that a criterion was used at least as part of a test case generation process in the scope of transition and state-based systems [1,7,9,12–14,16,17,20,26,31].

The results of the review show that most general-purpose test selection criteria may be applied to models of real-time systems. There are also specific criteria for real-time systems proposed in the literature. However, there is a lack of studies that investigate the theoretical and empirical relationship between criteria. The theoretical relationship could indicate the relative effort to satisfy a criterion, while the empirical evaluation could compare criteria effectiveness with respect to failure detection capability.

En-Nouaary [12] proposes a family of test selection criteria ordered by strict inclusion relation for Timed Input-Output Automata (TIOA). His family combines TRANSITION-BASED CRITERIA, REACTIVE SYSTEMS CRITERIA, and REAL-TIME SYSTEMS CRITERIA. But data-related criteria are not included because the TIOA model does not support data abstraction. Conversely, the TIOSTS model symbolically abstracts both time and data, thus data-related criteria can be applied to it. Furthermore, to the best of our knowledge, there is no work on test selection criteria for real-time systems at model level that evaluate the ability to reveal faults of selected criteria.

3   Towards a Family of Test Selection Criteria for TIOSTS

In this section, we propose a family of test selection criteria for TIOSTS models. We extend En-Nouaary's family [12] to include data-related criteria. We choose to include DATA-FLOW-ORIENTED CRITERIA, because they can be empirically evaluated with the same failure model employed to compare TRANSITION-BASED CRITERIA and REAL-TIME SYSTEMS CRITERIA in the next section. Thus our proposed family of criteria combines TRANSITION-BASED CRITERIA, REACTIVE SYSTEMS CRITERIA, REAL-TIME SYSTEMS CRITERIA and DATA-FLOW-ORIENTED CRITERIA. Table 1 describes the criteria we considered in this work.

Test selection criteria are often theoretically compared to each other by three relations: **strict inclusion**, **equivalence**, or **incompatibility** [23]. The relations are formalized in Definitions 6, 7 and 8 respectively.

Definition 5 (Inclusion Relation). *A criterion c_1 includes a criterion c_2 if any set of test cases that satisfies c_1 also satisfies c_2 [23].*   ◇

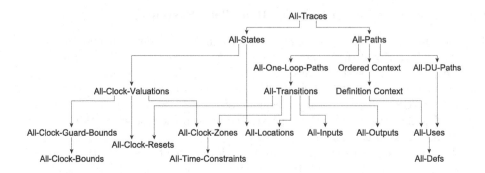

Fig. 3. Family of test selection criteria ordered by strict inclusion relation for TIOSTS models

Definition 6 (Strict Inclusion Relation). *A criterion c_1 strictly includes c_2, denoted by $c_1 \Rightarrow c_2$, if c_1 includes c_2 but there is a set of test cases that satisfies c_2 but does not satisfy c_1. Note that this is a transitive relation [23].* ⋄

Definition 7 (Equivalence Relation). *A criterion c_1 is equivalent to a criterion c_2 if c_1 includes c_2 and c_2 includes c_1.* ⋄

Definition 8 (Incompatible Relation). *A criterion c_1 is incompatible with a criterion c_2 if c_1 does not include c_2 and c_2 does not include c_1.* ⋄

Our goal is to produce a sound family of test selection criteria partially ordered by strict inclusion relation. We do not intend to prove all equivalences or incompatibilities between criteria. To accomplish this, our strategy is i) to reuse the proofs of strict inclusion relations from other formalisms if they are also valid for TIOSTS; ii) to prove new strict inclusion relations resulting from the combination of classes of criteria; iii) to prove the exclusion of strict inclusion relations valid for other formalisms but not valid for TIOSTS. The proposed family is formalized in Theorem 1.

Theorem 1. *The family of criteria for TIOSTS is partially ordered by strict inclusion as shown in Figure 3. Furthermore, $c_1 \Rightarrow c_2$ iff it is explicitly shown to be so in Figure 3 or follows from the transitivity of the relationship.*

Proof. We need to prove the relations ALL-STATES $\Rightarrow$ ALL-LOCATIONS, ALL-ONE-LOOP-PATHS $\Rightarrow$ ALL-TRANSITIONS, ALL-TRANSITIONS $\Rightarrow$ ALL-CLOCK-RESETS, and ALL-DU-PATHS $\not\Rightarrow$ ALL-TRANSITIONS. All other relations can be easily checked based on proofs already presented in the literature [12, 23, 29, 32].

1. ALL-STATES $\Rightarrow$ ALL-LOCATIONS. Proof follows directly from the definitions of the criteria. We recap that a state of a TIOSTS consists of a location, a specific valuation for all variables, and a valuation for all clocks. Since the ALL-STATES criterion demands the all states to be covered, thus ALL-STATES $\Rightarrow$ ALL-LOCATIONS.

Table 1. Test Selection Criteria for TIOSTS models

Criterion	Description
Transition-Based Criteria	
ALL-LOCATIONS [12, 16]	Every location of the model must be exercised by at least one test case.
ALL-PATHS [12, 14]	Every path of the model must be exercised by at least one test case.
ALL-ONE-LOOP-PATHS [29]	Every loop-free paths through the model must be exercised, plus all the paths that loop at least once.
ALL-TRANSITIONS [12, 16]	Every transition of the model must be exercised by at least one test case.
ALL-STATES [1, 12, 31]	Every state of the model must be exercised by at least one test case.
ALL-TRACES [12]	Every trace of the model must be included in the test suite.
Data-Flow-Oriented Criteria	
ALL-DEFS [29]	At least one def-use pair(d_v, u_v) for every definition d_v must be exercised by at least one test case, i.e. at least one path from every definition to one of its use must be covered.
ALL-DU-PATHS [29]	Every path for all def-use pairs(d_v, u_v) must be exercised by at least one test case, i.e. all paths from every definition d_v to every use u_v must be covered.
ALL-USES [29]	Every def-use pairs(d_v, u_v) must be exercised by at least one test case, i.e. at least one path from every definition d_v to every use u_v must be covered.
DEFINITION CONTEXT [14]	All paths from every context of definition of variable x to the definition of variable x must be exercised by at least one test case. The context of definition of the variable x are the transitions where the variables used to define the value of x are defined.
ORDERED CONTEXT [14]	Similar to DEFINITION CONTEXT, but the transitions context are listed in the order of their definitions.
Reactive Systems Criteria	
ALL-INPUTS [9, 12]	Every input action of the model must be exercised by at least one test case.
ALL-OUTPUTS [9, 12]	Every output action of the model must be exercised by at least one test case.
Real-Time Systems Criteria	
ALL-CLOCK-BOUNDS [12]	Every clock bound of the model must be exercised by at least one test case. The bound of a clock is the highest value that a clock can assume.
ALL-CLOCK-GUARD-BOUNDS [12]	Every clock guard bound of the model must be exercised by at least one test case. This criterion is similar to ALL-CLOCK-BOUNDS but considering only the time guards.
ALL-CLOCK-VALUATIONS [12]	Every clock valuation of the model must be exercised by at least one test case.
ALL-CLOCK-RESETS [12]	Every clock reset of the model must be exercised by at least one test.
ALL-CLOCK-ZONES [12, 26]	Every clock zone of the model must be visited through at least one test case, i.e. all transitions with clock resets or time guards must be covered.
ALL-TIME-CONSTRAINTS [12]	Every time guard of the model must be exercised by at least one test case.

Note: The criteria in this table are defined in terms of satisfiable paths, i.e. all data and time guards in a path must be satisfiable.

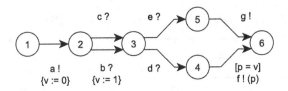

Fig. 4. A TIOSTS model to assist in the proof of ALL-DU-PATHS $\not\Rightarrow$ ALL-TRANSITIONS

2. ALL-ONE-LOOP-PATHS $\Rightarrow$ ALL-TRANSITIONS. Proof follows directly from the definitions of the criteria. The ALL-ONE-LOOP-PATHS criterion demands that all loop-free paths to be covered plus all loops at least one lap. Since all transitions must be either in a loop-free path or in a loop, thus ALL-ONE-LOOP-PATHS $\Rightarrow$ ALL-TRANSITIONS.
3. ALL-TRANSITIONS $\Rightarrow$ ALL-CLOCK-RESETS. Proof follows directly from the definitions of the criteria. A clock reset happens within the assignment of a transition. The ALL-TRANSITIONS criterion demand that all transitions to be covered. Since all transitions with clock resets are a subset of all transitions, thus ALL-TRANSITIONS $\Rightarrow$ ALL-CLOCK-RESETS.
4. ALL-DU-PATHS $\not\Rightarrow$ ALL-TRANSITIONS. Proof by contradiction. Let's assume that ALL-DU-PATHS $\Rightarrow$ ALL-TRANSITIONS. Consider the TIOSTS model in the Figure 4. The model has two def-use pairs: $\{(q_1, [true], a!, \{v := 0\}, \emptyset, q_2),$ $(q_4, [p = v], f!(p), \emptyset, \emptyset, q_6)\}$ and $\{(q_2, [true], b?, \{v := 1\}, \emptyset, q_3), (q_4, [p = v],$ $f!(p), \emptyset, \emptyset, q_6)\}$. The test cases[4] $\{\{a! \rightarrow c? \rightarrow d? \rightarrow f!(p)\}, \{a! \rightarrow b? \rightarrow d? \rightarrow f!(p)\}\}$ satisfy the ALL-DU-PATHS criterion for this model, but the transitions $(q_3, true, e?, \emptyset, \emptyset, q_5)$ and $(q_5, true, g!, \emptyset, \emptyset, q_6)$ are not covered. Thus our assumption is incorrect, and ALL-DU-PATHS $\not\Rightarrow$ ALL-TRANSITIONS. $\square$

It is important to remark that the relation ALL-USES $\Rightarrow$ ALL-TRANSITIONS does not hold for TIOSTS as it does for other models [23]. In fact, even ALL-DU-PATHS $\Rightarrow$ ALL-TRANSITIONS does not hold for TIOSTS. This happens because a transition in TIOSTS may have neither a definition nor a use of a variable. Thus not all transitions will be covered by the ALL-DU-PATHS criterion.

4   Empirical Study

In this section we present a controlled experiment to compare the effectiveness of selected criteria. We follow the guidelines given by Wohlin, Runeson, Höst and Ohlsson [30]. The main goal of the empirical study is to investigate test selection criteria for real-time systems by observing the test suite generated from TIOSTS models according to a given criterion with respect to their size and failure detection capability from the point of view of the tester in the context

---

[4] The last transition in the test case leads to the *Accept* location.

of model-based testing. The research hypothesis is that different criteria may generate different suites of different sizes that may reveal a number of different failures.

Planning. We conducted this experiment in a research laboratory — an offline study with a specific context. As independent variable, we have the test selection criterion. The treatments are: ALL-ONE-LOOP-PATHS (AOLP), ALL-TRANSITI-ONS (AT), ALL-LOCATIONS (AL), ALL-CLOCK-ZONES (ACZ), ALL-CLOCK-RE-SETS (ACR), ALL-DU-PATHS (ADUP), ALL-USES (AU), and ALL-DEFS (AD). Instead of evaluating all criteria of the family, we choose to evaluate the most used criteria found in our literature review. The selected criteria are representative of transition, time and data-related criteria.

The dependent variables are: i) size of the generated test suites (*Size*); and ii) failure detection capability, measured as the number of different failures that can be detected (*Failure*). From these dependent variables, for each treatment and object, we computed two values: i) the *percentage of failure*, defined as the relation between the *Failure* value and the total of possible failures; ii) the *density of failure* as the relation between the *Failure* and the *Size* values. For the sake of simplicity, the hypotheses of the study are formulated based on these measures only as follows. Let $\%failure_i = \frac{Failure_i}{TotalFailures}$ and $density_i = \frac{Failure_i}{Size_i}$, where i is a test criterion and $Failure_i$, $Size_i$ are the average value of the correspondent dependent variables for each of the considered objects. Based on statistical testing, the null hypothesis is defined as the equality of all criteria, whereas the alternative hypothesis is defined as the difference between all criteria.

Regarding experimental design, this study consists of one factor and eight levels (eight test criteria) with six repetitions corresponding to six different models from three applications of real-time systems presented in the literature. We considered a confidence of 95% when deciding on hypothesis rejection. As input, for each criterion, only TIOSTS models are required. Dependent variables are computed automatically. Therefore, there is no human intervention and no subjects to be considered. Since there are no random choices involved, there is no need to compute the number of replications required.

The objects (TIOSTS models) were obtained from 3 different applications: i) Alarm System — Monitoring and actuation system that can detect invasion and also the presence of intruders in a building through door, window and movement sensors [25]; ii) Aircraft Attack System — System that controls attacks to specific land targets and also threat detection from a missile or another aircraft [19]; and iii) Philips Audio Protocol — Protocol that defines control message exchanging for audio and video devices [8]. Moreover, collisions detection and delivery failure are handled. From these applications, we created six models and used them as input to the test case generator we implemented using a depth-first search-based algorithm. Table 2 presents the metrics of number of locations, transitions, transitions with time constraints, and transitions with data constraints of the considered models.

Table 2. Metrics of real-time system models used in the empirical study

Model	Loc.	Trans.	Trans. w/ time constraints	Trans. w/ data constraints
Alarm1	7	9	6	7
Alarm2	10	23	13	19
Aircraft1	11	13	8	6
Aircraft2	14	35	20	28
Protocol1	17	29	10	25
Protocol2	17	37	18	25

Notes. Alarm1: Alarm System without power failure. Alarm2: Simplified version of Alarm1 with power failure treatment. Aircraft1: Aircraft Attack System functionality only. Aircraft2: Simplified version of Aircraft1 with threat detection functionality. Protocol1: System without failure recovery. Protocol2: Simplified version of Protocol1 with failure recovery.

It is often difficult to associate a failure with a single fault at code level, because a failure may be caused by one or more faults. Therefore, for the purpose of this study and also to avoid undesired effects in the results, instead of the number of faults, we opt to measure failures — the number of different failures that can be detected by at least one test case in a given test suite. To allow for a reasonable sample of failures, we defined a failure model that contains potential failures which can be detected in a real-time system, particularly as a result of violation of time constraints. This model was based on previous studies such as the one performed by En-Nouaary, Khendek and Dssouli [11], and by Andrade and Machado [4]. Two basic types of failures were considered: time and behavior. The former is necessarily connected to non-conformity with time constraints, whereas the latter are more related to behavior non-conformity. For the sake of space, Table 3 presents only considered failures for the *Alarm2* model. Note that there is a different distribution of faults of the two types. The reason is that we do not aim to control this factor so that the distribution achieved is mostly a consequence of potential failures identified by considering each model.

Table 3. Failure Model for *Alarm2* model

Failure	Type	Description
F04	Time	When power failure occurs, sensor status does not change.
F05	Time	When power failure is detected, the system does not change power supply on time.
F06	Behavior	After handling power failure, system does not resume execution as expected.
F07	Time	When power failure occurs, status change of movement sensor is not detected.
F08	Time	When power failure occurs, status change of window sensor is not detected.
F09	Behavior	After power failure handling, system does not detect an invaded room.
F10	Behavior	After power failure handling, alarm starts without invasion detection.

Study execution was conducted according to the following process: 1) For each input model, a test suite was generated for each of the criteria; 2) For each test suite, each test case was analysed to determine whether it can fail according to the failure model; 3) For each test suite, failures from the failure model were marked when covered by the suite; 4) Data on study variables was collected; 5) *%failure* and *density* values were computed and analysis of results conducted.

Threats to Validity. Measures were rigorously taken regarding data treatment and assumption with a confidence level of 95% that is usually applied in comparing studies. Also, to avoid the influence on the kind of applications in the obtained results, we have chosen specifications constructed by different authors — the models have different structural elements as illustrated in Table 2. Moreover, correctness of the implementation of the algorithms is critical to assess whether the results are reliable. Therefore, validation was throughly performed and, to avoid an inconsistent generation of suites, all algorithms are based on the same basic strategy — a depth-first search — where each criterion is applied as a stop condition. Furthermore, models used in the study may not be representative of all kinds of real-time systems, therefore, results can only be interpreted as specific. However, it is important to remark that they may be considered as an evidence since results confirm properties already known, particularly for the general criteria.

Results and Analysis. Data collected in the study as well as test cases generated can be downloaded from the study web site[5]. Figure 5 shows the box plots for the percentage of failure values and Figure 6 shows the box plot for the density of failures values. As the values do not follow a normal distribution, the Kruskal-Wallis test was performed and we obtained a *p-value* of 0.0388 for the percentage of failures. This means that we can reject the null hypotheses: when compared together the criteria present a different failure detection capability. However, if we consider only "Time" failures, the *p-value* would be 0.1487. Therefore, we can observe that, for the considered criteria, significant differences of capability for this kind of failure cannot be observed.

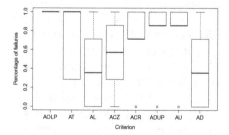 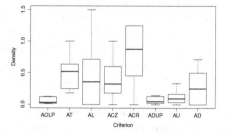

Fig. 5. Boxplot of percentage of failure detected for each criterion

Fig. 6. Boxplot of density of failure detected for each criterion

On the other hand, for the density of failure values, by applying the Kruskal-Wallis test we obtained a *p-value* of 0.0670. This means that we cannot reject the null hypotheses: we cannot observe a significant difference on the failure density for the considered criteria. It is also important to mention that no significant

---

[5] https://sites.google.com/a/computacao.ufcg.edu.br/rtscoverage/

correlation between the values of size and failure has been observed for any of the considered criteria.

General Remarks. From this study, we can observe that the more general criteria such as ALL-ONE-LOOP-PATHS and ALL-TRANSITIONS as well as ALL-DU-PATHS and ALL-USES present a better failure coverage even when only time failures are considered. The reason is that more test cases are generated when these criteria are considered. However, they do not always present the best failure density capacity. Which means that a number of test cases may be either useless or redundant for the purpose of detecting the considered failures. From the general criteria, ALL-USES (followed by ALL-DU-PATHS) seems to present more consistently the best relation between size and failure detection capability. The reason is that they can most effectively explore the relation between events that are related to a given variable, whereas the structural criteria such as ALL-TRANSITIONS and ALL-LOCATIONS can miss certain combinations. The clock related criteria ALL-CLOCK-ZONES and ALL-CLOCK-RESETS present considerably smaller test suites and good density failure capacity, particularly the second one. However, not all failures are covered, even time related ones. Consequently, these criteria may only be considered under severe project constraints. Otherwise, one might consider using both of them together in order to improve failure detection capability and still keep a reasonable failure density.

5   Related Work

Test selection criteria for different kinds of models of real-time systems have already been investigated in the literature. But most of works just describe a criterion or a set of criteria without proper theoretical and empirical evaluation.

En-Nouaary [12] proposes a family of test selection criteria ordered by strict inclusion relation criteria for TIOA models. Our proposal is an extension to his family including data-related criteria for TIOSTS models. We refine the relation between ALL-CLOCK-RESETS and the class of TRANSITION-BASED COVERAGE criteria. In his family, ALL-PATHS ⇒ ALL-CLOCK-RESETS, but we prove that the narrow relation ALL-TRANSITIONS ⇒ ALL-CLOCK-RESETS is true too. We introduce the relation ALL-STATES ⇒ ALL-LOCATIONS that was missing. En-Nouaary's family has neither the ALL-ONE-LOOP-PATHS criterion nor the class of DATA-FLOW-ORIENTED COVERAGE criteria. We introduce them below the ALL-PATHS criterion. Conversely, our family does not have the ALL-CLOCK-REGIONS criterion, because TIOSTS uses zones instead of regions. Finally, only we evaluate empirically the failure detection capability of eight criteria.

Zhu, Hall and May [32] surveys the literature for test selection criteria at source code level. They present several criteria applicable to unit testing, compare them using the strict inclusion relation and provide an axiomatic study of the properties of criteria. Our work is close to theirs because we also compare test selection criteria using the strict inclusion relation. But we work at model level instead of source code level, and we also perform an empirical study to compare selected criteria.

6   Concluding Remarks

In this paper we presented test selection criteria that can be applied to symbolic transition models of real-time systems, particularly, the TIOSTS model.

We investigated the literature for test selection criteria applicable to models of real-time systems. Next we selected the ones applicable to TIOSTS and formalized a family of 19 test selection criteria partially ordered by the strict inclusion relation.

We evaluated 8 criteria in an empirical study with six TIOSTS models. Our results showed that, even though there are differences on the criteria related to size and failure detection capability, the differences were not significant, particularly when considering time-related failures and cost-effectiveness measured as the rate of size by the number of failures.

In general, we can observe that current specific available criteria are still imprecise, because a number of failures were missed. General criteria were precise, but test suites were large, with a high percentage of test cases that did not fail. Therefore, we can conclude that more effective criteria for the model-based testing of real-time systems are still needed, particularly for symbolic models such as TIOSTS.

As future works, we plan to extend this study to include more test selection criteria, specially the CONTROL-FLOW-ORIENTED CRITERIA which exercise data and time guards thoroughly. Based on the analysis of advantages and weakness of the criteria in a new empirical study, we intend to propose more precise and effective criteria for TIOSTS.

Acknowledgments. This work was supported by the National Council for Scientific and Technological Development (CNPq) under grants 475710/2013-4, 484643/2011-8, and 560014/2010-4. This work was partially supported by the National Institute of Science and Technology for Software Engineering[6] of CNPq under grant 573964/2008-4. First author was also supported by CNPq. Finally, we thank the anonymous reviewers for their constructive comments.

References

1. Alagar, V.S., Ormandjieva, O., Zheng, M.: Specification-based testing for real-time reactive systems. In: Proceedings of the 34th International Conference on Technology of Object-Oriented Languages and Systems, pp. 25–36 (2000)
2. Almeida, D.R.: Critérios de Geração de Casos de Teste de Sistemas de Tempo Real. Master's thesis, Federal University of Campina Grande, Campina Grande, PB, Brazil (2012)
3. Alur, R., Dill, D.L.: A theory of timed automata. Theoretical Computer Science **126**(2), 183–235 (1994)
4. Andrade, W.L., Machado, P.D.L.: Testing interruptions in reactive systems. Formal Aspects of Computing **24**, 331–353 (2012)

---

[6] www.ines.org.br

5. Andrade, W.L., Machado, P.D.L.: Generating test cases for real-time systems based on symbolic models. IEEE Transactions on Software Engineering **39**(9), 1216–1229 (2013)
6. Andrade, W.L., Machado, P.D.L., Jéron, T., Marchand, H.: Abstracting time and data for conformance testing of real-time systems. In: Proceedings of the 8th Workshop on Advances in Model Based Testing, pp. 9–17 (2011)
7. Arcuri, A., Iqbal, M.Z., Briand, L.: Black-box system testing of real-time embedded systems using random and search-based testing. In: Petrenko, A., Simão, A., Maldonado, J.C. (eds.) ICTSS 2010. LNCS, vol. 6435, pp. 95–110. Springer, Heidelberg (2010)
8. Bengtsson, J., Griffioen, W.O.D., Kristoffersen, K.J., Larsen, K.G., Larsson, F., Pettersson, P., Yi, W.: Verification of an audio protocol with bus collision using UPPAAL. In: Alur, R., Henzinger, T.A. (eds.) CAV 1996. LNCS, vol. 1102, pp. 244–256. Springer, Heidelberg (1996)
9. Clarke, D., Lee, I.: Automatic test generation for the analysis of a real-time system: case study. In: Proceedings of the 3rd IEEE Real-Time Technology and Applications Symposium, pp. 112–124 (1997)
10. El-Far, I.K., Whittaker, J.A.: Model-based software testing. In: Marciniak, J.J. (ed.) Encyclopedia of Software Engineering, vol. 1, pp. 825–837. John Wiley & Sons, Inc. (2002)
11. En-Nouaary, A., Khendek, F., Dssouli, R.: Fault coverage in testing real-time systems. In: Proceedings of the 6th Real-Time Computing Systems and Applications, pp. 150–157 (1999)
12. En-Nouaary, A.: Test selection criteria for real-time systems modeled as timed input-output automata. International Journal of Web Information Systems **3**(4), 279–292 (2007)
13. En-Nouaary, A., Hamou-Lhadj, A.: A boundary checking technique for testing real-time systems modeled as timed input output automata. In: Proceedings of the 8th International Conference on Quality Software, pp. 209–215 (2008)
14. Hessel, A.: Model-Based Test Case Selection and Generation for Real-Time Systems. Ph.D. thesis, Uppsala University, Uppsala, Sweden (2007)
15. Jeannet, B., Jéron, T., Rusu, V., Zinovieva, E.: Symbolic test selection based on approximate analysis. In: Halbwachs, N., Zuck, L.D. (eds.) TACAS 2005. LNCS, vol. 3440, pp. 349–364. Springer, Heidelberg (2005)
16. Krichen, M., Tripakis, S.: Black-box conformance testing for real-time systems. In: Graf, S., Mounier, L. (eds.) SPIN 2004. LNCS, vol. 2989, pp. 109–126. Springer, Heidelberg (2004)
17. Krichen, M., Tripakis, S.: Conformance testing for real-time systems. Formal Methods in System Design **34**(3), 238–304 (2009)
18. Laplante, P.A.: Real-Time System Design and Analysis. John Wiley & Sons (2004)
19. Locke, C.D., Vogel, D.R., Lucas, L., Goodenough, J.B.: Generic avionics software specification. Software Engineering Institute, Carnegie Mellon University, Tech. rep. (1990)
20. Nielsen, B., Skou, A.: Test generation for time critical systems: tool and case study. In: Proceedings of the 13th Euromicro Conference on Real-Time Systems, pp. 155–162 (2001)
21. Peleska, J.: Industrial-strength model-based testing - state of the art and current challenges. In: Proceedings of the 8th Workshop on Model-Based Testing, pp. 3–28 (2013)

22. Pretschner, A., Slotosch, O., Aiglstorfer, E., Kriebel, S.: Model-based testing for real. International Journal on Software Tools for Technology Transfer **5**(2), 140–157 (2004)

23. Rapps, S., Weyuker, E.J.: Selecting software test data using data flow information. IEEE Transactions on Software Engineering **11**(4), 367–375 (1985)

24. Rusu, V., du Bousquet, L., Jéron, T.: An approach to symbolic test generation. In: Grieskamp, W., Santen, T., Stoddart, B. (eds.) IFM 2000. LNCS, vol. 1945, pp. 338–557. Springer, Heidelberg (2000)

25. Sommerville, I.: Software Engineering. International Computer Science Series, 9th edn. Addison-Wesley, Boston (2010)

26. Trab, M.S.A., Alrouh, B., Counsell, S., Hierons, R.M., Ghinea, G.: A multi-criteria decision making framework for real time model-based testing. In: Bottaci, L., Fraser, G. (eds.) TAIC PART 2010. LNCS, vol. 6303, pp. 194–197. Springer, Heidelberg (2010)

27. Tretmans, J.: Model-based testing and some steps towards test-based modelling. In: Bernardo, M., Issarny, V. (eds.) SFM 2011. LNCS, vol. 6659, pp. 297–326. Springer, Heidelberg (2011)

28. Tretmans, J.: Testing concurrent systems: a formal approach. In: Baeten, J.C.M., Mauw, S. (eds.) CONCUR 1999. LNCS, vol. 1664, pp. 46–65. Springer, Heidelberg (1999)

29. Utting, M., Legeard, B.: Practical Model Based Testing: A Tools Approach. Elsevier, San Francisco (2007)

30. Wohlin, C., Runeson, P., Höst, M., Ohlsson, M.C., Regnell, B., Wesslén, A.: Experimentation in Software Engineering. Springer, New York (2012)

31. Zheng, M., Alagar, V., Ormandjieva, O.: Automated generation of test suites from formal specifications of real-time reactive systems. Journal of Systems and Software **81**(2), 286–304 (2008)

32. Zhu, H., Hall, P.A.V., May, J.H.R.: Software unit test coverage and adequacy. ACM Computing Surveys **29**(4), 366–427 (1997)

Model-Driven Engineering
in the Heterogeneous Tool Set

Daniel Calegari[1]([envelope]), Till Mossakowski[2], and Nora Szasz[3]

[1] Universidad de la República, Montevideo, Uruguay
dcalegar@fing.edu.uy
[2] Otto-von-Guericke University Magdeburg, Magdeburg, Germany
mossakow@iws.cs.uni-magdeburg.de
[3] Facultad de Ingeniería, Universidad ORT Uruguay, Montevideo, Uruguay
szasz@ort.edu.uy

Abstract. We have defined a unified environment that allows formal verification within the Model-Driven Engineering (MDE) paradigm using heterogeneous verification approaches. The environment is based on the Theory of Institutions, which provides a sound basis for representing MDE elements and a way for specifying translations from these elements to other logical domains used for verification, such that formal experts can choose the domain in which they are more skilled to address a formal proof. In this paper we present how this environment can be supported in practice by the Heterogeneous Tool Set (HETS). We define semantic-preserving translations from the MDE elements to the core language of HETS, and we also show how it is possible to move from it to other logics, both to supplement the original specification with other verification properties and to perform a heterogeneous verification.

Keywords: Verification · Formal methods · Model-Driven Engineering

1 Introduction

The Model-Driven Engineering (MDE,[1]) paradigm is based on the construction of models representing different views of the system to be constructed, and model transformations as the main activity within the software development process. In this context, there are multiple properties that can be verified [2], from syntactic to semantic ones, and at different abstraction levels. Whenever formal verification is mandatory, there is a plethora of verification approaches with different objectives, formalisms and supporting tools, which are heterogeneous and not integrated. With an heterogeneous approach [3], different formalisms are used for expressing parts of a problem and semantic-preserving mappings allow the communication between these formalisms in order to compose different views to an overall specification of the whole problem. We have followed this approach by proposing a theoretical environment for the formal verification of different MDE aspects using heterogeneous verification approaches [4], based on the theory of

C. Braga and N. Martí-Oliet (Eds.): SBMF 2014, LNCS 8941, pp. 64–79, 2015.
DOI: 10.1007/978-3-319-15075-8_5

Institutions [5]. This environment proposes a generic representation of the MDE elements (by means of institutions) which can be formally (and automatically) translated into other formalisms, providing the "glue" that formal experts need to choose the formalism in which they are more skilled to address a formal proof.

In this paper we show how the environment can be supported in practice using the Heterogenous Tool Set (HETS,[3]) , which is meant to support heterogeneous multi-logic specifications. It also provides proof management capabilities for monitoring the overall correctness of a heterogeneous specification whereas different parts of it are verified using (possibly) different formalisms. We first define from a theoretical perspective how MDE elements can be integrated in this tool by defining semantic-preserving translations to the Common Algebraic Specification Language (CASL,[6]), which is the core language of HETS. The existent connections between CASL and other formalisms broadens the spectrum of formal domains in which verification can be addressed. We also detail the implementation of a prototype which allows us to specify MDE elements, supplement them with multi-logic properties, and perform a heterogeneous verification.

The remainder of the paper is structured as follows. In Section 2 we introduce the main concepts of MDE based on a running example, and in Section 3 we summarize how these elements can be represented within our institution-based environment. Then, in Section 4 we present how this environment can be formally connected with CASL, and in Section 5 we give details about an implementation of these ideas using HETS. Finally, in Section 6 we discuss related work and in Section 7 we present some conclusions and an outline of further work.

2   Model-Driven Engineering

In MDE there are two key elements: models specifying different views of the system to be constructed and model transformations allowing the (semi)automatic construction of the system by processing the models.

Every model *conforms* to a metamodel which introduces the syntax and semantics of certain kinds of models. The MetaObject Facility (MOF, [7]) is a standard language for metamodeling, basically defining hierarchical-structured classes with properties that can be attributes (named elements with an associated primitive type or class) or associations (relations between classes in which each class plays a role within the relation). Every property has a multiplicity which constraints the number of elements that can be related through it. If there are conditions that cannot be captured by the structural rules of this language, the Object Constraint Language (OCL, [8]) is used to specify them. These considerations allow defining conformance in terms of *structural* and *non-structural* conformance. Structural conformance with respect to a metamodel means that in a given model every object and link is well-typed and the model also respects the multiplicity constraints. Non-structural conformance means that a given model respects the invariants specified with the supplementary language.

Consider as an example a simplified version of the well-known Class to Relational model transformation [9]. The metamodel in the left side of Fig. 1 defines

UML class diagrams, where classifiers (classes and primitive types) are contained in packages. Classes can contain one or more attributes and may be declared as persistent, and each attribute is typed by a primitive type. Notice that a class must contain only one or two attributes, and also that the Classifier class is not abstract. We handle these aspects differently from UML class diagrams in order to have a more complete example. In the right side of Fig. 1 there is a model composed by a persistent class of name `ID` within a package of name `Package`. The class has an attribute of name `value` and type `String`.

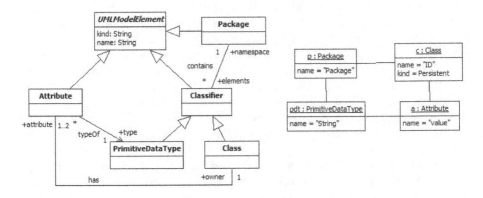

Fig. 1. Class metamodel and model of the example

A model transformation takes as input a model conforming to certain meta-model and produces as output another model conforming to another metamodel (possibly the same). Query/View/Transformation Relations (QVT-Relations, [9]) is a relational language which defines transformation rules as mathematical relations between source and target elements. A transformation is a set of interconnected relations: top-level relations that must hold in any transformation execution, and non-top-level relations that are required to hold only when they are referred from another relation. Every relation defines a set of variables, and source and target patterns which are used to find matching sub-graphs of elements in a model. Relations can also contain a **when** clause which specifies the conditions under which the relationship needs to hold, and a **where** clause which specifies the condition that must be satisfied by all model elements participating in the relation. The **when** and **where** clauses, as well as the patterns may contain arbitrary boolean OCL expressions and can invoke other relations.

The transformation of the example basically describes how persistent classes within a package are transformed into tables within a schema, and attributes of a class are transformed into columns of the corresponding table. Below we show an excerpt of this transformation. There are keys defined as the combination of those properties of a class that together can uniquely identify an instance of that class, e.g. there are no two tables with the same name within the same schema.

```
transformation uml2rdbms ( uml : UML , rdbms : RDBMS ) {
  key RDBMS::Table {name, schema};

  top relation PackageToSchema { ... }

  top relation ClassToTable {
    cn, prefix : String;
    checkonly domain uml c : UML::Class {
      namespace = p : UML::Package {}, kind = 'Persistent', name = cn
    };
    enforce domain rdbms t : RDBMS::Table {
      schema = s : RDBMS::Schema {}, name = cn
    };
    when { PackageToSchema(p, s); }
    where { AttributeToColumn(c, t);}
  }

  relation AttributeToColumn { ... }
}
```

3   An Institution-Based Environment for MDE

Our environment [4] is based on representing models (from now on SW-models to avoid confusion), metamodels, the conformance relation, transformations and verification properties in some consistent and interdependent way without depending on any specific logical domain. We follow an heterogeneous specification approach [3] which is based on providing *Institutions* [5] for representing the syntax and semantics of the elements. An institution is defined as:

- a category Sign of signatures (vocabularies for constructing sentences in a logical system) and signature morphisms (translations between vocabularies)
- a functor Sen : Sign → Set giving a set of sentences for each signature and a function $\text{Sen}(\sigma)$:$\text{Sen}(\Sigma_1)$→ $\text{Sen}(\Sigma_2)$ translating formulas to formulas for each signature morphism $\sigma : \Sigma_1 \rightarrow \Sigma_2$;
- a functor Mod : Sign^{op} → **Cat** , giving a category $\text{Mod}(\Sigma)$ of models (providing semantics) for each signature Σ and a reduct functor $\text{Mod}(\sigma)$:$\text{Mod}(\Sigma_2)$→ $\text{Mod}(\Sigma_1)$ translating models to models (and morphisms to morphisms) for each signature morphism;
- a satisfaction relation of sentences by models, such that when signatures are changed (by a signature morphism), satisfaction of sentences by models changes consistently, i.e. $M_2 \models_{\Sigma_2} \text{Sen}(\sigma)(\varphi)$ iff $\text{Mod}(\sigma)(M_2) \models_{\Sigma_1} \varphi$

We provide an institution $\mathcal{I}^Q$ for QVT-Relations check-only unidirectional transformations (which we called QVTR). This institution needs a representation of SW-models and metamodels, therefore we define an institution $\mathcal{I}^M$ for the structural conformance relation between them based on a simplified version of MOF (which we called CSMOF). Complete definitions can be found in [10].

The institution $\mathcal{I}^{\mathrm{M}}$ represents the MOF-based structural conformance relation between metamodels and SW-models. From any metamodel we can derive a signature $\Sigma = (\boldsymbol{C}, \alpha, \boldsymbol{P})$ declaring: a finite class hierarchy $\boldsymbol{C} = (C, \leq_C)$ (a partial order between classes representing the inheritance relation between them) extended with a subset $\alpha \subseteq C$ denoting abstract classes; and a properties declaration (attributes and associations) $\boldsymbol{P} = (R, P)$ where R is a finite set of role names with a default role name "$\_$", and P is a finite set of properties of the form $\langle r_1 : c_1, r_2 : c_2 \rangle$ representing a property and its opposite. The type c_i attached to the role r_i represents the type of the property, as well the type in the opposite side represents its owned class. By $\boldsymbol{T}(\boldsymbol{C})$ we denote the *type extension* of $\boldsymbol{C}$ by primitive types (e.g. Boolean) and type constructors (e.g. List). Formulas represent multiplicity constraints determining whether the number of elements in a property end is bounded (upper and/or lower). They are defined as follows: $\Phi ::= \#C \bullet R = \mathbb{N} \mid \mathbb{N} \leq \#C \bullet R \mid \#C \bullet R \leq \mathbb{N}$ The #-expressions return the number of links in a property when some role is fixed. The $\bullet$ operator represents the selection of the elements linked with another of class C through a role in R. An interpretation $\mathcal{I}$ (or model) contains a semantic representation for a SW-model, i.e. objects and links. It consists of a tuple $(\boldsymbol{V}_{\boldsymbol{C}}^{\boldsymbol{T}}(\boldsymbol{O}), \boldsymbol{A})$ where $\boldsymbol{V}_{\boldsymbol{C}}^{\boldsymbol{T}}(\boldsymbol{O}) = (V_c)_{c \in T(C)}$ is a $\boldsymbol{T}(\boldsymbol{C})$-object domain (a family of sets of object identifiers), $\boldsymbol{A}$ contains a relation $\langle r_1 : c_1, r_2 : c_2 \rangle^{\mathcal{I}} \subseteq V_{c_1} \times V_{c_2}$ for each relation name $\langle r_1 : c_1, r_2 : c_2 \rangle \in P$ with $c_1, c_2 \in T(C)$, and $c_2 \in \alpha$ implies $O_{c_2} = \bigcup_{c_1 \leq_C c_2} O_{c_1}$. Finally, an interpretation $\mathcal{I}$ satisfies a formula φ with some $c \bullet r$ if for any object of class c, the number of elements within $\mathcal{I}$ related through the role r (of a property of the class c) satisfies the multiplicity constraints. The satisfaction relation checks the multiplicity requirements of the structural conformance relation.

The institution $\mathcal{I}^{\mathrm{Q}}$ represents QVT-Relations transformations by extending the CSMOF institution. A signature is a pair $\langle \Sigma_1^{\mathrm{M}}, \Sigma_2^{\mathrm{M}} \rangle$ representing the source and target metamodels of the transformation, and an interpretation is a tuple $\langle \mathcal{M}_1^{\mathrm{M}}, \mathcal{M}_2^{\mathrm{M}} \rangle$ of disjoint $\mathrm{Sign}_i^{\mathrm{M}}$-interpretations that contains a semantic representation for the source and target SW-models. A formula φ^{K} represents a key constraint of the form $\langle c, \{r_1, ..., r_n\} \rangle$ $(1 \leq n)$ with $c \in C_i$ (i = 1..n) a class in one of the metamodels, $r_j \in R_i$ (j = 1..n) roles defined in properties in which such class participates (having such role or at the opposite side of it). Roles determine the elements within these properties that together can uniquely identify an instance of the class. A formula φ^{R} represents a set of interrelated transformation rules, such that, given variables $X^s = (X^s)_{s \in (\bigcup_i T(C_i))}$, the formula is a finite set of tuples representing rules of the form $\langle \mathrm{top}, \mathrm{VarSet}, \mathrm{ParSet}, \mathrm{Pattern}_1, \mathrm{Pattern}_2,$ when, where$\rangle$, where $\mathrm{top} \in \{true, false\}$ defines if the rule is a top-level relation or not, $\mathrm{VarSet} \subseteq X^s$ is the set of variables used within the rule, $\mathrm{ParSet} \subseteq \mathrm{VarSet}$ representing the set of variables taken as parameters when the rule is called from another one, $\mathrm{Pattern}_i$ (i = 1, 2) are the source and target patterns, and when/where are the **when**/**where** clauses of the rule, respectively. A pattern is a tuple $\langle E_i, A_i, Pr_i \rangle$ such that $E_i \subseteq (X^c)_{c \in C_i}$ is a set of class-indexed variables, A_i is a set of elements representing associations of the form $rel(p, x, y)$ with $p \in P_i$ and $x, y \in E_i$, and Pr_i is a predicate over these elements. A **when**/**where** clause is a pair $\langle \text{when}_c, \text{when}_r \rangle$ such that when_c is a predicate with variables in VarSet, and when_r is a set of pairs of transformation rules and their parameters. The satisfaction relation expresses that the target SW-model is the result of transforming the source SW-model (both within the interpretation) according to the transformation rules and also that key constraints hold (both represented as formulas).

Institutions can be formally connected by means of (co)morphisms. Then, by defining these semantic-preserving translations, it is possible to connect MDE elements to potentially several logics for formal verification. In this way, we just specify MDE elements once, then spread this information into other logics to supplement this specification with additional properties, and finally choose the verification approach we want to use. To the extent that there are many logics connected through comorphisms, the capabilities of our environment increases. The environment supports a separation of duties between software developers (MDE and formal methods experts) such that a formal perspective is available whenever it is required. Moreover, comorphisms can be automated, as we show in the following sections, thus the environment is scalable in terms of the rewriting of MDE elements in each logic. Although our proposal is aligned with OMG standards, this idea can be potentially formalized for any transformation approach and language. This allows extending the approach as far as necessary.

4   Borrowing Proof Capabilities

We make use of the possibility of connecting our institutions to potentially several host logics, each one with its own proof system. The host logic allows both to supplement the information contained within the MDE elements with properties specified in the host logic, and to borrow its proof calculus for formal verification. For this, we us *generalized theoroidal comorphisms* (GTC,[11]). A GTC between two institutions $\mathcal{I}$ and $\mathcal{J}$ consists of a functor $\Phi : \text{Th}^{\mathcal{I}} \to \text{Th}^{\mathcal{J}}$ translating theories (pairs of signatures and set of sentences), and a natural transformation $\beta : (\Phi)^{op}; \text{Mod}^{\mathcal{J}} \to \text{Mod}^{\mathcal{I}}$ translating models in the opposite direction.

We do not define GTC from the institutions defined in the last section, but from extended institutions $\mathcal{I}^{M^+}$ and $\mathcal{I}^{Q^+}$. We extend the definition of CSMOF formulas with a syntactic representation of SW-models as follows:

$$\Omega ::= x^c \mid \langle r_1, x_1{}^{c_1}, r_2, x_2{}^{c_2} \rangle \mid \Omega \oplus \Omega$$

with $x^c \in X^c$ a variable representing a typed element, $\langle r_1, x_1{}^{c_1}, r_2, x_2{}^{c_2} \rangle$ representing a link between two typed elements with their respective roles, and $\Omega \oplus \Omega$ the composition of these elements. In the case of QVTR, we extend QVTR formulas by including extended CSMOF formulas, i.e. now there is a representation of multiplicity constraints and SW-models, indexed by the institutions in which they are defined. These extensions make it possible to use a proof system such that it is possible to prove that constraints (as a formula) are derived from a syntactic representation of a SW-model, which is the context where the verification must be done. An exhaustive discussion on this topic can be found in [10].

We defined GTCs from our extended institutions to CASL, a general-purpose specification language. The institution $\mathcal{I}^C$ underlying CASL is the sub-sorted partial first-order logic with equality and constraints on sets $SubPCFOL^=$, a combination of first-order logic and induction with subsorts and partial functions. Since CASL has a sound proof calculus, and our comorphisms admit borrowing of entailment [3], we can translate our proof goals using the comorphism into CASL and use its proof calculus also for proving properties of our extended CSMOF and QVTR specifications. The importance of CASL is that it is the main language within the Heterogenous Tool Set (HETS, [3]), a tool meant to support heterogeneous multi-logic specifications. This comorphism not only allows us to have tool support for the verification of model transformation by using HETS (as will be introduced in Section 5) but also to move between the graph of logics within HETS to take advantage of the benefits of each logic.

In what follows we introduce CASL and resume the encoding of the main components of the extended institutions into it. An example of the encoding is given in Section 5, and a complete version can be found in [10].

4.1   Common Algebraic Specification Language

The institution $\mathcal{I}^C$ for CASL is defined as follows. Signatures consist of a set S of sorts with a subsort relation $\leq$ between them, together with a family $\{PF_{w,s}\}_{w \in S^*, s \in S}$ of partial functions, $\{TF_{w,s}\}_{w \in S^*, s \in S}$ of total functions and $\{P_w\}_{w \in S^*}$ of predicate symbols. Signature morphisms consist of maps taking sort, function and predicate symbols respectively to a symbol of the same kind in the target signature, and they must preserve subsorting, typing of function and predicate symbols and totality of function symbols.

For a signature Σ, terms are formed starting with variables from a sorted set X using applications of function symbols to terms of appropriate sorts, while sentences are partial first-order formulas extended with *sort generation constraints* which are triples (S', F', σ') such that $\sigma' : \Sigma' \to \Sigma$ and S' and F' are respectively sort and function symbols of Σ'. Models interpret sorts as non-empty sets such that subsorts are injected into supersorts, partial/total function symbols as partial/total functions and predicate symbols as relations.

The satisfaction relation is the expected one for partial first-order sentences. A sort generation constraint (S', F', σ') holds in a model M if the carriers of the reduct of M along σ' of the sorts in S' are generated by function symbols in F'.

4.2   Encoding CSMOF into CASL

We define a GTC between the extended CSMOF institution $\mathcal{I}^{M^+}$ and the institution $\mathcal{I}^C$ for $SubPCFOL^=$. The class hierarchy represented within a $\mathcal{I}^{M^+}$ signature is basically translated into a set of sorts complying with a subsorting relation, properties are translated into predicates, and an axiom is introduced to relate predicates derived from bidirectional properties. Formally, every $\mathcal{I}^{M^+}$ signature $\Sigma = (\boldsymbol{C}, \alpha, \boldsymbol{P})$ with $\boldsymbol{C} = (C, \leq_C)$ and $\boldsymbol{P} = (R, P)$ is translated into a theory $((S, TF, PF, P, \leq_S), E)$ such that:

- For every class name c in C, there is a sort name $c \in S$.
- For every $c_1 \leq_C c_2$ with $c_1, c_2 \in C$, we have $c_1 \leq_S c_2$ with $c_1, c_2 \in S$.
- For every $c \in \alpha$ there is an axiom in E stating that c is the disjoint embedding of its subsorts (sort generation constraint).
- For every $\langle r_1 : c_1, r_2 : c_2 \rangle \in P$, there are two predicates $r_1 : c_2 \times c_1$ and $r_2 : c_1 \times c_2 \in \Pi$, and an axiom in E stating the equivalence of the predicates, i.e. $r_1(x, y)$ iff $r_2(y, x)$ with $x \in S_1, y \in S_2$. In the case of predicates with the default role name _, we only generate the predicate in the opposite direction of the default role, i.e. if $\langle \_ : c_1, r_2 : c_2 \rangle$ or $\langle r_1 : c_1, \_ : c_2 \rangle$ we only have $r_2 : c_1 \times c_2$ or $r_1 : c_2 \times c_1$, respectively.

We consider the existence of a built-in extension of the institution $\mathcal{I}^C$, e.g. the CASL standard library. The sets of functions TF and PF within this extension contain those functions defined for built-in types (like $+$ for strings).

As an example, the signature corresponding to the class metamodel in Fig. 1 is translated into a theory such that there are sorts for each class, e.g. Package and UMLModelElement, within the subsorting relation, e.g. Package $\leq_S$ UMLModelElement; and there are predicates for each property, e.g. elements : Package $\times$ Classifier and name : UMLModelElement $\times$ String. There is a sort generation constraint stating that UMLModelElement is the disjoint embedding of its subsorts Attribute, Classifier, and Package. There are also axioms stating the equivalence of the predicates derived from bidirectional properties, e.g. $\forall x :$ Package, $y :$ Classifier. elements$(x, y) \Leftrightarrow$ namespace(y, x)

In the case of a SW-model formula Ω, each variable within the formula (representing an object) is translated into a total function of the corresponding type. We also add several axioms in order to represent implicit constraints in the $\mathcal{I}^{M^+}$ institution which are not necessarily kept when representing the basic elements in $SubPCFOL^=$, as for example the need of distinguishing between two different variables (functions in the target institution) and the specification of the cases in which a property holds (when there is a syntactic link represented within the formula Ω). Formally,

- For every $x^c \in \upsilon(\Omega)$ there is a total function $x : c \in TF$ with $c \in S$
- For every $\langle r_1, x^{c_1}, r_2, y^{c_2} \rangle \in \omega(\Omega)$ with $\langle r_1 : c_1, r_2 : c_2 \rangle \in P$, there is an axiom in E stating that the predicate $r_2 : c_1 \times c_2$ holds for $x : c_1, y : c_2 \in TF$. Notice that the opposite direction holds by the equivalence of predicates stated during the signature translation.
- E has some additional axioms:
  - Distinguishability: $\{x_i \neq x_j \mid i \neq j.\ x_i, x_j : c \in TF\}$ for all $c \in S$
  - Completeness of elements: for all $x : c$ we have that $x = o_i$ for some $o_i : c \in TF$. When c is a non-abstract class having sub-classes, completeness must be defined for $o_i : c' \in TF$ for all $c' \leq c$.
  - Completeness of relations: for all $x : c_1, y : c_2$ we have that $r(x, y)$ holds only if $x = o_1$ and $y = o_2$ for some $o_1 : c_1, o_2 : c_2$ for which $r(c_1, c_2)$ hold.

The "distinguishability" and "completeness of elements" axioms correspond to the "no junk, no confusion" principle: there are no other values than those denoted by the functions $x : c$, and distinct functions denote different values.

The variables within the class SW-model in Fig. 1 are translated into total functions, e.g. p : Package, c : Class and ID : String. Moreover, for every link there is an axiom stating that the corresponding predicate holds for the functions corresponding to the translated elements within the link. This axiom can be stated in conjunction with the "completeness of relations", e.g. $\forall\, x :$ Package, $y :$ Classifier. elements$(x, y) \Leftrightarrow (x = \mathrm{p} \;\wedge\; y = \mathrm{c}) \vee (x = \mathrm{p} \;\wedge\; y = \mathrm{pdt})$. In the case of the non-abstract class Classifier which has sub-classes, the "completeness of elements" constraint is stated by the axiom: $\forall\, x :$ Classifier. $x = \mathrm{c} \vee x = \mathrm{pdt}$. Finally, the "distinguishability" constraint must be stated between elements of sorts related by the subsorting relation. For example, in the case of the elements within the UMLModelElement hierarchy, we have the following constraint: $\neg(\mathrm{a} = \mathrm{c}) \wedge \neg(\mathrm{a} = \mathrm{p}) \wedge \neg(\mathrm{a} = \mathrm{pdt}) \wedge \neg(\mathrm{c} = \mathrm{p}) \wedge \neg(\mathrm{c} = \mathrm{pdt}) \wedge \neg(\mathrm{p} = \mathrm{pdt})$.

For the translation of a multiplicity constraint formula we define the following predicates for constraining the size of the set of elements in a relation:

- $min(n, R : D \times C)$ holds if for all $y : D$ there exists $x_1, ..., x_n : C$ such that $R(y, x_i)$ for all $i = \{1..n\}$, and $x_i \neq x_j$ for all $i = \{1..n - 1\}$, $j = i + 1$.
- $max(n, R : D \times C)$ holds if for all $y : D$ and $x_1, ..., x_{n+1} : C$, $Rel(y, x_i)$ for all $i = \{1..n + 1\}$ implies there is some $x_i = x_j$ with $i = \{1..n\}$, $j = i + 1$.

The first predicate states that there are at least n different elements related to every element y by the relation R, which represents a minimal cardinality for the relation. The other predicate states that there are no more than n elements related to any element y by the relation R, which represents a maximal cardinality for the relation. Using these predicates, we can translate any multiplicity constraint formula as follows:

- $n \leq \#D \bullet R$ is translated into $min(n, R : D \times C)$
- $\#D \bullet R \leq n$ is translated into $max(n, R : D \times C)$
- $\#D \bullet R = n$ is translated into $min(n, R : D \times C) \wedge max(n, R : D \times C)$

such that $Q : C \times D, R : D \times C \in \Pi$ are the predicates generated by the translation of the property $\langle R : C, Q : D\rangle$. If the multiplicity constraint involves the other end, i.e. $C \bullet Q$, the predicate $Q : C \times D$ is used instead of $R : D \times C$.

As an example, the formula $\#(\mathrm{UMLModelElement} \bullet \mathrm{name}) = 1$ derived from Fig. 1 is translated into the conjunction of

$$min(1, \mathrm{name} : \mathrm{UMLModelElement} \times \mathrm{String}) =$$
$$\forall\, x_1 : \mathrm{UMLModelElement}.\ \exists\, y_1 : \mathrm{String}.\ \mathrm{name}(x_1, y_1)$$
$$max(1, \mathrm{name} : \mathrm{UMLModelElement} \times \mathrm{String}) =$$
$$\forall\, x_1 : \mathrm{UMLModelElement}, y_2, y_1 : \mathrm{String}.$$
$$(\mathrm{name}(x_1, y_1) \wedge\ \mathrm{name}(x_1, y_2)) \Rightarrow y_1 = y_2$$

Given a $\mathcal{I}^{\mathrm{M}^+}$ theory $T = \langle \Sigma, \Psi\rangle$, a $\mathcal{I}^{\mathrm{C}}$ model M of its translated theory (Σ', E) is translated into a Σ-interpretation denoted $I = (V_C^T(O), A)$ such that: each non-empty carrier set $|M|_s$ with $s \in S$, is translated into the set V_c in the object domain $V_C^T(O)$, with s the translation of type $c \in T(C)$; and each relation p_M of a predicate symbol $r_2(c_1, c_2) \in P$ derived from the translation of a predicate $\langle r_1 : c_1, r_2 : c_2\rangle$, is translated into the relation $p^I \subseteq V_{c_1} \times V_{c_2} \in A$.

4.3   Encoding QVTR into CASL

We define a GTC between the extended QVTR institution $\mathcal{I}^{Q^+}$ and the institution $\mathcal{I}^C$ for $SubPCFOL^=$. Every $\mathcal{I}^{Q^+}$ signature $\langle \Sigma_1^M, \Sigma_2^M \rangle$ is translated by the functor Φ into a theory such that each signature Σ_i^M is translated as defined in the encoding of CSMOF into CASL. We assume that the institution $\mathcal{I}^E$ of the expressions language has a correspondence (via a comorphism) with the built-in extension of the institution $\mathcal{I}^C$.

Formulas representing keys and transformation rules are translated into named first-order formulas. Formulas will be of the form $P \Leftrightarrow F$ such that P is the predicate naming the formula, and F represents the conditions which must hold in order to satisfy a key constraint φ^K or transformation φ^R.

In the case of a formula φ^K, the formula F defines that there are not two different instances of that class with the same combination of properties conforming the key of such class. Formally, any formula $\langle C, \{r_1, ..., r_n\} \rangle$ is translated into a predicate key_C naming a key constraint definition, and a formula of the form $key\_C \Leftrightarrow \forall x, y \in C, v_j : T_j. \ x \neq y \rightarrow \bigwedge_{i,j} r_i(x, v_j) \rightarrow \bigvee_{i,j} \neg r_i(y, v_j)$, with $r_i(\_, \_)$ one of the two predicates from the translation of the property $\langle r_1 : C_1, r_2 : C_2 \rangle$ such that one of the roles is of type C and the other of type T_j.

The key formula in the example is translated into the expression

$$key\_Table \Leftrightarrow \forall x, y \in Table, v_1 : String, \ v_2 : Schema.$$
$$x \neq y \rightarrow name(x, v_1) \wedge schema(x, v_2) \rightarrow \neg name(y, v_1) \vee \neg schema(y, v_2)$$

In the case of a formula φ^R, the formula F declares that top-level relations must hold, and each individual rule is translated into the set of conditions stated by the checking semantics of QVT-Relations. Formally, every rule $Rule = \langle top, VarSet, ParSet, Pattern_i \ (i = 1, 2), when, where \rangle \in \varphi^R$ is translated into: a predicate $Rule : T_1 \times ... \times T_n \in P$ with $ParSet = \{T_1, .., T_n\}$, and a predicate Top_Rule without parameters (only if $top = true$), naming the formula; and a formula $\forall v_1 : T_1, ..., v_n : T_n. \ Rule(v_1, ..., v_n) \Leftrightarrow F$ such that $Rule(v_1, ..., v_n)$ is the predicate defined before. In the case of a top rule, there is also a formula $Rule \Leftrightarrow F$. For the formula F there are two cases corresponding to the checking semantics of QVT-Relations:

1. If WhenVarSet $= \emptyset$

$$\forall \ x_1, ..., x_n \in (VarSet \backslash 2\_VarSet) \backslash ParSet. \ (\Phi(Pattern_1) \rightarrow$$
$$\exists \ y_1, ..., y_m \in 2\_VarSet \backslash ParSet. \ (\Phi(Pattern_2) \wedge \ \Phi(where)))$$

2. If WhenVarSet $\neq \emptyset$

$$\forall \ z_1, ..., z_o \in WhenVarSet \backslash ParSet. \ (\Phi(when) \rightarrow$$
$$\forall \ x_1, ..., x_n \in (VarSet \backslash (WhenVarSet \cup 2\_VarSet)) \backslash ParSet.$$
$$(\Phi(Pattern_1) \rightarrow \exists \ y_1, ..., y_m \in 2\_VarSet \backslash ParSet.$$
$$(\Phi(Pattern_2) \wedge \ \Phi(where))))$$

The translation of $Pattern_i = \langle E_i, A_i, Pr_i \rangle$ is the formula $\bigwedge r_2(x,y) \wedge \Phi(Pr_i)$ such that $r_2(x,y)$ is the translation of predicate $p = \langle r_1 : C, r_2 : D \rangle$ for every $rel(p, x, y) \in A_i$ with $x : C, y : D$; and $\Phi(Pr_i)$ is the translation of the predicate into CASL. Moreover, the translation of $when = \langle when_c, when_r \rangle$ (or where) is the formula $\bigwedge Rule(v) \wedge \Phi(when_c)$ such that $Rule(v)$ is the parametric invocation of the rule $(Rule, v) \in when_r$, and $\Phi(when_c)$ is the translation of the predicate.

In the example, the relation `ClassToTable` is translated into CASL as follows:

```
Top_ClassToTable <=> forall p:Package; s:Schema . PackageToSchema(p,s) =>
    forall c:Class; cn:String . namespace(c,p) /\ kind(c,Persistent) /\
        name(c,cn) => exists t:Table . schema(t,s) /\
            name(t,cn) /\ AttributeToColumn(c,t)
```

The formula states that the relation holds whereas for every package and schema satisfying the relation `PackageToSchema`, if there is a persistent class within that package, there must exists a table in the corresponding schema with the same class name. Moreover, the attributes and columns of both elements must be in the relation `AttributeToColumn`.

Given a $\mathcal{I}^{Q^+}$ theory $T = \langle \Sigma, \Psi \rangle$, a model M of its translated theory (Σ', E) is translated into a Σ-model $\mathcal{M} = \langle \mathcal{M}_1^M, \mathcal{M}_2^M \rangle$ by constructing disjoint models with an interpretation of elements for each corresponding $\mathcal{I}^{M^+}$ theory.

5   The Environment in Action

We have implemented a prototype of our environment using the Heterogeneous Tools Set (HETS,[3]). HETS is an open source software providing a general framework for formal methods integration and proof management, based on the Theory of Institutions, as introduced above. Based on this foundation, HETS supports a variety of different logics. More specifically, HETS consists of logic-specific tools for the parsing and static analysis of basic logical theories written in the different involved logics (e.g. our extended CSMOF and QVTR institutions), as well as a logic-independent parsing and static analysis tool for structured theories and theory relations. Proof support for other logics can be obtained by using logic translations defined by comorphisms (e.g. from CSMOF to CASL). Our prototype and examples can be downloaded together with the HETS distribution.

Within this prototype, MDE experts can specify model transformations in their domain and such specifications can be complemented by verification experts with other properties to be verified, e.g. non-structural constraints. All this information is taken by HETS, which performs automatic translations of proof obligations into other logics and allows selecting the corresponding prover to be used, whilst a graphical user interface is provided for visualizing the whole proof. In other words, we provided to MDE practitioners the "glue" they need for connecting their domain with the logical domains needed for verification.

Our problem is represented as a heterogeneous specification using CASL structuring constructs, with three logics: CASL, CSMOF and QVTR. We also perform logic translations through the CSMOF2CASL and QVTR2CASL comorphisms. Next, there is an excerpt of the heterogeneous specification of the example.

```
(1)    logic CSMOF
       from QVTR/UML get UML |-> UMLMetamodel
       from QVTR/UML_WMult get UML |-> UMLConstraints

(2)    spec UMLProof = UMLMetamodel
       then %implies UMLConstraints end

(3)    logic QVTR
       from QVTR/uml2rdbms get uml2rdbms |-> QVTTransformation

(4)    logic CASL
       spec ModelTransformation = QVTTransformation with logic QVTR2CASL
       then %implies
         . key_RDBMS_Table
         . Top_PackageToSchema
         . Top_ClassToTable
       end
```

Within the CSMOF logic (1) we create two specifications from standard XMI files with the information of the class metamodel and SW-model in Fig. 1. This implies the creation of a representation of signatures and formulas according to the institution defined in Section 3. Another specification is created (2) by extending UMLMetamodel and stating that UMLConstraints is implied. This means that every formula (multiplicity constraint) in the second specification can be derived, thus there must be a proof of it. This is how the satisfaction relation of the CSMOF institution is checked. We also use the QVTR logic (3) to create a specification from a standard .qvt file according to the institution defined in Section 3. The only difference with respect to the QVT standard is that instead of using OCL as the expressions language, we use for now a very simple language containing boolean connectives, constants true and false, term equality, strings and variables. Finally, we move into CASL (using the comorphism QVTR2CASL) for creating another specification (4) in which the translation of key and rule formulas defined in Section 3 are implied by the transformation specification. When a proposition, e.g. Top_ClassToTable, is called from the CASL specification, a proof of the implication must be given. We can also translate our specifications and complement them with other constraints which cannot be stated as formulas of the former institutions, e.g. for stating that there cannot be two Classifiers with the same name in the UMLMetamodel specification. For this purpose we use the CSMOF2CASL comorphism as follows.

```
spec MoreProofs = UMLMetamodel with logic CSMOF2CASL
then %implies
   forall x,y:Classifier; str:String . name(x,str) /\ name(y,str) => x = y
end
```

Once our heterogeneous specification is processed, HETS constructs a development graph in which nodes correspond to specifications, some of them with open proof obligations, and arrows to dependencies between them. We have three proof obligations corresponding to those formulas marked as %implies within the specifications. Proof goals can be discharged using a logic-specific calculus, e.g. some prover for CASL in the example. The double arrows are heterogeneous theorem links, meaning that the logic changes along the arrow. In the example this corresponds to the extension of specifications by using the comorphisms. It can be noticed that we can use any other logic within the logics graph of HETS through comorphisms. This improves the proof capabilities of our environment.

5.1   Verification Properties

There are several properties that can be verified, some of them related to the computational nature of transformations and target properties of transformation languages, and other to the modeling nature of transformations [2]. The minimal requirement is conformance, i.e. that the source and target models (resp. the transformation specification) are syntactically well-formed instances of the source and target metamodels (resp. the transformation language). Our framework provides this verification in three parts. During the construction of CSMOF and QVTR theories, parsing and static analysis check whether signatures and formulas are well-formed, and (as we explained before) a SW-model within a signature is a structurally well-formed instance of the metamodel in the same signature, as well as a transformation specification given in a formula is well-formed with respect to the signature containing both source and target metamodels. Multiplicity constraints are verified when proving the satisfaction of CSMOF formulas. Finally, non-structural constraints are verified by extending both CSMOF and QVTR specifications using other logics, as CASL in the example. HETS also allows for disproving things using consistency checkers. This provides an additional point of view. In particular, we can check if a set of rules have contradictory conditions which could inhibit its execution.

In most cases a general-purpose logic, as provided by CASL, is enough to cover most of the verification approaches in [2]. The inclusion of OCL as an institution will provide additional support in this sense. However, the verification process may depend on the problem to verify, since it is well-known that there is a "state explosion" problem when using automated checkers. Thus, automatic proofs are not always possible. In HETS it is possible to choose the tool we want to use, e.g. not an automated theorem proving system but an interactive theorem prover.

Verification interests go beyond these kinds of problems. When verifying a model transformation we want to consider its elements as a whole and not individually. In this sense, sometimes the notion of a transformation model is used, i.e. a model composed by the source and target metamodel, the transformation specification and the well-formedness rules. We have a transformation model in a QVTR theory (QVTTransformation in the example) which allows to add other properties by combining elements from the source and target metamodels and SW-models. With this we can state model syntax relations, trying to ensure that certain elements or structures of any input model will be transformed into other elements or structures in the output model. This problem arises when, for example, these relations cannot be inferred by just looking at the individual transformation rules. We can also state model semantics relations, e.g. temporal properties and refinement. Besides further work is needed to evaluate the alternatives, there are languages and tools, as ModalCASL and VSE (based on dynamic logics) commonly used for verifying these kinds of things. We could also be interested in working at another abstraction level, i.e. not considering specific SW-models but only metamodels and the transformation specification. This can be useful, for example, for proving that a transformation guarantees some model syntax relations when transforming any valid source SW-model. The problem here is that we need another institutional representation, e.g. we need to consider an abstract representation of a SW-model instead of a fixed one.

6   Related Work

There are some works that define environments for the comprehensive verification of MDE elements based on a unified mathematical formalism, e.g. in [12] rewriting logic is used to analyze MOF-like and QVT-like elements. Since HETS integrates rewriting logic, we can use it instead of our comorphism into CASL. Nevertheless, since our institution is logic-independent it provides more flexibility for the definition of further specific comorphisms into other logics and languages (e.g. UML). In general, the use of a fixed unified mathematical formalism serving as a unique semantic basis can be quite restrictive. With our approach we can move between formalisms, and use a unified mathematical formalism if necessary (e.g. when transforming the whole specification into CASL).

In [13] the authors define a language-independent representation of metamodels and model transformations supporting many transformation languages. They also define mappings to the B and Z3 formalisms. Since they use only one generic language, only one semantic mapping needs to be defined for each target formalism. However, the semantic mapping should be semantics-preserving, and this aspect is not formally addressed in such work. In our case, comorphisms already preserve the semantics with respect to the satisfaction relation.

There are works representing the semantics of UML class diagrams with first-order logic, as in [14]. Since there are no so many alternatives for this representation, these works have similarities with our representation of extended CSMOF into CASL. In [15] the authors explain how class diagrams with OCL constraints can be translated into CASL. However, their definition is informally presented, and not in terms of a comorphism. In [16] the authors define a comorphism from UML class diagrams with rigidity constraints to ModalCASL (an extension of CASL). Since our $\mathcal{I}^{\mathrm{M}^+}$ institution is an adaptation of the institution for UML class diagrams, the comorphisms have some aspects in common, as the translation of formulas, but without the modal logic particularities.

There are several approaches to heterogeneous specification for traditional software development, but there is little tool support. CafeOBJ [17] is an institution-based approach providing a fixed cube of eight logics and twelve projections (formalized as institution morphisms), not allowing logic encodings (formalized as comorphisms). Thus, it is not an option for the definition of our environment.

Moreover, HeteroGenius [18] is another institution-based framework allowing the interaction between different external tools for performing hybrid analysis of a specification. However, the framework is not formally defined or available to be used as a basis for our environment.

7   Conclusions and Future Work

We have presented the implementation of an environment for the formal verification of different MDE aspects using heterogeneous verification approaches, which is based on the ideas introduced in [4]. The environment was integrated into HETS by defining comorphisms from institutions representing MDE elements to CASL, the core language of HETS. The existent connections between CASL and other logics within HETS broadens the spectrum of logical domains in which the verification of MDE elements can be addressed. The environment supports a separation of duties between software developers (MDE and formal methods experts) such that a formal perspective is available whenever it is required. A developer imports MDE elements, supplement them with verification properties specified using any other logic supported by HETS, and perform the heterogeneous verification assisted by the tool. Since the implementation can generate a heterogeneous specification from the same files used by MDE practitioners, and there is no need of rewriting MDE building block in each logic involved, the environment is scalable without human assistance.

A current drawback is the inexistence of an institution for OCL, in which QVT is strongly based. For now we have considered a very simple expressions language, but the definition of such institution is subject of further work. In the same sense, we expect to extend the institutions to include some elements not considered before. This will strengthen the formal environment for MDE. Since our institutions formalize languages strongly related with those in the UML ecosystem, it will be interesting to explore the possibility of integrating them with other languages, as those already defined as institutions in [19].

We need to continue bridging the gap between MDE and formal verification in terms of tool development in order to practitioners really be able to benefit from our approach. We can connect the definition of the MDE elements in any popular tool with an automatic generation of the heterogeneous specification. Moreover, we could perform an automated verification of some properties (if possible) by running HETS in background. We also need to improve feedback from existing formal tools, which needs better traceability between the problem definition and the results given by a verification tool. We can define some traceability links from comorphisms, interpret the output of the verification tool and return something that the MDE practitioner can interpret. Moreover, the environment deals with many verification properties, but a deeper understanding of this (as for example about the behavior of models) is a must. In this sense, we can use the knowledge in [2] to provide a guide for the selection of the "right" verification approach for the problem which is of interest to verify. We also need to apply our approach to industrial, real-size examples for strengthening the results.

References

1. Kent, S.: Model driven engineering. In: Butler, M., Petre, L., Sere, K. (eds.) IFM 2002. LNCS, vol. 2335, pp. 286–298. Springer, Heidelberg (2002)
2. Calegari, D., Szasz, N.: Verification of model transformations: A survey of the state-of-the-art. ENTCS **292**, 5–25 (2013)
3. Mossakowski, T.: Heterogeneous specification and the heterogeneous tool set. Technical report, Universitaet Bremen, Habilitation thesis (2005)
4. Calegari, D., Szasz, N.: Institution-based semantics for MOF and QVT-relations. In: Iyoda, J., de Moura, L. (eds.) SBMF 2013. LNCS, vol. 8195, pp. 34–50. Springer, Heidelberg (2013)
5. Goguen, J.A., Burstall, R.M.: Institutions: Abstract model theory for specification and programming. J. ACM **39**, 95–146 (1992)
6. Mossakowski, T., Haxthausen, A.E., Sannella, D., Tarlecki, A.: Casl - the common algebraic specification language: Semantics and proof theory. Computers and Artificial Intelligence **22**, 285–321 (2003)
7. OMG: Meta Object Facility (MOF) 2.0 Core Specification. Specification Version 2.0, Object Management Group (2003)
8. OMG: Object Constraint Language. Formal Specification Version 2.2, Object Management Group (2010)
9. OMG: Meta Object Facility (MOF) 2.0 Query/View/Transformation. Final Adopted Specification Version 1.1, Object Management Group (2009)
10. Calegari, D.: Heterogeneous Verification of Model Transformations. PhD thesis, Universidad de la República - PEDECIBA (2014). https://www.fing.edu.uy/inco/pedeciba/bibliote/tesis/tesisd-calegari.pdf
11. Codescu, M.: Generalized theoroidal institution comorphisms. In: Corradini, A., Montanari, U. (eds.) WADT 2008. LNCS, vol. 5486, pp. 88–101. Springer, Heidelberg (2009)
12. Boronat, A., Heckel, R., Meseguer, J.: Rewriting logic semantics and verification of model transformations. In: Chechik, M., Wirsing, M. (eds.) FASE 2009. LNCS, vol. 5503, pp. 18–33. Springer, Heidelberg (2009)
13. Lano, K., Rahimi, S.K.: Model transformation specification and design. Advances in Computers **85**, 123–163 (2012)
14. Shan, L., Zhu, H.: Semantics of metamodels in UML. In: Chin, W., Qin, S. (eds.) TASE 2009, pp. 55–62. IEEE Computer Society (2009)
15. Bidoit, M., Hennicker, R., Tort, F., Wirsing, M.: Correct realizations of interface constraints with OCL. In: France, R., Rumpe, B. (eds.) UML 1999. LNCS, vol. 1723, pp. 399–415. Springer, Heidelberg (1999)
16. James, P., Knapp, A., Mossakowski, T., Roggenbach, M.: Designing domain specific languages – a craftsman's approach for the railway domain using CASL. In: Martí-Oliet, N., Palomino, M. (eds.) WADT 2012. LNCS, vol. 7841, pp. 178–194. Springer, Heidelberg (2013)
17. Diaconescu, R., Futatsugi, K.: Logical foundations of CafeOBJ. Theor. Comput. Sci. **285**, 289–318 (2002)
18. Giménez, M., Moscato, M.M., Pombo, C.G.L., Frias, M.F.: Heterogenius: a framework for hybrid analysis of heterogeneous software specifications. In: Aguirre, N., Ribeiro, L. (eds.) LAFM 2013. EPTCS, Vol. 139, pp. 65–70 (2014)
19. Cengarle, M.V., Knapp, A., Tarlecki, A., Wirsing, M.: A heterogeneous approach to UML semantics. In: Degano, P., De Nicola, R., Meseguer, J. (eds.) Montanari Fest. LNCS, vol. 5065, pp. 383–402. Springer, Heidelberg (2008)

A Coinductive Animation of Turing Machines

Alberto Ciaffaglione[✉]

Dipartimento di Matematica e Informatica, Università di Udine, Udine, Italy
alberto.ciaffaglione@uniud.it

Abstract. We adopt corecursion and coinduction to formalize Turing
Machines and their operational semantics in the proof assistant `Coq`. By
combining the formal analysis of converging and diverging evaluations,
our approach allows us to certify the implementation of the functions
computed by concrete Turing Machines. Our effort may be seen as a
first step towards the formal development of basic computability theory.

1 Introduction

In this paper we present and discuss an encoding of *Turing Machines* (TMs) [12]
and their semantics in the `Coq` implementation of the *Calculus of (Co)Inductive
Constructions* ($CC^{(Co)Ind}$). Actually, we do not find in the literature much formalization work dealing with *computability theory*, a foundational, major area of
computer science, whereas several other domains have benefited, in recent years,
from formal developments carried out within mechanized environments.

As far as we know, the most recent contributions are [1,2,10,13]. Norrish
[10] develops a proof of equivalence between the recursive functions and the λ-
calculus computational models, and formalizes some computability theory results
in the `HOL4` system. The two works most related to the present one are those
focusing on TMs. Asperti and Ricciotti [1] develop computability theory up to
the existence of a universal machine, by carrying out their effort from a perspective oriented to complexity theory in `Matita`. Xu, Zhang and Urban [13] prove
the undecidability of the halting problem and relate TMs to register machines
and recursive functions by formalizing a universal TM in `Isabelle/HOL`.

Actually, TMs form an object system which is challenging in several respects.
First, TMs are *non-structured*. Second, the *tape*, used by TMs as workspace for
computing, is infinite in both directions. Third, the evaluation of TMs may give
rise to *diverging* computations. Therefore, TMs provide with a typical scenario
where the user is required to define and reason about *infinite* objects and concepts. To address formally such an object system, in this paper we settle within
Intuitionistic Type Theory. This framework makes available *coinductive types*,
i.e., types that have been conceived to provide finite representations of infinite
structures. In particular, a handy technique for dealing with *corecursive* definitions and *coinductive* proofs in $CC^{(Co)Ind}$ was introduced by Coquand [4] and
refined by Giménez [6]. Such an approach is particularly appealing, because
proofs carried out by coinduction are accommodated as any other infinite, core-
cursively defined object. This technique is mechanized in the `Coq` system [11].

C. Braga and N. Martí-Oliet (Eds.): SBMF 2014, LNCS 8941, pp. 80–95, 2015.
DOI: 10.1007/978-3-319-15075-8_6

The present work is in fact a departure from the two cited formalizations of TMs, due to the following reasons. On the one hand, we adopt corecursion as *definition* principle and coinduction as *proof* principle (while the alternative contributions do not employ coinductive tools). On the other hand, inspired by our previous effort on unlimited register machines [2], we encode TMs and their operational semantics from the perspective of *program certification*: *i.e.*, we introduce and justify a methodology to prove the correctness of concrete TMs.

The motivations to carry out our formalization of TMs in Coq are the following. As it is well-known, traditional papers and textbooks about TMs treat the topic at a more superficial level of detail, and in particular the arguments why individual TMs are correct are often left out. Therefore, the mechanization effort in a proof assistant, besides offering the possibility to discover errors, may typically improve the confidence on the subject (*e.g.*, the correctness proofs for concrete TMs in [13], developed to formalize the undecidability of the halting problem, are acknowledged as the most important contribution). Besides being intellectually stimulating, our work has also the educational objective of popularizing corecursion and coinduction, an aim which is pursued by justifying the formalization methodology in an analytical way and via suggestive examples.

We have used, as starting point for our development, the textbooks by Cutland [5] and by Hopcroft et al. [7]. As an effort towards a broader audience, we display rarely Coq code in this paper, but present the encoding at a more abstract level (however, the formalization is available as a web appendix [3]).

Synopsis. In the next section we recall TMs, then in the two following sections we introduce their formalization and illustrate the implementation of coinduction in Coq. In the two central sections 5 and 6 we define a big-step operational semantics for TMs and address its adequacy via a small-step semantics, respectively. In the core Section 7 we prove the correctness of three sample TMs, then we state final remarks and discuss related and future work.

2   Turing Machines

Turing Machines (TMs), one among the frameworks proposed to set up a formal characterization of the intuitive ideas of computability and decidability, perform algorithms as carried out by a human agent using paper and pencil. In this work we address *deterministic*, single tape TMs, as introduced by Cutland [5].

Alphabet and tape. TMs operate on a *paper tape*, which is *infinite* in both directions and is divided into single squares along its length. Each square is either blank or contains a symbol from a *finite* set of symbols $s_0, s_1, \ldots, s_n$, named the *alphabet* $\mathcal{A}$ (in fact, the "blank" B is counted as the first symbol s_0).

Specification and computation. At any time, TMs both scan a single square of the tape (via a *reading/writing head*) and are in one of a *finite* number of states $q_1, \ldots, q_m$. Depending on the current state q_i and the symbol being scanned s_h, TMs take *actions*, as indicated by a *specification*[1], *i.e.* a *finite*

---

[1] As said above, we deal with deterministic TMs, *i.e.*, *non-ambiguous* specifications: for every pair q_i, s_h there is at most one quadruple of the form $\langle q_i, s_h, x, q_j \rangle$.

collection of quadruples $\langle q_i, s_h, x, q_j \rangle$, where $i, j \in [1..m]$, $h \in [0..n]$, $x \in \{R, L\} \cup \mathcal{A}$:

$\langle q_i, s_h, x, q_j \rangle \triangleq$ 1) if $x=R$ then move the head one square to the right
else if $x=L$ then move the head one square to the left
else if $x=s_k$ ($k \in [0..n]$) then replace s_h with s_k
2) change the state from q_i into q_j

When provided with a tape, a specification becomes an *individual TM*, which is capable to perform a *computation*: it keeps carrying out actions by starting from the initial state q_1 and the symbol scanned by the initial position of the head.

Such a computation is said to *converge* if and only if, at some given time, there is no action specified for the current state q_i and the current symbol s_h (that is, there is no quadruple telling what to do next). On the other hand, if this never happens, such a computation is said to *diverge*.

Computable functions. TMs may be regarded as devices for computing numerical *functions*, according to the following conventions. A natural number m is represented on a tape by an amount of $m+1$ *consecutive* occurrences of the "tally" symbol 1 (in such a way, the representation of the $0 \in \mathbb{N}$ is distinguished from the blank tape). Then, a machine M computes the *partial* function $f : \mathbb{N} \rightharpoonup \mathbb{N}$ when, for every $a, b \in \mathbb{N}$, the computation under M, starting from its initial state and the leftmost 1 of the a representation, stops with a tape that contains a *total* of b symbols 1 (not necessarily consecutive) *if and only if* $a \in dom(f)$ and $f(a)=b$ (therefore f is undefined on all inputs a that make the computation diverge). n-ary partial functions $g : \mathbb{N}^n \rightharpoonup \mathbb{N}$ are computed in a similar way, where the representations of the n inputs are separated by single blank squares.

Consequently, computability theory can be developed via TMs, leading to the well-known characterization of the class of effectively computable functions.

3   Turing Machines in Coq

As described in the previous section, TMs are formed by two components: the specification and the tape, whose content in fact instantiates the former, making it executable. Specifications and tapes actually work together, but are evidently independent of each other from the point of view of the formalization matter.

Our encoding of TMs in Coq reflects such an independence: in the present work we are mainly interested in the formal treatment of the tape, which is more problematic and particularly delicate; conversely, we do not pursue the specification-component management (*automata* are actually supported by Coq's library), thus keeping that part of the formalization down to a minimum.

Specification and Tape. Concerning the *specification* part, we represent states via natural numbers (reserving the 0 for the halting state, for which no transition is provided), while alphabet symbols and operations performed by the head are finite collections of elements (we fix the alphabet by adding the "mark" symbol 0 to the "blank" B and the "tally" 1 of previous section). Finally, specifications are finite sequences (*i.e.*, lists) of actions (*i.e.*, quadruples)[2]:

$$
\begin{array}{llll}
State : p, q, i & \in \mathbb{N} = \{0, 1, 2, \ldots\} & & \text{state} \\
Sym \ : a, b & \in \{B, 1, 0\} & & \text{alphabet symbol} \\
Head : x, y & \in \{R, L, W(a)\} & & \text{head operation} \\
Act \ \ : \alpha & \in State \times Sym \times State \times Head & & \text{action} \\
Spec \ : T, U, V & ::= (\iota \mapsto \alpha_\iota)^{\iota \in [0..n]} \ (n \in \mathbb{N}) & & \text{specification}
\end{array}
$$

To formalize the *tape*, whose squares are scanned by the head and contain the alphabet symbols, we adopt a pair of *streams* (*a.k.a.* infinite sequences), a datatype borrowed from the `Haskell` community, where is named "zipper":

$$
\begin{array}{lll}
HTape : l, r & ::= (\iota \mapsto a_\iota)^{\iota \in [0..\infty]} & \text{half tape (stream)} \\
Tape \ \ : s, t, u & ::= \langle\!\langle \, l, r \, \rangle\!\rangle & \text{full tape (zipper)}
\end{array}
$$

The intended meaning of this encoding is that the second stream ($r = r_0{:}r_1{:}\ldots$) models the infiniteness of the tape towards the right, while the first stream ($l = l_0{:}l_1{:}\ldots$) is infinite towards the left. At any time, the head "$\Downarrow$" will be scrutinizing the first symbol of r, which corresponds physically to:

$$
\Downarrow
$$
$$
\cdots \mid l_1 \mid l_0 \mid r_0 \mid r_1 \mid \cdots
$$

This representation allows for a direct access to the content of the tape, an operation which has therefore constant complexity (see the next section).

Transitions. To make specifications concretely compute, it is necessary, given the current state and tape symbol, to extract from such lists the corresponding target state and head operation. In our encoding, this task is carried out by a *transition* function $tr\colon Spec \to State \to Sym \to (State * Head)$.

In fact, we delegate to this transition function the responsibility to guarantee the *determinism* of TMs. We implement tr as a recursive function that scans a list-like specification T: given an input pair (p, a), the target state and head operation are obtained from the *first* quadruple of shape $\langle p, a, q, x \rangle$ found in T (no matter if there are other ones with form $\langle p, a, i, y \rangle$); if, on the other hand, there is no corresponding quadruple in T, tr returns an "halting" output:

Parameter halt: (State * Head).

The motivation for this naïve encoding of determinism is, as said at the beginning of the section, to keep the formalization as minimal as possible, being the modelling and the management of the tape the focus of our investigation.

4   Coinduction in `Coq`

The proof assistant `Coq` supports the formal treatment of circular, infinite data and relations by means of the mechanism of *coinductive types*.

First of all, one may formalize concrete, infinite *objects* (*i.e.*, data) as elements of coinductive *sets*[3], which are fully described by a set of *constructors*. From a

---

[2] The middle columns display the metavariables and the datatypes they range over.
[3] Coinductive sets are coinductive types whose type is the sort `Set`.

pure logical point of view, the constructors can be seen as *introduction rules*; these are interpreted coinductively, that is, they are applied infinitely many times, hence the type being defined is inhabited by infinite objects:

$$\frac{a \in Sym \quad h \in HTape}{a{:}h \in HTape} \ (HTape)_\infty$$

In this example we have formalized (via the *cons* constructor) infinite sequences, *i.e.*, streams, of symbols in the alphabet $Sym=\{B, 1, 0\}$, the coinductive set *HTape* which we have introduced in the Section 3 to model the tape of TMs.

Once a new coinductive type is defined, the system supplies automatically the *destructors*, that is, an extension of the native pattern-matching capability, to *consume* the elements of the type itself. Therefore, coinductive types can also be viewed as the *largest* collection of objects closed *w.r.t.* the destructors. We use here the standard *match* destructor to extract the *head* and *tail* from streams:

$$head(h) \triangleq \text{match } h \text{ with } a{:}k \Rightarrow a \qquad tail(h) \triangleq \text{match } h \text{ with } a{:}k \Rightarrow k$$

However, the destructors *cannot* be used for defining functions by *recursion* on coinductive types, because it is not possible to consume their elements down to a base case. In fact, the natural way to allow self-reference with coinductive types is the *dual* approach of *building* objects that belong to them. Such a goal is fulfilled by defining *corecursive* functions, like, *e.g.*, the following ones:

$$Bs \triangleq B{:}Bs \qquad same(a) \triangleq a{:}same(a) \qquad blink(a, b) \triangleq a{:}b{:}blink(a, b)$$
$$merge(h, k) \triangleq \text{match } h \text{ with } a{:}h' \Rightarrow \text{match } k \text{ with } b{:}k' \Rightarrow a{:}b{:}merge(h', k')$$

Corecursive functions yield infinite objects and may have any type as domain (notice that in the last definition the two parameters are infinite objects as well). To prevent the evaluation of corecursive functions from infinitely looping, their definition must satisfy a *guardedness condition*: every corecursive call has to be guarded by *at least* one constructor ("`:`" in the definitions above) and by *nothing but* constructors[4]. In fact, corecursive functions are never unfolded in Coq, unless their elements are explicitly needed, "on demand", by a destruction operation. This way of regulating the implementation of corecursion is inspired by *lazy* functional languages, where the constructors do not evaluate their arguments.

Given a coinductive set (such as *HTape* above), no *proof principle* can be automatically generated by the system: actually, proving properties about infinite objects requires the potential of building *proofs* which are infinite too. What is needed is the design of *ad-hoc* coinductive *predicates* (*i.e.*, relations)[5]; these types are in fact inhabited by infinite *proof terms*. The traditional example is *bisimilarity*, that we define on streams and name $\simeq \ \subseteq HTape \times HTape$:

$$\frac{a \in Sym \quad h, k \in HTape \quad h \simeq k}{a{:}h \simeq a{:}k} \ (\simeq)_\infty$$

---

[4] Syntactically, the constructors guard the corecursive call "on the left"; this captures the intuition that infinite objects are built via the repetition of a productive step.

[5] Coinductive predicates are coinductive types whose type is the sort Prop.

Two streams are bisimilar if we can observe that their heads coincide and, recursively, *i.e.*, *coinductively*, their tails are bisimilar. Once this new predicate is defined, the system provides a corresponding proof principle, to carry out proofs about bisimilarity: such a tool, named "guarded induction" principle [4,6], is particularly appealing in a context where proofs are managed as any other infinite object. In fact, a bisimilarity proof is just an infinite proof term built by corecursion (hence, it must respect the same guardedness constraint that corecursive functions have to). The guarded induction principle provides a handy technique for building proofs inhabiting coinductive predicates, as such proofs can be carried out *interactively* through the cofix tactic[6]. This tactic allows the user to yield proof terms as *infinitely regressive* proofs, by assuming the thesis as an extra hypothesis and using it later with care, *i.e.*, provided its application is guarded by constructors. In this way the user is not required to pick out any bisimulation beforehand, but may build it incrementally, via tactics.

To illustrate the support provided by the cofix tactic, we display below the proof of the property $\forall a, b \in Sym.\ merge(same(a), same(b)) \simeq blink(a, b)$, in *natural deduction* style[7]. By mimicking Coq's top-down proof practice, first the coinductive hypothesis is assumed among the hypotheses[8]; then, the corecursive functions *same*, *blink* and *merge*, in turn, are unfolded to perform a computation step; finally, the constructor $(\simeq)_\infty$ is applied twice. Hence, the initial goal is reduced to $merge(same(a), same(b)) \simeq blink(a, b)$, *i.e.*, an instance of the coinductive hypothesis. Therefore, the user is eventually allowed to exploit (*i.e.*, discharge) such a hypothesis, whose application is now guarded by the constructor $(\simeq)_\infty$. The application of the coinductive hypothesis in fact completes the proof, and intuitively has the effect of repeating ad infinitum the initial fragment of the proof term, thus realizing the "and so on forever" motto:

$$[\forall a, b \in Sym.\ merge(same(a), same(b)) \simeq blink(a, b)]_{(1)}$$
$$\vdots$$

$$\cfrac{\cfrac{\cfrac{\cfrac{merge(same(a), same(b)) \simeq blink(a, b)}{a{:}b{:}merge(same(a), same(b)) \simeq a{:}b{:}blink(a, b)}\ (\simeq)_\infty, twice}{merge(a{:}same(a), b{:}same(b)) \simeq a{:}b{:}blink(a, b)}\ (def{:}\ merge)}{merge(same(a), same(b)) \simeq blink(a, b)}\ (def{:}\ same,\ blink)}{\forall a, b \in Sym.\ merge(same(a), same(b)) \simeq blink(a, b)}\ \begin{matrix}(1), (introduction)\end{matrix}$$

with $a, b \in Sym$

5 Operational Semantics

As stressed in Sections 2 and 3, the semantics of TMs' specifications is parametric *w.r.t.* tapes: computations, induced by specifications, may either converge or

---

[6] A tactic is a command to solve a goal or decompose it into simpler goals.

[7] As usual, local hypotheses are indexed with the rules they are discharged by.

[8] According to Gentzen's notation, we write such an hypothesis (among the leaves of the proof tree) within square brackets, to bear in mind that it can be *discharged*, *i.e.*, cancelled, in the course of a formal proof, as it represents a *local* hypothesis.

diverge, depending on the tape that is coupled to them and the initial position of the head (while the initial state is $1{\in}\mathbb{N}$). In Section 3 we have also chosen an encoding for tapes (via a zipper, made of two streams) such that the position of the head is implicit within the tape itself. Therefore, the semantics of TMs may be defined by considering configurations (T, p, s), where T is a specification, p a state, and $s{=}\langle\!\langle l, r{=}r_0{:}r_1{:}\ldots\rangle\!\rangle$ a tape. Some configurations make actually a computation stop, because there is no action specified by T for the current state p and symbol r_0: these configurations will play the role of the *values* of our semantics. In the following, we will denote with $tr(T, p, s)$ the application of the transition function tr, introduced in Section 3: in particular, we will write $tr(T, p, s){=}\downarrow$ for (tr T p r0)=halt, and $tr(T, p, s){=}\langle i, x\rangle$ for (tr T p r0)=(i,x).

In this section we define a *big-step* semantics for TMs, which will play the role of our main tool throughout the rest of the paper. The *potential* divergence of computations provides us with a typical scenario which may benefit from the use of *coinductive* specification and proof principles. In fact, a faithful encoding has to reflect the separation between converging and diverging computations, through two different judgments. Hence, we define the *inductive* predicate $b_* \subseteq Spec{\times}Tape{\times}State{\times}Tape{\times}State$ to cope with converging evaluations, and the *coinductive* $b_\infty \subseteq Spec{\times}Tape{\times}State$ to deal with diverging ones.

Definition 1. *(Evaluation) Assume $T{\in}Spec$, $s{=}\langle\!\langle l{=}l_0{:}l_1{:}\ldots, r{=}r_0{:}r_1{:}\ldots\rangle\!\rangle$ and $t{\in}Tape$, $p, q, i{\in}State$. Then, b_* is defined by the following inductive rules:*

$$\frac{tr(T, p, s)=\downarrow}{b_*(T, s, p, s, p)} \; (stop) \qquad \frac{tr(T, p, s)=\langle i, R\rangle \quad b_*(T, \langle\!\langle r_0{:}l, tail(r)\rangle\!\rangle, i, t, q)}{b_*(T, \langle\!\langle l, r\rangle\!\rangle, p, t, q)} \; (right)_*$$

$$\frac{tr(T, p, s)=\langle i, L\rangle \quad b_*(T, \langle\!\langle tail(l), l_0{:}r\rangle\!\rangle, i, t, q)}{b_*(T, \langle\!\langle l, r\rangle\!\rangle, p, t, q)} \; (left)_*$$

$$\frac{tr(T, p, s)=\langle i, W(a)\rangle \quad b_*(T, \langle\!\langle l, a{:}tail(r)\rangle\!\rangle, i, t, q)}{b_*(T, \langle\!\langle l, r\rangle\!\rangle, p, t, q)} \; (write)_*$$

And b_∞ is defined by the following rules, (this time) interpreted coinductively[9]:

$$\frac{tr(T, p, s)=\langle q, R\rangle \quad b_\infty(T, \langle\!\langle r_0{:}l, tail(r)\rangle\!\rangle, q)}{b_\infty(T, \langle\!\langle l, r\rangle\!\rangle, p)} \; (right)_\infty$$

$$\frac{tr(T, p, s)=\langle q, L\rangle \quad b_\infty(T, \langle\!\langle tail(l), l_0{:}r\rangle\!\rangle, q)}{b_\infty(T, \langle\!\langle l, r\rangle\!\rangle, p)} \; (left)_\infty$$

$$\frac{tr(T, p, s)=\langle q, W(a)\rangle \quad b_\infty(T, \langle\!\langle l, a{:}tail(r)\rangle\!\rangle, q)}{b_\infty(T, \langle\!\langle l, r\rangle\!\rangle, p)} \; (write)_\infty$$

Notice that in the rules above we write r_0 and l_0 for head(r) and head(l), respectively (see Section 4 for the definitions of the head *and* tail *functions).* □

---

[9] The relation b_∞ is the greatest fixed-point of the above rules, or, equivalently, amounts to the conclusions of infinite derivation trees built from such rules.

In our semantics, given a specification T, a tape s and a state p, we capture on the one hand the *progress* of both the head and the states transitions, and on the other hand the *effect* of the operations performed by the head itself.

In detail, the intended meaning of $b_*(T, s, p, t, q)$ is that the computation under the specification T, by starting from the tape s and the state p, *stops* in the state q, transforming s into t. Conversely, $b_\infty(T, s, p)$ asserts that the computation under T, by starting from the tape s and the state p, *loops*: *i.e.*, there exist a state i and a pattern-tape u (reachable from p and s) such that, afterwards, the computation gets again to the state i with a tape fulfilling u after a non-zero, finite number of actions. Therefore, a *final* tape cannot exist for b_∞, because the initial s is scrutinized (and possibly updated) "ad infinitum".

Since TMs are not structured, we have embedded in the big-step semantics an alternative *structuring criterion*, *i.e.*, the number of evaluation steps implicit amount. In fact, we have defined a base (*i.e.*, non-recursive) rule for b_* (the computation stops because no next action exists) and (co)inductive rules for both b_* and b_∞, to address how moving the head and writing on the tape is carried out within a converging computation and a diverging one, respectively.

We remark again that the benefit of the zipper encoding of tapes (introduced in Section 3) is that every operation of the head may be carried out via basic functions on streams, whose complexity is minimal and constant.

6   Adequacy

To argue that our big-step semantics for TMs is appropriate, we introduce here a *small-step* semantics *à la* Leroy [9], and prove that they are equivalent.

We first define a *one-step* reduction concept, to express the three basic actions of TMs (*i.e.*, moving the reading head and writing on the current square). Formally, it is defined as a predicate $\to \subseteq Spec \times Tape \times State \times Tape \times State$, that we write more suggestively as $(T, s, p) \to (T, t, q)$. Note (again) that, since TMs are not structured, we do not need to define *contextual* reduction rules.

Now we can formalize the small-step semantics as reduction sequences: *finite* reductions $\overset{*}{\to}$, defined by *induction*, are the reflexive transitive closure of $\to$, while *infinite* reductions $\overset{\infty}{\to}$, defined by *coinduction*, its transitive closure.

Definition 2. *(Reduction) Assume $T \in Spec$, $s = \langle\!\langle l, r \rangle\!\rangle \in Tape$, and $p, q \in State$. Then, the* one-step *reduction $\to$ is defined by the following rules:*

$$\frac{tr(T, p, s) = \langle q, R \rangle}{(T, \langle\!\langle l, r \rangle\!\rangle, p) \to (T, \langle\!\langle r_0{:}l, tail(r) \rangle\!\rangle, q)} \ (\to_R)$$

$$\frac{tr(T, p, s) = \langle q, L \rangle}{(T, \langle\!\langle l, r \rangle\!\rangle, p) \to (T, \langle\!\langle tail(l), l_0{:}r \rangle\!\rangle, q)} \ (\to_L)$$

$$\frac{tr(T, p, s) = \langle q, W(a) \rangle}{(T, \langle\!\langle l, r \rangle\!\rangle, p) \to (T, \langle\!\langle l, a{:}tail(r) \rangle\!\rangle, q)} \ (\to_W)$$

For $t, u \in Tape$, $i \in State$, finite *reduction* $\overset{*}{\to}$ is defined by induction, via the rules:

$$\frac{}{(T,s,p) \overset{*}{\to} (T,s,p)} \; (\overset{*}{\to}_0) \qquad \frac{(T,s,p) \to (T,u,i) \quad (T,u,i) \overset{*}{\to} (T,t,q)}{(T,s,p) \overset{*}{\to} (T,t,q)} \; (\overset{*}{\to}_+)$$

And infinite *reduction* $\overset{\infty}{\to}$ is defined by the following coinductive rule:

$$\frac{(T,s,p) \to (T,t,q) \quad (T,t,q) \overset{\infty}{\to}}{(T,s,p) \overset{\infty}{\to}} \; (\overset{\infty}{\to}_\infty)$$

We can prove that evaluation and reduction are equivalent concepts, both in their converging and diverging versions. We remark that our proofs are *constructive*, whereas Leroy [9] had to postulate the "excluded middle" for divergence.

Proposition 1. *(Equivalence) Let be $T \in Spec$, $s, t, u \in Tape$, and $p, q, i \in State$.*

1. *If $(T, s, p) \to (T, u, i)$ and $b_*(T, u, i, t, q)$, then $b_*(T, s, p, t, q)$*
2. *If $(T, s, p) \overset{*}{\to} (T, u, i)$ and $b_*(T, u, i, t, q)$, then $b_*(T, s, p, t, q)$*
3. *$b_*(T, s, p, t, q)$ if and only if $(T, s, p) \overset{*}{\to} (T, t, q)$ and $tr(T, q, t) = \downarrow$*
4. *$b_\infty(T, s, p)$ if and only if $(T, s, p) \overset{\infty}{\to}$*

Proof. 1) By inversion of the first hypothesis. 2) By structural induction on the derivation of $(T, s, p) \overset{*}{\to} (T, u, i)$, and point 1. 3) Both directions are proved by structural induction on the hypothetical derivation, but the direction ($\Leftarrow$) requires also point 1. 4) Both directions by coinduction and hypothesis inversion. □

The above result points out that the proof practice of reduction and evaluation is very similar in Coq. In fact, the small-step predicate $\overset{*}{\to}$ is slightly less handy, because, to perform a TM action, the user is required to exhibit the witness tape, besides the target state; obviously, the small-step version lacks the "halting" concept (*i.e.*, $tr(T, q, t) = \downarrow$), which is internalized by the big-step judgment.

Streams vs. Lists. We complete this section with a digression about a different encoding for tapes, that we pursued in a preliminary phase of our research.

Even if streams are a datatype which captures promptly and naturally the infiniteness of tapes, a formalization approach via (finite) *lists* may also be developed: in this case, the empty list is intended to represent an infinite sequence of blanks. The choice of lists makes explicit the assumption about TMs that, when a computation starts, only a finite number of squares can contain non-blank symbols (in fact, the representation of numerical functions in Cutland's setting, that we have adopted at the end of Section 2, respects such a constraint).

Therefore, we proceed by encoding the tape through a pair of lists:

$$HTape_L : ll, rl ::= (\iota \mapsto a_\iota)^{\iota \in [0..n]} \qquad \text{half tape (list, } n \in \mathbb{N})$$
$$Tape_L \; : sl, tl ::= \langle\!\langle \, ll, rl \, \rangle\!\rangle \qquad \text{full tape (list-pair)}$$

Afterwards, big-step semantics predicates, playing the role of the ones that deal with streams in Section 5, can be introduced. However, since lists (conversely to streams) might be empty, such predicates must take into consideration this extra pattern and manage it via additional rules. Without going into the full details (for lack of space), we display here the rules for the move-R action[10]:

$$\frac{bL_*(T,\langle\!\langle\, B{:}ll,[\,]\,\rangle\!\rangle,i,t,q)}{bL_*(T,\langle\!\langle\, ll,[\,]\,\rangle\!\rangle,p,t,q)}\ (r_{[]})_* \qquad \frac{bL_*(T,\langle\!\langle\, a{:}ll,rl\,\rangle\!\rangle,i,t,q)}{bL_*(T,\langle\!\langle\, ll,a{:}rl\,\rangle\!\rangle,p,t,q)}\ (r_L)_*$$

The inductive convergence predicate $bL_* \subseteq Spec \times Tape_L \times State \times Tape_L \times State$ has the same intended meaning of b_*. The coinductive divergence predicate $bL_\infty \subseteq Spec \times Tape_L \times State$, corresponding to b_∞, is defined analogously.

By using the predicates bL_* and bL_∞, we can prove that the semantics with streams may mimic that with lists, and a limited form of the opposite result (in the Proposition below we denote with Bs the stream of blank symbols and with "$::$" a recursive function that appends a list in front of a stream).

Proposition 2. *(Tape) Let be $T \in Spec$, $ll, rl, ll', rl' \in HTape_L$, and $p, q \in State$.*

1. *If $bL_*(T,\langle\!\langle\, ll,rl\,\rangle\!\rangle,p,\langle\!\langle\, ll',rl'\,\rangle\!\rangle,q)$,*
   then $b_*(T,\langle\!\langle\, ll{::}Bs, rl{::}Bs\,\rangle\!\rangle,p,\langle\!\langle\, ll'{::}Bs, rl'{::}Bs\,\rangle\!\rangle,q)$
2. *$bL_\infty(T,\langle\!\langle\, ll, rl\,\rangle\!\rangle,p)$ if and only if $b_\infty(T,\langle\!\langle\, ll{::}Bs, rl{::}Bs\,\rangle\!\rangle,p)$*

Proof. 1) By structural induction on the hypothetical derivation. 2) Both the directions are proved by coinduction and hypothesis inversion. □

The difficulty of proving the reverse implication of point 1 above depends on the fact that the representation of the tape through lists is not unique, because one may append to any list blank symbols at will; hence, it is necessary to introduce an *equivalence* relation on list-tapes to develop their metatheory. For this reason (and because lists demand to double the length of proofs, as their predicates have two constructors for any action), we prefer working with streams.

7 Certification

In this section we use the big-step predicates b_* and b_∞, introduced in Section 5 and justified in Section 6, to address the *certification* of the partial functions computed by *individual* TMs. This "algorithmic" approach, which exploits corecursion and coinduction in an involved setting, is significant as it provides a foundation methodology for the formal development of computability theory.

The divergence of TMs may be caused by different kinds of behavior. Clearly, it is easy to manage the scenario where a finite portion of the tape is scanned. The interesting case is when TMs scrutinize an infinite area of it; this may happen by moving the head infinitely either just in one direction or in both directions. In this section we address one example for each pattern of behavior, to convey to the reader the confidence that we can master all of them.

---

[10] We omit from both the rules the transition conditions, that is, the premise $tr(T,p,\langle\!\langle\, ll,[\,]\,\rangle\!\rangle)=\langle i,R\rangle$ from $(r_{[]})_*$ and $tr(T,p,\langle\!\langle\, ll,a{:}rl\,\rangle\!\rangle)=\langle i,R\rangle$ from $(r_L)_*$.

First Example: R Moves. The first partial function that we work out computes the half of *even* natural numbers, and is not defined on *odd* ones:

$$div2(n) \triangleq \begin{cases} n/2 & \text{if } n \in \mathbb{E} \\ \uparrow & \text{if } n \in \mathbb{O} \end{cases}$$

One algorithm that implements the *div2* function is conceived as follows. Erase the first "1" (which occurs by definition) and move the head to the right; then try to find pairs of consecutive "1": if this succeeds, erase the second "1" and restart the cycle, otherwise (a single "1" is found) move indefinitely to the right.

Such an algorithm can be realized, *e.g.*, by the following specification T:

$$\{\langle 1, 1, W(B), 1 \rangle, \langle 1, B, R, 2 \rangle, \langle 2, 1, R, 3 \rangle, \langle 3, B, R, 3 \rangle, \langle 3, 1, W(B), 4 \rangle, \langle 4, B, R, 2 \rangle\}$$

This implementation of the *div2* function is certified through the predicates b_* and b_∞; the computation starts from the state 1 and the following tape[11]:

$$\overset{\Downarrow}{-\mid B\mid 1\mid \underbrace{1\mid - \mid 1}_{n}\mid B\mid -} \tag{1}$$

which is formalized as $\forall n. \langle\!\langle Bs,\ 1{:}ones(n){::}Bs \rangle\!\rangle$, where Bs is the stream of blank symbols, $ones(n)$ a list of n consecutive "1" symbols, "::" a recursive function that appends a list in front of a stream, and ":" the *cons* constructor on streams.

To fulfill our goal we carry out, via tactics, a top-down formal development that simulates the computation of the TM at hand. First, we perform a write-B and a move-R action from the starting *configuration*[12] (state 1 and tape (1), that represents the input n), thus reaching the state 2 with the tape:

$$\overset{\Downarrow}{-\mid B\mid \underbrace{1\mid - \mid 1}_{n}\mid B\mid -} \tag{2}$$

Proving the *divergence* requires a combination of coinductive and inductive reasoning. The core property is the divergence when proceeding from the state 3 and a right-hand blank tape, a lemma which is proved by coinduction[13]:

$$\cfrac{l \in HTape \quad \cfrac{\cfrac{tr(T, 3, \langle\!\langle l, B{:}Bs \rangle\!\rangle)=\langle 3, R \rangle \quad b_\infty(T, \langle\!\langle B{:}l, Bs \rangle\!\rangle, 3)}{b_\infty(T, \langle\!\langle l, B{:}Bs \rangle\!\rangle, 3)} \ (right)_\infty}{b_\infty(T, \langle\!\langle l, Bs \rangle\!\rangle, 3)} \ (def{:}\ Bs)}{\forall l \in HTape.\ b_\infty(T, \langle\!\langle l, Bs \rangle\!\rangle, 3)} \ (1), (introduction)$$

$$[\forall l \in HTape.\ b_\infty(T, \langle\!\langle l, Bs \rangle\!\rangle, 3)]_{(1)}$$
$$\vdots$$

$$\tag{3}$$

---

[11] From now on, we will use "$a \mid -$" to represent an infinite amount of "a" symbols.

[12] Given a specification T, a configuration will be a pair $\langle state, tape \rangle$ from now on.

[13] Like at the end of Section 4, we display coinductive proofs in natural deduction-style: the coinductive hypothesis is indexed with the rule it is discharged by.

If n is *odd*, we prove by induction on k that the tape (2) leads to divergence:

$$\forall l \in HTape. \; b_\infty(T, \langle\!\langle\, l, \, ones(2k+1)::Bs \,\rangle\!\rangle, 2)$$

If $k=0$, carry out a move-R and apply the lemma (3) above; if $k=h+1$, complete a cycle (by erasing the second "1") and conclude via the induction hypothesis.

We address the *convergence* in the complementary scenario (an *even* input n in (2)) by proving the following property, again by induction on k:

$$\forall l \in HTape. \; b_*(T, \langle\!\langle\, l, \, ones(2k)::Bs \,\rangle\!\rangle, 2, \langle\!\langle\, rpt(k)::l, \; Bs \,\rangle\!\rangle, 2)$$

where $rpt(k)$ in the final tape stands for a list of k consecutive pairs "B:1".   □

Second Example: R and L Moves. The second sample function that we choose is partially defined on input *pairs*, and may be named "partial minus":

$$pminus(m,n) \triangleq \begin{cases} m-n & \text{if } m \geq n \\ \uparrow & \text{if } m < n \end{cases}$$

To compute it, we devise the following algorithm. First scan the tape towards the right till reaching the B that separates the two inputs; then erase the leftmost "1" from the representation of n and the rightmost "1" from that of m (both the "1s" must occur) by replacing them, respectively, with a mark symbol "0" (on the right, for n) and a B (on the left). The core of the computation is repeating this cycle, which leads to one of two possible situations: if the end of n is reached (*i.e.*, we are scanning the first B on the right of a 0-block), then stop; on the other hand, replacing m with B symbols may cause that the head (looking for "1s") moves indefinitely on the left. The specification is the following:

$$U \triangleq \{\langle 1,1,R,1\rangle, \langle 1,B,R,2\rangle, \langle 2,0,R,2\rangle, \langle 2,1,W(0),3\rangle, \langle 3,0,L,3\rangle,$$
$$\langle 3,B,L,4\rangle, \langle 4,B,L,4\rangle, \langle 4,1,W(B),5\rangle, \langle 5,B,R,5\rangle, \langle 5,0,R,2\rangle\}$$

The initial part of the formal development (erasing the first pair of "1s", so moving from state 1 to 5) is common to the divergence and convergence cases[14]:

$$\Downarrow \qquad\qquad\qquad\qquad\qquad\qquad\qquad\qquad\qquad \Downarrow$$
$$-\,|\,B\,|\,\underbrace{1\,|-|\,1}_{m+1}\,|\,B\,|\,\underbrace{1\,|-|\,1}_{n+1}\,|\,B\,|\,- \;\overset{*}{\Longrightarrow}\; -\,|\,B\,|\,1^m\,|\,B\,|\,B\,|\,0\,|\,1^n\,|\,B\,|\,-$$

At this point of the proof, the key pattern to be mastered is shaped as follows:

$$\Downarrow$$
$$-\,|\,B\,|\,\underbrace{1\,|-|\,1}_{m}\,|\,\underbrace{B\,|-|\,B}_{k+2}\,|\,\underbrace{0\,|-|\,0}_{k+1}\,|\,\underbrace{1\,|-|1}_{n}\,|\,B\,|\,- \qquad\qquad (4)$$

---

[14] Informally, we represent with $\Longrightarrow$ the effect of a finite number of actions on a tape. Moreover, we denote with 1^m a block of m consecutive squares with the "1" symbol.

Starting from this tape and the state 5, we can discriminate between divergence and convergence by distinguishing the case $m<n$ from $m\geq n$. Notice that we have introduced the variable k to obtain a more general induction hypothesis.

When we come to the state 5 and an instance (for $k=1$) of the above tape (4) we prove the *divergence*, under the hypothesis $m<n$, by nested induction on n and m. This proof requires auxiliary lemmas, to scan 0-blocks and B-blocks (by induction on k) and for assuring the divergence from the state 4 with the tape Bs towards the left. One key point is that we can use the predicate b_∞ in a *compositional* way: *i.e.*, when carrying out a divergence proof in top-down fashion, we can perform a preliminary finite number of actions, thus reducing to a different goal. In fact, this amounts to split a divergent computation into a convergent one, easily provable, plus another divergent one, which becomes our goal; *e.g.*, we scan, by moving the head to the right, a 0-block (of length k, formalized by the *blanks* function) via the lemma (proved by induction on k):

$$\forall k \in \mathbb{N}, \forall l, r \in HTape. \ b_\infty(U, \langle\!\langle blanks(k)::l, r \rangle\!\rangle, 5) \Rightarrow b_\infty(U, \langle\!\langle l, blanks(k)::r \rangle\!\rangle, 5)$$

Conversely, it is *not* possible to use the predicate b_* in a compositional way to manage the *convergence* scenario. The problem is that b_* requires to exhibit the final tape, but in this case, due to the complexity of the proof, we cannot master it *tout-court* as we have done in the first example. Therefore, we need an extra tool to accomplish the convergence. Actually, such a tool is provided by the *small-step* predicate $\xrightarrow{*}$: by applying the Proposition 1.2, we may decompose a convergent computation and address separately the intermediate steps. In the end, we carry out the proof from (4), under the hypothesis $m\geq n$, by nested induction on n and m, and by means of lemmas similar to those used for b_∞.   □

Third Example: R and L Moves, Infinitely. In this example we consider the unary function $f_\emptyset$, undefined on every input, for which we devise an implementation that points out a problem that involves the mechanization of coinduction.

In fact, our algorithm to compute $f_\emptyset$ is very simple: first scan the 1-block towards the right and replace the first blank with a "1"; then move the head towards the left till reaching the first blank and replace it again with a "1"; proceed infinitely in the same way. The specification we pick out is minimal:

$$V \triangleq \{\langle 1, 1, R, 1 \rangle, \langle 1, B, W(1), 2 \rangle, \langle 2, 1, L, 2 \rangle, \langle 2, B, W(1), 1 \rangle\}$$

The idea beneath the formal divergence proof is nesting a couple of inductions inside the main coinduction; that is, by using the notation introduced in the previous example to display the modification of the tape, we want to perform the two computations (passing to state 2 and then coming back to state 1):

$$\Downarrow \qquad\qquad\qquad \Downarrow \qquad\qquad\qquad \Downarrow$$

$$-\,|\,B\,|\,\underbrace{1\,|-|\,1}_{n+1}\,|\,B\,|\,- \xRightarrow{*} -\,|\,B\,|\,\underbrace{1\,|-|\,1}_{n+2}\,|\,B\,|\,- \xRightarrow{*} -\,|\,B\,|\,\underbrace{1\,|-|\,1}_{n+3}\,|\,B\,|\,-$$

It is apparent that, to accommodate this proof, we may assume the coinductive hypothesis for the initial configuration (state 1 and leftmost tape above) and then carry out two finite computations, thus reducing to a configuration (state 1 and rightmost tape) which is an instance of the coinductive hypothesis itself.

Nevertheless, the application of the coinductive hypothesis is *not* allowed by Coq, because the whole proof (*i.e.*, the proof term built interactively through tactics, and mainly via cofix) is recognized as *non-guarded* by constructors. Essentially, this is caused by the fact that the syntactic check does not accept an induction (*i.e.*, a lemma) nested inside the coinductive development[15].

To circumvent the problem, we introduce here a new small-step divergence predicate. The idea is very direct: divergence may be characterized as the *coinductive* transitive closure of the *inductive* non-reflexive transitive closure of $\rightarrow$.

Definition 3. *(Extra reduction) Assume $T \in Spec$, $s, t, u \in Tape$, $p, q, i \in State$. Then, finite positive reduction $\xrightarrow{+}$ is defined by induction, via the rules:*

$$\frac{(T,s,p) \rightarrow (T,t,q)}{(T,s,p) \xrightarrow{+} (T,t,q)} \ (\xrightarrow{+}_1) \qquad \frac{(T,s,p) \rightarrow (T,u,i) \quad (T,u,i) \xrightarrow{+} (T,t,q)}{(T,s,p) \xrightarrow{+} (T,t,q)} \ (\xrightarrow{+}_+) \ .$$

And infinite split reduction $\overset{\infty}{\Rightarrow}$ *is defined by the following coinductive rule:*

$$\frac{(T,s,p) \xrightarrow{+} (T,t,q) \quad (T,t,q) \overset{\infty}{\Rightarrow}}{(T,s,p) \overset{\infty}{\Rightarrow}} \ (\overset{\infty}{\Rightarrow}_\infty)$$

Proposition 3. *(Equivalence, bis) Let be $T \in Spec$, $s \in Tape$, and $p \in State$.*

1. *If $(T,s,p) \xrightarrow{+} (T,u,i)$ and $(T,u,i) \xrightarrow{+} (T,t,q)$, then $(T,s,p) \xrightarrow{+} (T,t,q)$*
2. *If $(T,s,p) \overset{\infty}{\Rightarrow}$, then $(T,s,p) \xrightarrow{\infty}$*
3. *$b_\infty(T,s,p)$ if and only if $(T,s,p) \overset{\infty}{\Rightarrow}$*

Proof. 1) By structural induction on the derivation of $(T,s,p) \xrightarrow{+} (T,u,i)$. 2) By coinduction and hypothesis inversion. 3) ($\Rightarrow$) By coinduction and hypothesis inversion. ($\Leftarrow$) By Proposition 1.4 and point 2. ☐

Since the reduction predicate $\overset{\infty}{\Rightarrow}$ turns out to be equivalent to b_∞, we adopt the former to carry out our divergence proof. Actually, $\overset{\infty}{\Rightarrow}$ does not suffer from the non-guardedness problem, as it is apparent from the following proof tree[16]:

$$[\forall n \in \mathbb{N}. \ (V,s,1) \overset{\infty}{\Rightarrow}]_{(1)}$$
$$\vdots$$
$$\frac{n \in \mathbb{N} \quad \dfrac{(V,s,1) \xrightarrow{+} (V,t,1) \qquad (V,t,1) \overset{\infty}{\Rightarrow}}{(V,s,1) \overset{\infty}{\Rightarrow}} \ (\overset{\infty}{\Rightarrow}_\infty)}{\forall n \in \mathbb{N}. \ (V,s,1) \overset{\infty}{\Rightarrow}} \ (1), (introduction)$$

The proof of the premise $(V,s,1) \xrightarrow{+} (V,t,1)$ relies on the transitivity of $\xrightarrow{+}$ (Proposition 3.1) and on two auxiliary lemmas, argued by induction on n. ☐

---

[15] See [8] for a recent proposal of an alternative, *semantic* guardedness checking.
[16] We write s for $\langle\!\langle \, Bs, \ ones(n+1)::Bs \, \rangle\!\rangle$ and t for $\langle\!\langle \, Bs, \ ones(n+3)::Bs \, \rangle\!\rangle$.

8   Conclusion

In the present contribution we have formalized TMs and their (big-step and small-step) operational semantics in the Coq proof assistant. Our key choices are the encoding of tapes as pairs of *streams* (managed by means of corecursion) and a clear distinction between *converging* computations (modeled via inductive predicates) and *diverging* ones (formalized through coinductive predicates). In the previous, core section we have pointed out the potential of our machinery, by proving the correctness of representative TMs (that is, by certifying the implementation of the partial functions computed by them).

Our encoding provides a completely mechanized management of the transitions (via the auto tactic), with the benefit that we may concentrate on the formal treatment of the tape and the logic of proofs. *Divergence* can be proved very often in a compositional way, via the sole big-step coinductive predicate. When "non-guardedness" complications arise (essentially because induction is nested inside coinduction), alternative, equivalent small-step coinductive predicates may be employed, by taking advantage of their close relationship with the main big-step predicate. On the other hand, it is not always possible to master *convergence* proofs by compositionality. When this is not feasible (due to the difficulty of the proof at hand), the small-step semantics predicates may be used again as an auxiliary tool, to perform intermediate computation steps.

We note also that, in order to carry out either divergence or convergence proofs, often the user has the responsibility to figure out how to decompose the main goal. As usual, it is sometimes necessary to generalize the statements to obtain sufficiently powerful (co)inductive hypotheses. Moreover, some proofs require a subtle combination of inductive and coinductive reasoning.

Related Work. The contributions of the literature most related to the present one are those by Asperti and Ricciotti in Matita [1], Xu, Zhang and Urban in Isabelle/HOL [13], and Leroy in Coq [9]. Both the first two works address TMs, achieving the ambitious goals we have reported in Section 1.

Asperti and Ricciotti formalize the tape as a triple, made of two lists plus the square currently scrutinized. The non-termination is managed by requiring that the total computation function returns an optional value, when it meets an upper bound of iterations without reaching a final state. The semantics is defined through a relation between tapes, (weakly) "realized" by TMs.

Xu, Zhang and Urban represent the tape via a pair of lists. They handle the non-termination in a similar way, *i.e.*, via the condition that there is no transition into a halting state. The semantics is defined by means of Hoare-rules.

None of the above two works makes use of coinductive tools (that we have exploited to deal with stream-tapes and divergence); from this perspective, our paper is more related to that of Leroy [9], who adopts coinduction in Coq to capture infinite evaluations and reductions of a call-by-value λ-calculus.

Future Work. We believe that the main result achieved by our work (*i.e.*, the development of a technology for proving the correctness of concrete TMs, via several versions of big-step and small-step semantics) is a promising tool to pursue more advanced goals which are outside the scope of the present paper.

In particular, our effort may be seen as a first step towards the development of computability theory, as the construction of "brick" TMs and their composition at higher-levels of abstraction is the natural progress of this contribution.

It would be also stimulating to relate the present formalization to that of unlimited register machines, that we have addressed in a previous work [2].

Acknowledgments. The author is very grateful to the anonymous referees for their helpful, constructive reviews.

References

1. Asperti, A., Ricciotti, W.: Formalizing turing machines. In: Ong, L., de Queiroz, R. (eds.) WoLLIC 2012. LNCS, vol. 7456, pp. 1–25. Springer, Heidelberg (2012)
2. Ciaffaglione, A.: A coinductive semantics of the unlimited register machine. In: Yu, F., Wang, C. (eds.) INFINITY. Electronic Proceedings in Theoretical Computer Science, vol. 73, pp. 49–63 (2011)
3. Ciaffaglione, A.: The Web Appendix of this paper. Università di Udine, Italia (2014). http://users.dimi.uniud.it/~alberto.ciaffaglione/Turing/
4. Coquand, T.: Infinite objects in type theory. In: Barendregt, H., Nipkow, T. (eds.) TYPES 1993. LNCS, vol. 806, pp. 62–78. Springer, Heidelberg (1994)
5. Cutland, N.J.: Computability: An Introduction to Recursive Function Theory. Cambridge University Press (1980)
6. Giménez, E.: Codifying guarded definitions with recursive schemes. In: Dybjer, P., Nordström, B., Smith, J. (eds.) TYPES 1994. LNCS, vol. 996, pp. 39–59. Springer, Heidelberg (1995)
7. Hopcroft, J.E., Motwani, R., Ullman, J.D.: Introduction to Automata Theory, Languages, and Computation. Addison-Wesley (2003)
8. Hur, C.-K., Neis, G., Dreyer, D., Vafeiadis, V.: The power of parameterization in coinductive proof. In: Giacobazzi, R., Cousot, R. (eds.) POPL, pp. 193–206. ACM (2013)
9. Leroy, X.: Coinductive big-step operational semantics. In: Sestoft, P. (ed.) ESOP 2006. LNCS, vol. 3924, pp. 54–68. Springer, Heidelberg (2006)
10. Norrish, M.: Mechanised computability theory. In: van Eekelen, M., Geuvers, H., Schmaltz, J., Wiedijk, F. (eds.) ITP 2011. LNCS, vol. 6898, pp. 297–311. Springer, Heidelberg (2011)
11. The Coq Development Team. The Coq Proof Assistant, version 8.4. INRIA (2012). http://coq.inria.fr
12. Turing, A.M.: On computable numbers, with an application to the Entscheidungsproblem. Proc. Lond. Math. Soc. **42** (1936)
13. Xu, J., Zhang, X., Urban, C.: Mechanising turing machines and computability theory in Isabelle/HOL. In: Blazy, S., Paulin-Mohring, C., Pichardie, D. (eds.) ITP 2013. LNCS, vol. 7998, pp. 147–162. Springer, Heidelberg (2013)

Towards Completeness
in Bounded Model Checking Through
Automatic Recursion Depth Detection

Grigory Fedyukovich[(✉)] and Natasha Sharygina

Faculty of Informatics, University of Lugano,
Via Guiseppe Buffi 13, CH-6904 Lugano, Switzerland
grigory.fedyukovich@usi.ch

Abstract. The presence of recursive function calls is a well-known bottleneck in software model checking as they might cause infinite loops and make verification infeasible. This paper proposes a new technique for sound and complete Bounded Model Checking based on detecting depths for all recursive function calls in a program. The algorithm of detection of recursion depth uses over-approximations of function calls. It proceeds in an iterative manner by refining the function over-approximations until the recursion depth is detected or it becomes clear that the recursion depth detection is infeasible. We prove that if the algorithm terminates then it guarantees to detect a recursion depth required for complete program verification. The key advantage of the proposed algorithm is that it is suitable for generation and/or substitution of function summaries by means of Craig Interpolation helpful to speed up consequent verification runs. We implemented the algorithm for automatic detection of recursion depth on the top of our SAT-based model checker FunFrog and demonstrate its benefits on a number of recursive C programs.

1 Introduction

Model checking plays an important role in both proving program correctness and finding bugs. It provides a powerful fully automated engine which is able to search for an assertion violation among all possible combinations of the input values. These advantages are however hindered by the high complexity of analysis, known as the state-space explosion phenomenon. To combat this problem, many effective state-space reduction solutions have been developed to allow model checking to scale to verification of complex systems. The most successful solutions are symbolic model checking among which are Bounded Model Checking (BMC) [2], and abstraction-based approaches such as predicate abstraction [8], interpolation-based reasoning [11], and function summarization [1,12,13,19].

BMC has been shown to be particularly successful in safety analysis of software. The state-of-the-art BMC-based tools such as CBMC [3], LLBMC [14], VeriSoft [9], FunFrog [18], just to name a few, have been successfully applied to verification of industrial-size programs. The well-known limitation of BMC is

© Springer International Publishing Switzerland 2015
C. Braga and N. Martí-Oliet (Eds.): SBMF 2014, LNCS 8941, pp. 96–112, 2015.
DOI: 10.1007/978-3-319-15075-8_7

that it is aimed at searching for errors in a program within the given number (bound) of loop iterations and recursion depth. For this reason, BMC is suitable only for program falsification, while for complete verification it requires finding a sufficient bound. This problem remains open: the BMC tools analyze an under-approximation of a program using some particular bound, defined a priori by the user or set by the tool to some constant, and check the program only up to this bound.

There exists a number of (direct and indirect) solutions for the automatic loop bound detection (i.e., constant propagation, k-induction, loop summarization, etc). However, dealing with recursive function calls is more complicated and more expensive in practice. This paper proposes an approach for the automatic recursion depth detection in BMC and shows its applicability in practice.

In particular, we present a BMC algorithm enhanced with automated construction of the sufficient unwinding[1]. The algorithm iteratively explores the program calltree and over-approximates recursive function calls while treating precisely the other ones. The entire abstraction of the calltree is then checked on-the-fly with respect to a given assertion. If the assertion holds in the current level of abstraction then the corresponding unwinding is sufficient to guarantee complete verification (and the length of the longest unwinding chain constitutes the recursion depth). Otherwise, the algorithm identifies which over-approximated function calls are responsible for the assertion violation. These function calls are going to be refined and the algorithm goes to the next iteration.

Our approach is developed to reach efficiency in BMC. At each iteration, it refines only a minimal set of over-approximated function calls, i.e., only those responsible for spuriousness of the error on the previous iteration. Clearly, the algorithm is not guaranteed to terminate when there are unbounded sequences of recursive calls in the program. But if for every possible value of input parameters, every recursive function in the real program is called a fixed number of times, the algorithm automatically detects this number and terminates.

We further demonstrate how our algorithm can be made practical by extending our earlier work on construction and reusing of interpolation-based function summaries in BMC [19] for checking different assertions. In the current work, aside from checking user-provided assertions, we use a heuristic called *assertion decomposition* to artificially implant *helper*-assertions into the recursive program. These assertions are then checked incrementally to generate function summaries that will be reused to speed up verification of the user-provided assertions.

We implemented the approach on the top of FunFrog BMC, previously restricted to work only for a user-supplied recursion depth. We evaluated it on a range of academic and industrial recursive programs requiring bitwise and non-linear reasoning. Our experimentation confirmed that the summarization-based recursion depth detection in many cases makes BMC complete and dramatically improves its performance compare to the classical BMC approach (e.g., CBMC).

---

[1] The algorithm relies on the output of a loop bound detection routine (e.g., conversion loops to recursion) done by an external tool or set by the user.

Algorithmically, the closest body of work is the `Corral` [10] tool (see related work section for detailed comparison). It is a solver for a restricted version of the reachability-modulo-theories problem, and it also uses summaries in its bounded analysis to guarantee a practical solution. Unlike in our approach, in the `Corral`, 1) the depth of recursion is bounded by a user-supplied recursion depth and 2) an external tool [7] is used to generate function summaries which in general may not be helpful to verify the given assertion. Our approach is able to generate relevant function summaries by itself. Moreover, it forces summaries to be bit-precise and highly related to the given assertion. It makes our algorithm converge more effectively and faster.

The rest of the paper is structured as follows. Sect. 2 defines the notation and presents background on BMC, function summarization and refinement. Sect. 3 presents the BMC algorithm with automatic detection of recursion depth, proves its correctness and demonstrates its application to function summarization-based model checking. Sect. 4 discusses different experimentation scenarios of the approach including the assertion decomposition heuristic. Sect. 5 provides a comparison with the related work and Sect. 6 concludes the paper.

2   Preliminaries and Previous Work

We first define basic constructs required to present the new algorithm. In particular, we explicitly define recursion, function summaries and basic BMC steps.

2.1   Programs, Function Calls, Recursion Depth

Definition 1 (cf. [19]). *An* unwound program *for a depth ν is a tuple $P_\nu = (\hat{F}_\nu, \hat{f}_{main}, child)$, such that $\hat{F}_\nu$ is a finite set of function calls, unwound up to the depth ν, $\hat{f}_{main} \in \hat{F}_\nu$ is a program entry point and child $\subseteq \hat{F}_\nu \times \hat{F}_\nu$ relates each function call $\hat{f}$ to all function calls invoked directly from it.*

There is a fixed set F to represent functions declared in the program and a possibly unbounded set $\hat{F}$ to represent function calls. A call $\hat{f} \in \hat{F}$ corresponds to a call of a target function, determined by a mapping $target : \hat{F} \to F$. A subset $\hat{F}_\nu \subseteq \hat{F}$ is introduced to help handling recursion. There is exactly one call of function f_{main}, but there may be several calls of the other functions. For simplicity, later we will use primes (i.e., $\hat{f}'$, $\hat{f}''$,..) and indexes (i.e., $\hat{f}_1$, $\hat{f}_2$,..) to differentiate the calls of the same function $f \in F$ in the unwound program.

The set of function calls $\hat{F}$ together with the relation *child* can be represented by a corresponding calltree with the root $\hat{f}_{main}$. We also use relation *subtree* $\subseteq \hat{F} \times \hat{F}$, a reflexive transitive closure of *child*. Now we can define recursive functions using this notation.

Definition 2. *A function f is* recursive *if for every call $\hat{f}_i$, there is another call $\hat{f}'_i$ in its subtree, and $target(\hat{f}_i) = target(\hat{f}'_i) = f$.*

According to Def. 2, the calltree of a program with recursive functions is infinite. As detailed later in this section, for classical BMC it has to be bounded.

A recursive function f is unwound ν times if there is a sequence of function calls (later called an *unwinding chain*) $\hat{f}_0$, $\hat{f}_1$,.. $\hat{f}_\nu$, where $1 \leq i \leq \nu$, $target(\hat{f}_i) = f$, and each $\hat{f}_{i+1}$ is in the subtree of $\hat{f}_i$. The set of function calls $\hat{F}_\nu$ and the relation *child* define a finite corresponding calltree. If there are no recursive function calls in the program $P_\nu = (\hat{F}, \hat{f}_{main}, child)$ then $\hat{F}_\nu \equiv \hat{F}$ for any ν.

BMC is aimed at checking assertions in a program within the given bound of loop iterations and recursion depth. If the unwinding number ν is provided a priori, BMC unrolls the loops and recursion up to ν, encodes the program symbolically and delegates the checking to a SAT solver. If the number is not provided a priori, BMC may go into an infinite loop and not terminate. Typically in the absence of the number or when the number is set too high, a predefined timeout is used to cope with this problem.

BMC encodes the program into the Static Single Assignment (SSA) form, where each variable is assigned at most once. The SSA form is then conjoined with the negation of the assertion condition and converted into a logical formula, called a *BMC formula*. The BMC formula is checked for satisfiability, and every its satisfying assignment identifies an error trace. Otherwise, the program is safe up to ν. Notably, this unwinding number may not be sufficient for complete verification. A program can be proven safe for ν, but buggy for $\nu + 1$.

```
int f(int a) {
    if (a < 10)
        return f (a + 1);
    return a - 10;
}

void main() {
    int y = 1;
    int x = nondet();

    if (x > 5)
        y = f(x);

    assert(y >= 0);
}
```

(a) C code

```
y0 = 1;
x0 = nondet();
if (x0 > 5) {
    a0 = x0;
    // f (unwind 1)
    if (a0 < 10)
        // f (unwind 2)
        ...
        // end f (unwind 2)
        ret0 = ...;
    else
        ret1 = a0 - 10;
    ret2 = phi(ret0, ret1);
    // end f (unwind 1)
    y1 = ret2;
}
y2 = phi(y0, y1);
assert(y2 >= 0);
```

(b) SSA form

$y_0 = 1 \wedge$

$x_0 = nondet_0 \wedge$

$a_0 = x_0 \wedge$

$ret_0 = ... \wedge$

$... \wedge$

$ret_1 = a_0 - 10 \wedge$

$(x_0 > 5 \wedge a_0 < 10 \Rightarrow$
$\qquad ret_2 = ret_0) \wedge$

$(x_0 > 5 \wedge a_0 \geq 10 \Rightarrow$
$\qquad ret_2 = ret_1) \wedge$

$y_1 = ret_2 \wedge$

$(x_0 > 5 \Rightarrow y_2 = y_1) \wedge$

$(x_0 \leq 5 \Rightarrow y_2 = y_0) \wedge$

$y_2 < 0$

(c) BMC formula

Fig. 1. BMC formula generation

Fig. 1 illustrates BMC encoding for a simple C program (Fig. 1a) with a recursive function f. For this example, the recursion depth $\nu = 5$ guarantees complete verification.[2] In this setting, it is assumed that this recursion depth is

---

[2] See more details on termination in Sect. 3.1.

given a priori. During unwinding (Fig. 1b), a call of function f is substituted by its body. There will be five such nested substitutions, and the sixth call is simply skipped in the example. The encoded BMC formula is shown on Fig. 1c.

Classical BMC algorithms use a monolithic BMC formula, as described in details in [3]. For specialized BMC algorithms (such as in our earlier work on function summarization [19] and upgrade checking [6], and the new algorithm for automatic detection of recursion depth) it is convenient to use a so called *Partitioned* BMC formula, which is going to be presented in Sect. 2.2.

2.2 PBMC Encoding

Definition 3 (cf. [19]). *Let $\hat{F}_\nu$ be an unwound calltree, π encodes an assertion, $\phi_{\hat{f}}$ symbolically represent the body of a function f, a target of the call $\hat{f}$. Then a partitioned BMC (PBMC) formula is constructed as $\neg\pi \wedge \bigwedge_{\hat{f}\in\hat{F}_\nu} \phi_{\hat{f}}$.*

Fig. 2 demonstrates creation of a PBMC formula for the example from Fig. 1a. In the example program, unwound 5 times, the partitions for function calls $f_1, f_2, ..f_5$ and main are generated separately. They are bound together using a special boolean variable $callstart_{\hat{f}}$ for every function call $\hat{f}$. Intuitively, $callstart_{\hat{f}}$ is equal to *true* iff the corresponding function call $\hat{f}$ is reached. Note that the assertion π is not encoded inside $\phi_{\hat{f}_{main}}$, as in classical BMC, but separated from the rest of the formula, such that it helps interpolation.[3]

Formula $\phi_{\hat{f}_1}$ that encodes the function call f_1 aims to symbolically represent the function output argument ret_0 by means of the function input argument a_0, symbolically evaluated in $\phi_{\hat{f}_{main}}$. At the same time, $\phi_{\hat{f}_1}$ relies on the value of ret_3 defined in $\phi_{\hat{f}_2}$ by means of a_1. Similar reasoning is applied to create each of the following partitions: $\phi_{\hat{f}_2}, ... \phi_{\hat{f}_5}$.

$$y_0 = 1 \wedge$$
$$x_0 = nondet_0 \wedge$$
$$a_0 = x_0 \wedge$$
$$x_0 > 5 \Leftrightarrow callstart_{\hat{f}_1} \wedge$$
$$y_1 = ret_0 \wedge$$
$$(x_0 > 5 \Rightarrow y_2 = y_1) \wedge$$
$$(x_0 \leq 5 \Rightarrow y_2 = y_0)$$

(a) formula $\phi_{\hat{f}_{main}}$

$$y_2 \geq 0 \Leftrightarrow \pi$$

(b) definition of π

$$(a_0 < 10 \Leftrightarrow callstart_{\hat{f}_2}) \wedge$$
$$a_1 = a_0 + 1 \wedge$$
$$ret_1 = ret_3 \wedge$$
$$ret_2 = a_0 - 10 \wedge$$
$$(callstart_{\hat{f}_1} \wedge a_0 < 10 \Rightarrow$$
$$ret_0 = ret_1) \wedge$$
$$(callstart_{\hat{f}_1} \wedge a_0 \geq 10 \Rightarrow$$
$$ret_0 = ret_2)$$

(c) formula $\phi_{\hat{f}_1}$

Fig. 2. PBMC formula generation

---

[3] See more details on interpolation in Sect. 2.3.

2.3   Craig Interpolation and Function Summarization

Definition 4 (cf. [4]). *Given formulas A and B, such that $A \wedge B$ is unsatisfiable. Craig Interpolant of A and B is a formula I such that $A \rightarrow I$, $I \wedge B$ is unsatisfiable and I is defined over the common alphabet to A and B.*

For mutually unsatisfiable formulas A and B, an interpolant always exists [4]. For quantifier free propositional logic, an interpolant can be constructed from a proof of unsatisfiability [16]. Interpolation is used to generate function summaries to speed up incremental verification (see our earlier work [18,19]).

Definition 5 (cf. [19]). *Function summary is an over-approximation of the function behavior defined as a relation over its input and output variables.*

A summary contains all behaviors of the function and (due to its over-approximating nature) possibly more. The infeasible behaviors (detected during analysis of abstract models) have to be refined by means of the automated procedure, as will be described in Sect. 2.4.

If the program is safe with respect to an assertion π, then the PBMC formula representing the program is unsatisfiable. The interpolation procedure is applied repeatedly for each function call $\hat{f}$. It splits the PBMC formula into two parts, $\phi_{\hat{f}}^{subtree}$ and $\phi_{\hat{f}}^{env}$ (1). The former encodes the subtree of $\hat{f}$. The latter corresponds to the rest of the encoded program including a negation of assertion π.

$$\phi_{\hat{f}}^{subtree} \equiv \bigwedge_{\hat{g} \in \hat{F}:subtree(\hat{f},\hat{g})} \phi_{\hat{g}} \qquad \phi_{\hat{f}}^{env} \equiv \neg\pi \wedge \bigwedge_{\hat{h} \in \hat{F}:\neg subtree(\hat{f},\hat{h})} \phi_{\hat{h}} \qquad (1)$$

Since $\phi_{\hat{f}}^{subtree} \wedge \phi_{\hat{f}}^{env}$ is unsatisfiable, the proof of unsatisfiability can be used to extract an interpolant $I_{\hat{f}}$ for $\phi_{\hat{f}}^{subtree}$ and $\phi_{\hat{f}}^{env}$. Such formula $I_{\hat{f}}$ is then considered as a summary for the function call $\hat{f}$. While verifying another assertion π', the entire part $\phi_{\hat{f}}^{subtree}$ of the PBMC formula will be replaced by the summary formula $I_{\hat{f}}$.

2.4   Counter-Example Guided Refinement

Definition 6 (cf. [19]). *A substitution scenario for function calls is a function $\Omega : \hat{F} \rightarrow \{\text{inline, sum, havoc}\}$.*

For each function call, a substitution scenario determines a level of approximation as one of the following three options: *inline* when it processes the whole function body; *sum* when it substitutes the call by an existing summary, and *havoc* when it treats the call as a nondeterministic function. Since *havoc* abstracts away the function call, it is equivalent to using a summary *true*.

In the incremental abstraction-driven analyses [6,19], substitution scenarios are defined recurrently. Algorithms start with the least accurate *initial* scenario

Ω_0, and iteratively *refine* it. In (2) and (3), we adapt the definitions from [19] to the recursive case.

$$\Omega_0(\hat{f}) = \begin{cases} sum, & \text{if there exists a summary of } \hat{f} \\ inline, & \text{if } \hat{f} \text{ is not recursive or } \nu \text{ is not exceeded} \\ havoc, & \text{if } \hat{f} \text{ is recursive and } \nu \text{ is exceeded} \end{cases} \quad (2)$$

$$\Omega_{i+1}(\hat{f}) = \begin{cases} inline, & \text{if } \Omega_i(\hat{f}) \neq inline \text{ and } callstart_{\hat{f}} = true \\ \Omega_i(\hat{f}), & \text{otherwise} \end{cases} \quad (3)$$

When a substitution scenario Ω_i leads to a satisfiable PBMC formula (i.e., there exists an error trace ϵ), an analysis of ϵ is required to shows that the error is either real or spurious. By construction of the PBMC formula, for each function call $\hat{f}$, a variable $callstart_{\hat{f}}$ is evaluated to *true* iff $\hat{f}$ appears along ϵ. Consequently, each $\hat{f}$ might be responsible for spuriousness of ϵ if $\hat{f}$ was not precisely encoded and $callstart_{\hat{f}} = true$. If there is no function call, satisfying the above mentioned conditions, ϵ is real and must be reported to the user.

3   Bounded Model Checking with Automated Detection of Recursion Depth

This section presents an iterative abstraction-refinement algorithm for BMC with automated detection of recursion depth. We first present a basic algorithm, where all function calls are treated nondeterministically (Sect. 3.1). Then we strengthen this algorithm to support generation and use of interpolation-based function summaries (Sect. 3.2).

3.1   Basic Algorithm

An overview of the algorithm is depicted in Alg. 1. The algorithm starts with a preset recursion depth ν^4 and iterates until it detects the actual recursion depth, needed for complete proof of the program correctness, or a predefined timeout is reached. Notably, at each iteration of the algorithm, ν gets updated and is equal to the length of the longest unwinding chain of recursive function calls. In the end of the algorithm, all recursive calls are unwound exactly same number of times as they would be called during the execution of the program.

The details of the computation are given below. First, the algorithm aims to construct a PBMC formula ϕ using the sets $\hat{F}_\nu$ and $\mathbb{T}$. Every function call $\hat{f} \in \hat{F}_\nu$ is encoded precisely, every function call $\hat{g} \in \mathbb{T}$ is treated nondeterministically. In particular, bodies of function calls from set $\hat{F}_\nu$ are encoded into the SSA forms

---

[4] The algorithm can be initialized with any number value as demonstrated in our experiments.

Algorithm 1. BMC with automatic detection of recursion depth

Input: Initial recursion depth: ν; Program unwound ν times: $P_\nu = (\hat{F}_\nu, \hat{f}_{main}, child)$;
Assertion to be checked: π; *TimeOut*
Output: Verification result: $\{SAFE, BUG, TimeOut\}$; Detected recursion depth: ν; Error
trace: ϵ
Data: PBMC formula: ϕ; temporary set of function calls to be refined: $\mathbb{T}$

```
 1  while (¬TimeOut) do
 2      𝕋 ← {ĝ ∉ F̂ν | child(f̂, ĝ), f̂ ∈ F̂ν};                      // get refinement candidates
 3      φ ← ¬π ∧ ⋀f̂∈F̂ν CreateFormula(f̂) ∧ ⋀ĝ∈𝕋 Nondet(ĝ);
 4      result, sat_assignment ← Solve(φ);                           // run SAT solver
 5      if (result = UNSAT) then
 6          return SAFE, ν;
 7      else
 8          ε ← extract_CE(sat_assignment);                          // extract error trace
 9          𝕋 ← 𝕋 ∩ extract_calls(ε);          // filter out calls which do not affect SAT
10          if (𝕋 = ∅) then
11              return BUG, ν, ε;
12          else
13              F̂ν ← F̂ν ∪ 𝕋;                            // unwind the calltree on demand
14              ν ← max_chain_length(F̂ν);                            // update the depth
15  end
16  return TimeOut
```

(i.e., method `CreateFormula`) and put together into separate partitions (one partition per each function call) of ϕ (line 3). At the same time, all function calls from $\mathbb{T}$ are replaced by *true* (i.e., method `Nondet`). In total, ϕ encodes a program abstraction containing precise and over-approximated parts, conjoined by negation of an assertion π (line 3). Fig. 3a demonstrates a calltree of a program with a single recursive function called twice at the first iteration of the algorithm. In the example, $\hat{F}_\nu = \{\hat{f}_{main}, \hat{g}_1, \hat{h}_1, \hat{f}_1, \hat{f}_2\}$ (grey nodes) are encoded precisely, and $\mathbb{T} = \{\hat{f}_3, \hat{f}_2\}$ (white nodes) are treated nondeterministically.

After the PBMC formula ϕ is constructed, the algorithm passes it to a SAT solver. If ϕ is satisfiable, and the SAT solver returns a satisfying assignment (line 7), function calls from $\mathbb{T}$ are considered as candidate calls to be refined. To refine, the satisfying assignment is used to restrict $\mathbb{T}$ on the calls, appeared along the error trace ϵ (i.e., in the satisfying assignment) (line 9). In the next iteration of the algorithm, the calls from $\mathbb{T}$ are encoded precisely in the updated PBMC formula. Technically, the algorithm extends $\hat{F}_\nu$ by adding function calls from $\mathbb{T}$ (line 13), as shown, for example, on Fig. 3b. There, $\hat{f}_2'$ appears along ϵ and therefore it has to be refined; $\hat{f}_3$ does not appear in ϵ, so it will be encoded nondeterministically. If $\mathbb{T} = \varnothing$ then no nondeterministically treated recursive calls were found along the error trace, so the real bug is found (line 11), and the algorithm terminates.

If the SAT solver proves unsatisfiability of ϕ then the program abstraction, and consequently the program itself, are safe (line 6). This case is represented on Fig. 3c. The final recursion depth ν is detected, and the algorithm terminates.

Theorem 1. *Given the program P and an assertion π, if Alg. 1 terminates with an answer SAFE (BUG) then π holds (does not hold) for P.*

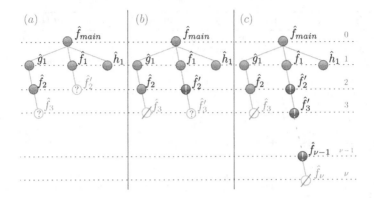

Fig. 3. Illustration of the individual steps of the Alg. 1 on the example with a single recursive function f, called twice.

a) First iteration: $\hat{F}_\nu = \{\hat{f}_{main}, \hat{g}_1, \hat{h}_1, \hat{f}_1, \hat{f}_2\}$ (grey nodes) are encoded precisely, $\mathbb{T} = \{\hat{f}_3, \hat{f}_2'\}$ (white "?" nodes) are treated nondeterministically; the initial recursion depth is equal to 1.

b) Second iteration: solver returns SAT (corresponding to error trace $\epsilon = \{\hat{f}_{main}, \hat{f}_1, \hat{f}_2'\}$), set $\mathbb{T}$ is updated to contain only one function call ($\{\hat{f}_2'\}$ (black "!" nodes)). All calls from $\mathbb{T}$ are added to current $\hat{F}_\nu$. The current recursion depth is incremented, and equal to 2.

c) Final iteration: solver returns UNSAT or $\mathbb{T} = \varnothing$, the detected recursion depth is equal to $\nu - 1$.

Proof (Proof sketch). The proof is divided into two parts, for *SAFE* (line 6) and *BUG* (line 11) outputs of the algorithm (and respectively, the PBMC formula ϕ proven UNSAT or SAT).

   Case **SAFE**. In this case ϕ is unsatisfiable. The formula ϕ represents some abstraction of P which contains precise and over-approximated components (as described in section 3.1). Since every abstracted formula can be strengthened and turned into the corresponding precise encoding, and since unsatisfiability of a weaker formula implies unsatisfiability of a stronger formula, then the PBMC formula ϕ^{inline} encoding P without abstraction is also unsatisfiable, i.e., π holds.

   Case **BUG**. In this case, ϕ is satisfiable, and the satisfying assignment represents an error trace. At the same time, the algorithm did not detect any nondeterministically treated recursive function calls along the error trace (line 10). It means that π is indeed violated within the current recursion depth.   □

Note on Termination. The algorithm is guaranteed to terminate within a given timeout when it finds an error or proves that the assertion holds. Similar to classical BMC, Alg. 1 terminates if the recursion depth is sufficient to disprove the assertion. Classical BMC can prove the assertion up to some fixed recursion depth, but the result might be incomplete if the recursion depth is insufficient. In contrast, by Theorem 1, if our algorithm does not yield a timeout, it guarantees that the detected recursion depth is complete to prove (disprove) the assertion.

Algorithm 2. Summarization in BMC with Automatic Detection of Recursion Depth

---

Input: Initial recursion depth ν; Program unwound ν times: $P_\nu = (\hat{F}_\nu, \hat{f}_{main}, child)$;
       Assertion to be checked: π; Set of summaries: *summaries*; *TimeOut*
Output: Verification result: $\{SAFE, BUG, TimeOut\}$; Error trace: ϵ
Data: PBMC formula: ϕ; set of function calls: $\mathbb{T}$; substitution scenario: Ω

1   $\phi \leftarrow \neg\pi;$ *// initialize ϕ*

2   $\mathbb{T} \leftarrow \hat{F}_\nu \cup \{\hat{g} \notin \hat{F}_\nu \mid child(\hat{f}, \hat{g}), \hat{f} \in \hat{F}_\nu\};$ *// unwind the calltree initially*

3   $\Omega \leftarrow init;$ *// use (2) from Sect. 2.4 to create initial scenario*

4   **while** ($\neg TimeOut$) **do**

5       $\phi \leftarrow \phi \wedge \bigwedge_{\hat{f} \in \mathbb{T}: \Omega(\hat{f}) = inline} \textsf{CreateFormula}(\hat{f}) \wedge \bigwedge_{\hat{g} \in \mathbb{T}: \Omega(\hat{g}) = sum} \textsf{ApplySummaries}(\hat{g}) \wedge$
        $\bigwedge_{\hat{h} \in \mathbb{T}: \Omega(\hat{h}) = havoc} \textsf{Nondet}(\hat{h});$ *// add partitions to ϕ (inline, summarize, havoc)*

6       $result, proof, sat\_assignment \leftarrow \textsf{Solve}(\phi);$

7   **if** ($result = UNSAT$) **then**

8   **foreach** ($\hat{f} \in \mathbb{T}$) **do**   *// split $\phi \equiv \phi_{\hat{f}}^{subtree} \wedge \phi_{\hat{f}}^{env}$ as in Sect. 2.3*

9              $summaries(\hat{f}) \leftarrow \textsf{Interpolate}(proof, \hat{f});$

10   **end**

11   **return** $SAFE;$

12   **else**

13          $\epsilon \leftarrow \textsf{extract\_CE}(sat\_assignment);$

14   **if** ($\varnothing = \{\hat{f} \in \textsf{extract\_calls}(\epsilon) \mid \Omega(\hat{f}) \neq inline\}$) **then**

15   **return** $BUG, \epsilon;$

16   **else**

17             $\Omega \leftarrow \textsf{Refine}(\Omega, \mathbb{T}, \textsf{extract\_calls}(\epsilon));$ *// use (3) in Sect. 2.4*

18             $\mathbb{T} \leftarrow \mathbb{T} \cup \{\hat{g} \notin \mathbb{T} \mid child(\hat{f}, \hat{g}), \hat{f} \in \mathbb{T}, \Omega(\hat{f}) = inline\};$ *//*
                                                         // unwind the calltree on demand

19 **end**

20 **return** $TimeOut$

The other benefit of our algorithm is that it does not require the recursion depth to be given a priori, but instead it is detected automatically.

Based on our observations, termination of Alg. 1 depends on the termination of the recursive program it was applied to. For example, the program with one single recursive function from Fig. 1a terminates for any values of input data. The recursion termination condition, $\neg(\texttt{a < 10})$ defines the upper bound 10 for the value of $\texttt{a}$, and at the same time the function $\texttt{f}$ monotonically increments the value of $\texttt{a}$. Hence, the recursive function $\texttt{f}$ is called a fixed number of times and the program eventually terminates. Clearly, for complete analysis of this program it is enough to consider the maximum possible number of recursive function calls for every initial value of $\texttt{a}$ which in this example is equal to 5. At the same time, it introduces an upper bound for the size of the constructed PBMC formula which is a sufficient condition to the SAT solver to terminate while solving it.

3.2 Optimizations and Applications of Alg. 1

Incremental Formula Construction and Refinement. Possible optimizations of Alg. 1 are 1) the incremental construction of the PBMC formula ϕ and 2) more efficient handling of a set of the refinement candidates, $\mathbb{T}$.

In the first optimization, ϕ is created in an incremental manner. At each iteration, ϕ is not recomputed from scratch, but gets conjoined with new partitions.

These partitions precisely encode the refined function calls from the set $\mathbb{T}$. In this manner the PBMC formula is updated at the beginning of each iteration.

In the second optimization, the set of refinement candidates $\mathbb{T}$ is merged with the whole set of unwound function calls $\hat{F}_\nu$. Instead of handling those two sets, it is enough to handle one. To distinguish function calls which were present in $\mathbb{T}$ from the others present in $\hat{F}_\nu$ the substitution scenario Ω is used.

Summarization. The proposed algorithm for recursion depth detection can be exploited for efficient incremental program verification (i.e., verification of the same program with respect to different assertions [19].[5] In this setting, function summaries are computed by means of Craig Interpolation.

Alg. 2 shows how the optimized Alg. 1 can be integrated with summarization-based verification. Interpolating procedure (line 9), that employs the PBMC formula ϕ and its proof of unsatisfiability, is run after each assertion is proven. The use of summaries makes the verification more flexible. Instead of treating recursive function calls nondeterministically, the algorithm might apply existent summaries, thus making entire program abstraction more accurate. Moreover, the use of substitution scenario (line 5)enables summarization of any (not necessarily recursive) function calls.

4   Experimental Evaluation

We implemented the automatic Recursion Depth Detection (RDD) and Summarization-based RDD (SRDD) inside of the BMC tool FunFrog [18] and make its binary (FunFrog+(S)RDD) available[6]. FunFrog supports interpolation-based function summarization for C programs and uses the SAT-solver PeRIPLO [17] for solving propositional formulas, proof reduction and interpolation. FunFrog follows CProver's[7] paradigm. In particular, it accepts a precompiled goto-binary, a representation of the C program in an intermediate goto-cc language, and runs the analysis on it.

We evaluated the new algorithms on a set of various recursive C programs (taken from the SVCOMP'14[8] set (Ackermann X McCarthy, GCD, EvenOdd), obtained from industry[9] (P2P_Joints X), crafted by USI students for evaluation of interpolation-based abstractions). We provide two verification scenarios to evaluate the algorithms. In the first one, FunFrog+RDD verifies a single assertion in each benchmark and detects the recursion depth. In the second one, FunFrog+SRDD incrementally verifies a set of assertions and reuses function summaries between its checks. In our experiments loop handling was done by means of CProver (see Sect. 5 for more details).

---

[5] Recall that the analysis in [19] is restricted to programs, unwound fixed number of times (i.e., without recursion).

[6] http://www.inf.usi.ch/phd/fedyukovich/funfrog_srdd.tar.gz

[7] http://www.cprover.org

[8] http://sv-comp.sosy-lab.org/2014/

[9] In scope of FP7-ICT-2009-5 — project PINCETTE 257647.

Table 1. Verification statistics for various BMC tools with and without automated detection of recursion depth

benchmark				FunFrog+RDD											FunFrog	CBMC
				In≡1					1 ¡ In ¡ ν			In≡ ν				
name	#R	T	Result	In	Time	#It	ν	#Calls	In	Time	#It	In	Time	#It	Time	Time
Array A	5	a	SAFE	1	664.02	15	15	75	10	513.986	6	15	121.381	1	3600+	3600+
Array B	12	a	SAFE	1	777.432	24	24	71	2	1781.92	23	24	3600+	—	3600+	3600+
Array C	3	a	SAFE	1	1113.68	27	16	106	14	991.724	3	16	557.281	1	3600+	3600+
Ackermann A	2	b	SAFE	1	55.758	34	20	2169	7	3493.64	10	20	3600+	—	3600+	3600+
Ackermann B	2	b	BUG	1	56.772	30	17	1942	7	3547.29	10	17	3600+	—	3600+	3600+
Alternate A	2	c	SAFE	1	35.068	50	50	100	30	22.206	20	50	0.902	1	3600+	3600+
Alternate B	2	c	BUG	1	92.314	77	77	154	50	53.315	28	77	1.681	1	3600+	3600+
Multiply	10	a	SAFE	1	710.517	110	110	110	7	569.559	4	10	226.659	1	3600+	3600+
InterleaveBitsRec	1	a	SAFE	1	150.053	33	33	33	15	125.241	19	33	8.188	1	3600+	3600+
BitShiftRec A	1	a	SAFE	1	128.074	64	64	64	20	13.416	45	64	2.413	1	3600+	3600+
BitShiftRec B	2	b	SAFE	1	65.537	12	12	4285	3	65.399	10	12	3600+	—	3600+	3600+
P2P_Joints A	1	a	SAFE	1	1234.71	4	4	4	2	1195.31	3	4	1092.26	1	3600+	3600+
P2P_Joints B	1	a	BUG	1	1266.38	4	4	4	2	1222.11	3	4	1120.03	1	3600+	3600+

4.1 Evaluating RDD

Table 1 summarizes the verification statistics of a set of benchmarks with different types (**T**) of recursion (a - single recursion, b - multiple recursion, c - indirect recursion). The number of recursive functions present in each benchmark is depicted in the column marked #**R**. Each benchmark was verified using CBMC, FunFrog[10] without recursion depth detection and 3 different versions of FunFrog+RDD. The first configuration of FunFrog+RDD performs the algorithm with the initial recursion depth set to 1 (denoted as **In** $\equiv$ **1** in the table), detects recursion depth (ν) and also reports the number of unwound recursive calls as #**Calls**. Then, in purpose of comparison, the second and the third configurations perform the same algorithm with the another values of the initial recursion depths (**1 ¡ In ¡ ν** and **In** $\equiv$ ν respectively). For each experiment, we report total verification time (in seconds) and a number of iterations of FunFrog+RDD (#**It**). The verification results (SAFE/BUG) were identical for experiments with all configurations and we placed them in the table in the section describing the benchmarks.

Notably, for all different types of recursion, the experiments with CBMC and pure FunFrog failed as they reached the timeout (**3600+**) of 1 hour without producing the result. This in general was not a problem for any of the experiments when FunFrog+RDD was used. We compare different configurations of FunFrog+RDD in order to demonstrate possible behaviors of FunFrog+RDD depending on the structure of benchmarks. The benchmarks Multiply, Alternate A/B, Array A/C, InterleaveBitsRec and BitShiftRec A witness the overhead of the procedure. In InterleaveBitsRec and BitShiftRec A there is a single recursive function called one time; in Multiply and Alternate A/B there are several recursive calls requiring the same recursion depth; in Array A and Array C there are several recursive calls requiring different, but relatively close recursion depths. That is, if we compare the first configuration with the

---

[10] CBMC and FunFrog were run with default parameters.

Table 2. Verification statistics of `FunFrog+RDD` and `FunFrog+SRDD`

benchmark					FunFrog+RDD			FunFrog+SRDD			
name	#R	T	Result	ν	In	TotalTime	#It	In	#A	TotalTime	ItpTime	#It
Arithm	1	a	SAFE	100	1	128.47	100	1	20	9.676	2.036	119
McCarthy	2	b	SAFE	11	1	3600+	—	1	5	10.495	4.859	24
GCD	3	b	SAFE	11	1	145.381	64	1	4	54.185	0.409	37
EvenOdd	2	c	SAFE	25	1	38.621	50	1	8	27.99	4.49	82
P2P_Joints C	1	a	SAFE	4	1	1531.38	4	1	4	1151.72	68.10	4
P2P_Joints D	1	a	SAFE	4	1	1192.28	4	1	4	1089.04	87.08	4

third one, we can see that such overhead exists. The first configuration takes more time to complete verification than the second one, and the second configuration takes more time to complete verification than the third one. This is because `FunFrog+RDD` executes more iterations in the first configuration than in the second one and more iterations in the second configuration than in the third one. Again, the difference and the advantage is in the fact that the first and the second configurations do not know the recursion depth needed for verification and the third one gets it provided (as an initial recursion depth for `FunFrog+RDD`). Therefore, for the third configuration it is always enough to execute one iteration.

The benchmarks `Array B`, `Ackerman A/B` and `BitShiftRec B` show the opposite behavior, where the first configuration takes less time to complete than the second and the third ones. These cases demonstrate the benefits of using *minimality* feature of the `FunFrog+RDD`, since they require different recursion depths for each recursive function call appearing in the code. In all configurations we specify **In** by a fixed number which may fit well some of the recursive calls, but for other ones it may be bigger than needed. In this case, `FunFrog+RDD` creates unnecessary PBMC partitions, blows up the formula and consequently slows down the verification process. While using **In** = 1, incremental unwinding automatically finds depths for each recursive function call. It means that for such cases the new approach for BMC not only detects the recursion depth sufficient for verification but that it also performs it efficiently and allows to slice out parts of the system which are redundant for verification purpose.

Interesting results are demonstrated by experimentation with the industrial benchmark `P2P_Joints A/B`. It contains expensive nonlinear computations, a complex calltree structure with relatively trivial recursion requiring unrolling 4 times. The experiments show that the difference in timings between different `FunFrog+RDD` configurations is minor.

4.2 Evaluating SRDD

Another set of experiments of verifying recursive programs by applying `FunFrog +SRDD` is summarized in Table 2. There are two configurations of `FunFrog` compared in the table. The first one, **FunFrog+RDD**, is similar to the first configuration in Table 1. The second one, **FunFrog+SRDD**, is SRDD driven by *assertion decomposition*.

We explain the idea of assertion decomposition on the example from Fig. 1. The assertion `assert(y >= 0)` ($A1$) can be used to derive a set the following *helper*-assertions `assert(x < 5 || y >= 0)` ($A2$), `assert(x < 7 || y >= 0)` ($A3$) and so on. It is clear that if $A1$ holds, then both $A2$ and $A3$ hold as well; and if $A2$ holds then $A3$ holds as well. We will say that $A3$ is *weaker* than $A2$, and $A2$ is *weaker* than $A1$.

In this experiment, we derive helper-assertions (number of them is denoted **#A** in the table) by guessing values of the input parameters of recursive functions, then order assertions by strength and begin verification from the weakest one. If the check succeeds, the summaries of all (even recursive) functions are extracted. They will be reused in verification of stronger assertions. This procedure is repeated until the original assertion is proven valid. We summarize total timings (**TotalTime**) for verification of each weaker assertion, which includes the timings for interpolation (**ItpTime**).

For all benchmarks in the table, `FunFrog+SRDD` outperforms `FunFrog+RDD`. Technically, it means that checking a single assertion may be slower than checking itself and also several other assertions.[11] The strongest result, we obtained, is verifying a well-known `McCarthy` function. Running `FunFrog+SRDD` for it takes around 10 seconds, while `FunFrog+RDD`, pure `FunFrog` and CBMC exceed timeout. Notably, the interpolation may take up to a half of whole verification time. In some cases, summarization increases the number of iterations. But in total, `FunFrog+SRDD` remains more efficient that `FunFrog+RDD`.

5   Related Work

To the best of our knowledge, there is very little support for computing recursion depths in BMC algorithms. One of the most successful BMC tools, CBMC [3], attempts to find unwinding recursion depths using constant propagation. This approach works only if the number of recursive calls is explicitly specified in the source code (i.e., as a constant number in a termination condition of a recursive call). If it cannot be detected by constant propagation, the tool gets into an infinite loop and fails to complete verification. CBMC also supports explicit definition of a recursion depth ν which may lead to incomplete verification results. In order to check correctness of the current unwinding, CBMC inserts and checks so called *unwinding assertions*. If all unwinding assertions hold, the currently used recursion depth is sufficient. If there is a violated unwinding assertion, the current recursion depth has to be increased. To our knowledge, CBMC does not have the refinement procedure and error trace analysis to make the recursion depth detection complete.

The idea of processing function calls on demand was also researched by [10] in the tool `Corral`. The method, called *stratified inlining*, relies on substituting bodies of function calls by summaries, and checking the resulting program using a theorem prover. If the given level of abstraction is not accurate enough, the

---

[11] A reader can find all these benchmarks with already inserted helper-assertions at http://www.inf.usi.ch/phd/fedyukovich/funfrog_srdd.tar.gz

algorithm refines function calls in a similar way to our refinement. Despite some similarity to Alg. 1, `Corral` relies on the external tool [7] to generate function summaries. In contrast, our method automatically generates summaries using Craig Interpolation inside Alg. 2 after an assertion is successfully checked, and use already constructed summaries to check other assertions.

There are techniques designed to deal with recursion. For instance, [20] is able to verify recursive programs in milliseconds, but it is limited only to functional programs. BMC, in contrast, is not designed to deal with recursion, but it has been applied to a wide range of verification tasks. `FunFrog+(S)RDD` itself is not a standalone recursive model checker, but an extension of the existent SAT-based BMC tool. In our previous work [18], it was already shown applicable to verify industrial-size programs, supporting complete ANSI C syntax. Conversion to SAT formulas allows to perform bit-precise checks, i.e., verify assertions in the programs using bitwise operators.

Craig Interpolation is applicable to verification of recursive programs in a rather different scenario. In `Whale` [1], it is used to guess summaries generated from under-approximations of the function bodies behavior. Unfortunately, the tool is not available for use, so we are unable to compare it with `FunFrog+(S)RDD`.

k-induction [5,15] is another under-approximation-driven technique for checking recursion. First, it proves an induction base (i.e., that there is no assertion violation in the unwinding chain with the length k). Then, if successful, it proves an induction step (i.e., whenever the assertion holds in an unwinding chain with the length k, it also holds in the unwinding chain with the length $(k+1)$). Finally, the approach is able to find an inductive invariant, which can be treated as function summary. To our knowledge, there is no incremental model checker based on k-induction which (re-)uses function summaries.

The overview of other summarization approaches to program analysis can be found in our earlier work published at [19].

6   Conclusion and Future Work

This paper presented the new approach to automatically detect recursion depths for BMC and applies it to function summarization-based approaches to model checking. In principle, a similar idea may be applied to solve the problem of loop bound detection where an algorithm abstracts away loop bodies and iteratively refines one more body at a time. One can develop such algorithm in future. We believe, there is a strong mapping between program termination and analysis termination which can be investigated in future. In cases of multiple recursion, the algorithm may be improved by using SAT solvers with support for Minimal SAT. The approach of the summarization-based BMC might be extended to support SMT theories. This way, the analysis in general might become more efficient, but will lose bit-precision.

Acknowledgments. We thank Antti Hyvärinen for his notable contribution during the work on this paper.

References

1. Albarghouthi, A., Gurfinkel, A., Chechik, M.: WHALE: An interpolation-based algorithm for inter-procedural verification. In: Kuncak, V., Rybalchenko, A. (eds.) VMCAI 2012. LNCS, vol. 7148, pp. 39–55. Springer, Heidelberg (2012)
2. Biere, A., Cimatti, A., Clarke, E., Zhu, Y.: Symbolic model checking without BDDs. In: Cleaveland, W.R. (ed.) TACAS 1999. LNCS, vol. 1579, pp. 193–207. Springer, Heidelberg (1999)
3. Clarke, E., Kroning, D., Lerda, F.: A tool for checking ANSI-C programs. In: Jensen, K., Podelski, A. (eds.) TACAS 2004. LNCS, vol. 2988, pp. 168–176. Springer, Heidelberg (2004)
4. Craig, W.: Three uses of the Herbrand-Gentzen theorem in relating model theory and proof theory. J. of Symbolic Logic, 269–285 (1957)
5. Donaldson, A.F., Haller, L., Kroening, D., Rümmer, P.: Software verification using k-induction. In: Yahav, E. (ed.) SAS 2011. LNCS, vol. 6887, pp. 351–368. Springer, Heidelberg (2011)
6. Fedyukovich, G., Sery, O., Sharygina, N.: eVolCheck: incremental upgrade checker for C. In: Piterman, N., Smolka, S.A. (eds.) TACAS 2013. LNCS, vol. 7795, pp. 292–307. Springer, Heidelberg (2013)
7. Flanagan, C., M. Leino, K.R.: Houdini, an annotation assistant for ESC/Java. In: Oliveira, J.N., Zave, P. (eds.) FME 2001. LNCS, vol. 2021, pp. 500–517. Springer, Heidelberg (2001)
8. Graf, S., Saidi, H.: Construction of abstract state graphs with PVS. In: Grumberg, O. (ed.) CAV 1997. LNCS, vol. 1254, pp. 72–83. Springer, Heidelberg (1997)
9. Ivancic, F., Yang, Z., Ganai, M.K., Gupta, A., Ashar, P.: Efficient SAT-based bounded model checking for software verification. Theor. Comput. Sci. **404**, 256–274 (2008)
10. Lal, A., Qadeer, S., Lahiri, S.K.: A solver for reachability modulo theories. In: Madhusudan, P., Seshia, S.A. (eds.) CAV 2012. LNCS, vol. 7358, pp. 427–443. Springer, Heidelberg (2012)
11. McMillan, K.L.: Applications of craig interpolants in model checking. In: Halbwachs, N., Zuck, L.D. (eds.) TACAS 2005. LNCS, vol. 3440, pp. 1–12. Springer, Heidelberg (2005)
12. McMillan, K.L.: Lazy abstraction with interpolants. In: Ball, T., Jones, R.B. (eds.) CAV 2006. LNCS, vol. 4144, pp. 123–136. Springer, Heidelberg (2006)
13. McMillan, K.L.: Lazy annotation for program testing and verification. In: Touili, T., Cook, B., Jackson, P. (eds.) CAV 2010. LNCS, vol. 6174, pp. 104–118. Springer, Heidelberg (2010)
14. Merz, F., Falke, S., Sinz, C.: LLBMC: Bounded model checking of C and C++ programs using a compiler IR. In: Joshi, R., Müller, P., Podelski, A. (eds.) VSTTE 2012. LNCS, vol. 7152, pp. 146–161. Springer, Heidelberg (2012)
15. Morse, J., Cordeiro, L., Nicole, D., Fischer, B.: Handling unbounded loops with ESBMC 1.20. In: Piterman, N., Smolka, S.A. (eds.) TACAS 2013. LNCS, vol. 7795, pp. 619–622. Springer, Heidelberg (2013)
16. Pudlák, P.: Lower bounds for resolution and cutting plane proofs and monotone computations. Journal of Symbolic Logic. **62**, 981–998 (1997)

17. Rollini, S.F., Alt, L., Fedyukovich, G., Hyvärinen, A.E.J., Sharygina, N.: PeRIPLO: A framework for producing effective interpolants in SAT-based software verification. In: McMillan, K., Middeldorp, A., Voronkov, A. (eds.) LPAR-19 2013. LNCS, vol. 8312, pp. 683–693. Springer, Heidelberg (2013)
18. Sery, O., Fedyukovich, G., Sharygina, N.: FunFrog: bounded model checking with interpolation-based function summarization. In: Chakraborty, S., Mukund, M. (eds.) ATVA 2012. LNCS, vol. 7561, pp. 203–207. Springer, Heidelberg (2012)
19. Sery, O., Fedyukovich, G., Sharygina, N.: Interpolation-based function summaries in bounded model checking. In: Eder, K., Lourenço, J., Shehory, O. (eds.) HVC 2011. LNCS, vol. 7261, pp. 160–175. Springer, Heidelberg (2012)
20. Unno, H., Terauchi, T., Kobayashi, N.: Automating relatively complete verification of higher-order functional programs. In: POPL, pp. 75–86. ACM (2013)

A Probabilistic Model Checking Analysis of a Realistic Vehicular Networks Mobility Model

Bruno Ferreira$^{(\boxtimes)}$, Fernando A.F. Braz, and Sérgio V.A. Campos

Department of Computer Science, Federal University of Minas Gerais,
Avenida Antônio Carlos, 6627, Pampulha, 30123-970 Belo Horizonte, Brazil
{bruno.ferreira,fbraz,scampos}@dcc.ufmg.br

Abstract. Vehicular Ad-Hoc Networks (VANET) are a special type of network where its nodes are vehicles that move according to specific patterns. This network is based on wireless communication, presenting new challenges, such as how it will be tested in realistic scenarios. Currently, simulations are widely used. However, they have limitations, such as local minima. Another approach is model checking, which has been used in only a few studies, often overlooking mobility and signal propagation issues. This work provides a realistic mobility model using probabilistic model checking to describe an overtake scenario involving three vehicles in a short distance. Our analysis has shown 98 % of accident chance in this situation. However, the main result is providing an example to represent the mobility aspect which can be connected with other models such as signal propagation and the network itself. Therefore, VANETs can now be tested using methods closer to the reality.

Keywords: Model Checking · Vehicular Ad-Hoc Networks · Mobility

1 Introduction

Intelligent Traffic Systems (ITS) are a response to reduce the number of traffic accidents, the cost of transportation and the volume of CO_2 emissions [11]. These systems make intensive use of communication among vehicles, which is possible using Vehicular Ad-Hoc Networks (VANETs), a particular class of Mobile Ad-Hoc Networks (MANETs). VANETs are distributed and self-organized communication networks, characterized by their high speed and mobility, which brings several challenges to the academic community [13].

Current research in this field frequently analyzes the behavior of VANETs using simulators. However, simulation methods examine only a subset of possible scenarios, which can lead to an incomplete – or even worse, an incorrect – analysis [14]. Furthermore, works such as [1] and [3] have reported that VANET simulators, despite their constant evolution, have not reached an ideal point, because they need to integrate the mobility of the nodes, the communication protocols (network model) and the signals propagation.

© Springer International Publishing Switzerland 2015
C. Braga and N. Martí-Oliet (Eds.): SBMF 2014, LNCS 8941, pp. 113–129, 2015.
DOI: 10.1007/978-3-319-15075-8_8

A complementary approach to simulation is the use of probabilistic model checking (PMC) [8,19]. PMC is a technique for the automatic analysis of systems, which verifies properties in probabilistic logic by exhaustively enumerating all reachable states. PMC can answer questions such as "What is the probability of the occurrence of a certain event?". This approach is ideal for dynamic and stochastic systems, such as VANETs. PMC verification is performed by (1) specifying what are the properties that the system must obey, (2) constructing the formal model of the system, which should capture all the essential properties and (3) finally, running the verifier to validate the specified properties.

Verification techniques can be useful to assess the efficiency and correctness of MANETs. The results obtained can be used to improve a wide range of systems. Despite its benefits, model checking is rarely used in VANETs. Also, the few studies (e.g. [4] and [21]) do not address uncertainty caused by the dynamism of the nodes. Thus, the non-determinism of the message delivery caused by the mobility of vehicles is not being represented, which is an underlying factor in VANETs. [20] uses simulation of Markov chains to represent planned trajectories of autonomous vehicles. The tool which we have used for analysis also represents its model with this technique, however, it uses a formal approach, finding exact probabilities and estimates, besides, other resources such as multi-terminal binary decision diagrams are used [19] and our work benefits from these features.

It is important to verify networks considering not only the network itself, but also its additional functionalists. Thus, it is often necessary to model the communication and other important system components [7]. Therefore, building complete models considering the traffic flow, network and radio propagation are necessary and rarely explored in model checking. We have proposed the first step for completely modeling VANETs presenting a motion aspect which will be coupled with the traditional network analysis.

Nevertheless, this work has the objective of representing mobility models in VANETs using PMC. The proposed model follows practices and concepts already used in simulation methods to model an overtake situation involving three vehicles. However, it uses the benefits of automatic and exhaustive verification provided by PMC. Thus, the application of model checking in VANETs can be extended in the future to describe network and mobility models.

We have used PRISM, a probabilistic model checker for formal modelling and analysis. This tool can represent systems that exhibit random or probabilistic behaviour. It has been used to analyze many different application domains from communication protocols to biological systems [18]. We have modeled an overtake scenario involving three vehicles in a short distance. The model shows that there is a huge chance of an accident (98% in some scenarios), however counter-examples to a safe overtake are presented.

This paper is organized as follows: Section 2 presents important concepts of VANET analysis; PMC is defined in Section 3; Section 4 shows our mobility model; Section 5 discusses the results of the model; finally, conclusions and future works are presented in Section 6.

2 VANET Analysis

In order to validate the effectiveness of Intelligent Traffic Systems, it is necessary to evaluate their performance and communication protocols in real test environments. However, there are logistic difficulties, economic questions and technological limitations which make simulations a good choice for testing and validation of these protocols. The fields of computer networks and traffic engineering make extensive use of simulators. There are long established software such as NS-2 (The Network Simulator)[1] and SUMO (Simulation of Urban Mobility)[2]. Since the introduction of vehicular networks, the integration of these two fields has recently become necessary [14].

This integration is required due to inherent features of the strong coupling between communication and mobility in VANETs. Communication modifies mobility patterns, on the other hand, correct message reception is affected by vehicular movement. However, three distinct aspects must work together in order to achieve realistic tests [3]: (1) **Mobility Models** represent the vehicle movement, including mobility patterns and the interaction between vehicles (e.g. crossroad control); (2) **Network Models** describe the data exchanged between vehicles, including MAC, routing and superior protocol layers; (3) **Signal Propagation Models** reproduce the environment modeling involving fixed and mobile obstacles during the communication. For further details on these mobility and signal propagation techniques, we refer to [13] and [17], respectively.

Mobility models, the main subject of this work, can be described in two points [12]: (1) **Freedom of movement**, responsible for describing the motion constraint to each vehicle. These representations have been improved from simplified models such Manhattan grid [2] to real world maps (e.g. [6] and [22]) and (2) **Interaction among vehicles** which modeling the behavior of a vehicle that is a direct consequence of the interaction with the other vehicles on the road. This includes microscopic aspects, such as lane changing and decreasing/increasing the speed due to the surrounding traffic.

Regarding this microscopic implementation, Car Following Models (CFMs) are the most used type of driver model. CFMs usually represent time, position, speed, and acceleration as continuous functions. However, CFMs have been extended to include discrete formulations [14]. Commonly used models are (as described by [15]): the cellular automata models, follow-the-leader models and intelligent driver model (IDM). The next subsections describe two CFM models chosen for their simplicity, efficiency and realism.

2.1 Intelligent Driver Model

The Intelligent Driver Model (IDM) shows a crash-free collective dynamic, exhibits controllable stability properties, and implements a braking strategy with smooth transitions between acceleration and deceleration behavior [16].

---

[1] NS-2 . http://www.isi.edu/nsnam/ns/. Access date: November 4, 2014.

[2] SUMO. http://sumo.sourceforge.net/. Access date: November 4, 2014.

The IDM acceleration is a continuous function incorporating different driving modes for all velocities of freeway and city traffic. The distance s (bumper-to-bumper) to the leading vehicle is given by $s = x_l - x - e$, where x_l and x are the coordinates and e is the extent of vehicle. IDM also takes into account the velocity difference (approaching rate) to the leading vehicle, given by $\Delta v = v - v_l$. The IDM acceleration function is given by the Equations 1 and 2.

$$a_{IDM}(s, v, \Delta v) = a \left[1 - \left(\frac{v}{v_0} \right)^\delta - \left(\frac{s^*(v, \Delta v)}{s} \right)^2 \right] \tag{1}$$

$$s^*(v, \Delta v) = s_0 + vT + \frac{v\Delta v}{2\sqrt{ab}} \tag{2}$$

This expression combines the free-road acceleration strategy, given by:

$$a_{free}(v) = a[1 - (v/v_0)^\delta]$$

with a deceleration strategy, given by:

$$a_{brake}(s, v, \Delta v) = -a(s^*/s)^2$$

The deceleration strategy becomes relevant when the gap to the leading vehicle is not significantly larger than the "desired (safe) gap", given by $s^*(v, \Delta v)$. The free acceleration is denoted by the desired speed v_0, the maximum acceleration is a, and the exponent δ indicates how the acceleration decreases with velocity ($\delta = 1$ corresponds to a linear decrease, while $\delta \rightarrow \infty$ denotes a constant acceleration).

The effective minimum gap s^* is composed of the minimum distance s_0 (which is relevant for low velocities only), the velocity dependent distance vT, which corresponds to following the leading vehicle with a constant desired time gap T, and a dynamic contribution which is only active in non-stationary traffic corresponding to situations in which $\Delta v \neq 0$. This latter contribution implements an "intelligent" driving behavior that, in normal situations, limits braking decelerations to a comfortable deceleration b. In critical situations, however, the IDM deceleration becomes significantly higher, making the IDM collision-free [24]. The IDM parameters v_0, T, s_0, a and b are shown in Table 1.

Calculating the acceleration at a time t, the new position and speed or deceleration distance can be given by traditional kinematics' equations.

Table 1. Parameters of the Intelligent Driver Model. Adapted– [16].

Parameter	Car	Truck
Desired speed v_0	120 km/h	85 km/h
Free acceleration exponent δ	4	4
Desired time gap T	1.5	2.0
Jam distance s_0	2.0	4.0
Maximum acceleration a	1.4 m/s^2	0.7 m/s^2
Desired deceleration b	2.0 m/s^2	2.0 m/s^2
Changing threshold Δ_{th}	0.1 m/s^2	0.1 m/s^2

2.2 Minimizing Overall Braking Induced by Lane Change

A general model to represent lane-changing rules was proposed by [9]. The model is called Minimizing Overall Braking Induced by Lane Change (MOBIL). The utility and risk associated of a given lane are determined in terms of longitudinal accelerations calculated by microscopic car-following models as IDM. The previous vehicle deceleration in the target lane can not exceed a given safe limit b_{safe}. Risk criterion prevents critical lane changes and collisions, while the incentive criterion takes into account the advantages and disadvantages of other drivers associated with a lane change via the "politeness factor" p.

A lane change is shown in Figure 1. The MOBIL model depends on the two previous vehicles in the current and the target lanes, respectively. Thus, for a vehicle c considering a lane change, the previous vehicles in the target and current lanes are represented by n and o, respectively. The acceleration a_c denotes the acceleration of vehicle c on the current lane, and $\tilde{a}_c$ refers to the situation in the target lane, that is, to the new acceleration of vehicle c in the target lane. Likewise, $\tilde{a}_o$ and $\tilde{a}_n$ denote the acceleration of old and new previous vehicles after the lane change of vehicle c [9].

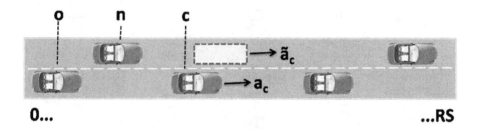

Fig. 1. Mobil notations. Adapted from [9].

According to [9], the incentive criterion determines if the lane change is better or not to a driver. In this model, the incentive is generalized to include the immediately affected neighbors. The politeness factor p determines to which degree these vehicles influence the lane- changing decision. Thus, the incentive criterion is given by the Equation 3.

$$\underbrace{\tilde{a}_c - a_c}_{\text{driver}} + p \left(\underbrace{\tilde{a}_n - a_n}_{\text{new behind}} + \underbrace{\tilde{a}_o - a_o}_{\text{old behind}} \right) > \Delta a_{th} \qquad (3)$$

The first two terms of the Equation 3 denote the advantage of a possible lane change to the driver. The change is good if the driver can go faster in the new lane. The third term denotes the total advantage of the two immediately affected neighbors multiplied by the politeness factor p. The Δa_{th} term on the right-hand side represents a certain inertia and prevents lane changes if the overall advantage is only marginal compared with a "keep lane" directive.

2.3 Framework for Realistic Vehicular Mobility Models

For the purpose of guiding the developers through various challenges and options during the modeling, the authors of [13] propose a concept map for a comprehensible representation of a realistic vehicular mobility model. As can be seen in Figure 2, the concept map is organized around two major modules, **motion constraints** and the **traffic generator**. Additional modules such as **time** and **external influences** are also required for a fine tuning of the mobility patterns. The main modules (gray blocks) are implemented through several auxiliary modules (white ones), which are added according to the desired detail level. These last ones can be more explored in the original work. The main modules description are as follows [13]:

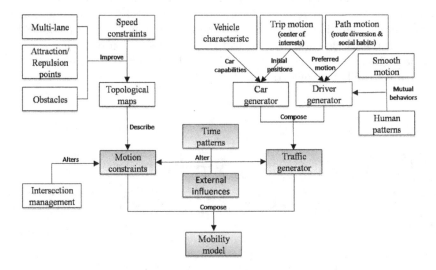

Fig. 2. Concept map of realistic mobility models. Adapted from [13].

- **Motion constraints** describe the relative degree of freedom available for each vehicle. Restrictions can be streets, buildings, vehicles and pedestrians.
- **Traffic generator** defines different kinds of vehicles, and handles their interactions according to the environment under study. Macroscopically, it models traffic densities, speeds and flows, while microscopically, it deals with properties such as the distance between cars, acceleration, braking, and overtaking.
- **Time** describes different mobility configurations for a specific time of the day. Traffic density is not uniform during a day. Peak times, such as rush hours or during special events, can be observed. This block influences the motion constraints and the traffic generator functional blocks.
- **External influences** model the impact of a communication protocol or any other source of information on the motion patterns. This block models the impact of accidents, temporary road works, or real-time knowledge of the traffic status on the motion constraints and the traffic generator blocks.

3   Probabilistic Model Checking

Probabilistic model checking is a formal, exhaustive and automatic technique for modeling and analyzing stochastic systems. PMC checks if the model satisfies a set of properties given in special types of logics.

A stochastic system M is usually a Markov chain or a Markov decision process. This means that the system must satisfy the Markov property, i.e., its behavior depends only on its current state and not on the whole system history, and each transition between states occurs in real-time.

Given a property ϕ expressed as a probabilistic temporal logic formula, PMC attempts to check whether a model of a stochastic system M satisfies the property ϕ with a probability $p \geq \theta$, for a probability threshold $\theta \in [0, 1]$.

Tools called model checkers such as PRISM [19] solve this problem. It requires two inputs: a modeling description of the system, which defines its behavior (for example, through the PRISM language), and a probabilistic temporal logic specification of a set of desired properties (ϕ).

The model checker builds a representation of the system M, usually as a graph-based data structure called Binary Decision Diagrams (BDDs), which can be used to represent boolean functions. States represent possible configurations, while transitions are changes from one configuration to another. Probabilities are assigned to the transitions between states, representing rates of negative exponential distributions.

Properties can be expressed quantitatively as "What is the shortest time which occurs overtaking?" or qualitatively as "Is overtake maneuver successful?", offering valuable insight over the system behavior.

Let $\mathbb{R}_{\geq 0}$ be the set of positive reals and AP be a fixed, finite set of atomic propositions used to label states with properties of interest. A labeled CTMC $\mathcal{C}$ is a tuple $(S, \bar{s}, \mathbf{R}, L)$ where:

- S is a finite set of states;
- $\bar{s} \in S$ is the initial state;
- $\mathbf{R} : S \times S \to \mathbb{R}_{\geq 0}$ is the transition rate matrix, which assigns rates between each pair of states;
- $L : S \to 2^{\mathrm{AP}}$ is a labeling function which labels each state $s \in S$ the set $L(s)$ of atomic propositions that are true in the state.

The probability of a transition between states s and s' being triggered within t time units is $1 - e^{-\mathbf{R}(s,s') \cdot t}$. The elapsed time in state s, before a transition occurs, is exponentially distributed with the *exit rate* given by $E(s) = \sum_{s' \in S} R(s, s')$. The probability of changing to state s' is given by $\frac{\mathbf{R}(s,s')}{E(s)}$.

Properties are specified using the Continuous Stochastic Logic (CSL) [23], which is based on the Computation Tree Logic (CTL) and the Probabilistic CTL (PCTL). The syntax of CSL formulas is the following:

$$\Phi ::= true \mid a \mid \neg\Phi \mid \Phi \wedge \Phi \mid \mathcal{P}_{\unlhd p}[\phi] \mid \mathcal{S}_{\unlhd p}[\phi]$$
$$\phi ::= \mathbf{X}\,\Phi \mid \Phi\,\mathbf{U}^I\,\Phi$$

where a is an atomic proposition, $\unlhd \in \{>, <, \geq, \leq\}$, $p \in [0, 1]$ and $I \in \mathbb{R}_{\geq 0}$.

There are two types of CSL properties: transient ($\mathcal{P}_{\unlhd p}$) and steady-state ($\mathcal{S}_{\unlhd p}$). In this work we are interested in transient or time related properties. A formula $\mathcal{P}_{\unlhd p}[\phi]$ states that the probability of the formula ϕ being satisfied from a state respects the bound $\unlhd p$. Path formulas use the **X** (next) and the $\mathbf{U}^I$ (time-bounded until) operators. For example, formula $\mathbf{X}\,\varPhi$ is true if $\varPhi$ is satisfied in the next state.

This can be applied to check if a probability p is met for one property leading to other, such as $\mathcal{P}_{\unlhd p}[\varPhi_1 => \mathbf{X}\,\varPhi_2]$, where $\varPhi_1$ and $\varPhi_2$ could be the properties "car reaches twice the truck's speed" and "*car* overtakes *truck* in 150 meters".

PRISM allows including **rewards** in the model, which are structures used to quantify states and transitions by associating real values to them. The state rewards are counted proportionately to the elapsed time in the state, while transition rewards are counted each time the transition occurs. In PRISM, rewards are described using the syntax:

rewards *"reward name"*

...

endrewards

Each reward is specified using the multiple reward commands syntax:

$$[sync]\, guard : reward;$$

Reward commands describe state and transition rewards. The *guard* predicate must be true. The *sync* is a label used to synchronize commands into a single transition. The *reward* is an expression that counts for the reward.

Reward properties can be used in states and transitions, e.g. "What is the expected reward (speed or throttle) for the car to travel 200 meters at time T?".

This reward can be instantaneous, obtaining its value at the given time through the property $\mathcal{R}_{=?}[\mathcal{I}^{=t}]$, or accumulated, calculating its value until the given time, using the property $\mathcal{R}_{=?}[\mathcal{C}^{<=t}]$. One can obtain the probability of a state reward by dividing it to the sum of all state rewards. The same procedure can be applied to transitions.

Rewards of paths in a Continuous-time Markov chain are summations of state rewards along the path and transition rewards for each transition between these states. State rewards are interpreted as the rate at which rewards are accumulated, essentially counting them, i.e. if t time units are spent in a state with state-reward r, the accumulated reward in that state is $r \times t$.

Another interesting PRISM feature, when reporting the result of model checking, is the ability to customize properties to obtain different results. This is done using filters, which use the following syntax:

$$filter(op, prop, states);$$

PRISM usually has to compute values for all states simultaneously, thus a specific point or all initial states can be selected. In the syntax, **op** is the filter operator (e.g. max, min, avg), **prop** is any PRISM property and **states** is a Boolean-valued expression identifying a set of initial states to apply the filter.

4   Mobility VANET Model

Our model was created with a microscopic focus. The idea is to show the representation of movement of nodes through the analytical Equations 1, 2 and 3, previously described in Section 2.1. Signal propagation and communication have been abstracted. Our microscopic model take into account position, speed, and acceleration of the vehicles. For this, a overtaking vehicle scenario is implemented using the PRISM language. This has been done to demonstrate the viability of PMC usage to check microscopic aspects. Fragments of the models are presented below and the complete version can be found in the supplementary material and website [10].

Figure 3 illustrates the proposed scenario. There are three vehicles involved. The car $c1$ will overtake the truck, called **Leader**, which travels slower. However, the vehicle $c2$ is coming in the opposite direction. In this situation, $c1$ can not see $c2$, due to weather conditions or lack of attention. This scenario will happen in a 250 meters road. Thus, the model should answer questions such as "What is the probability of a collision?".

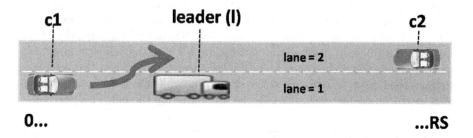

Fig. 3. Overtaking vehicle scenario

The Figure 6 depicts the $c1$'s variables (other vehicles are similar). Each vehicle maintains its current position and velocity. The variable *lane* informs where $c1$ is located. If the lane is equal to 1, then the vehicle is on right-hand side (default value), otherwise the car is on left-hand side. In other words, the vehicle is trying to overtake. The constants `desired_speed_car`, `desired_speed_truck` and `RS` (road side) constrain the model and they are respectively represented in m/s, m/s and m. The `carCrash` variable indicates whether $c1$ and $c2$ collided at some point in time.

An interesting feature of the model is that it does not have a specific initial state. This is achieved by the code shown in Figure 4. The restriction implemented states that vehicles $c1$ and $c2$ in opposite directions are separated by `RS` meters and that there is a leader (truck) between them, which will be overtaken by $c1$. However, the leader position and the initial speed of all involved can be a combination of values. This creates several scenarios to be automatically explored. An interesting abstraction was adopted to $c2$'s position. It starts in *one*, however, its real location on the road is given by $RS - pos\_c2$.

```
init
  (pos_l >= truck_size + min_gap_car) & (pos_c1 = 1) & (pos_c2=1) &
  (lane = ( (v_c1>pos_l) | (a_c1 <= 0) ? 2 : 1) ) &
  (v_c1 >= 0 & v_c1 <= desired_speed_car) &
  (v_c2 >= 0 & v_c2 <= desired_speed_car) &
  (v_l >=0 & v_l <= desired_speed_truck) &
  (carCrash = false)
endinit
```

Fig. 4. Initial states for the model

The vehicles position is given by $x = x_i + vt + (a/2)t^2$, implemented in the PRISM language, which involves the initial position x_i, velocity vt, acceleration a, and time t. Each transition of the model represents a time period that is defined by the constant t. The acceleration of the vehicles are calculated by the IDM model previously presented in Section 2.1. The new speed is given by $v = v_i + at$ and it also depends on the vehicle acceleration. The Figure 5 describes a fragment of the model responsible for calculating the acceleration and position of vehicle $c1$. The formulas are similar for other vehicles.

As mentioned in Section 2.1, the IDM expression combines the free-road acceleration strategy, given by $a_{free}(v) = a[1 - (v/v_0)^\delta]$, with a deceleration strategy, given by $a_{brake}(s, v, \Delta v) = -a(s^*/s)^2$. Therefore, the Equation 1 has been algebraically split during implementation, because the vehicles do not suffer deceleration when there are no obstacles ahead. Thus, when the vehicle $c1$ overtakes the leader, $c1$ does not suffer slowdown, while the truck's acceleration, which used to have free way, starts to be influenced by the new $c1$'s position.

Acceleration and Position Formulas

```
formula a_c1_free = AM_car - AM_car * pow(v_c1 / desired_speed_car, exponent);
formula a_c1_obst = a_c1_free - a_brake_c1;
formula a_c1 = (overtook|lane=2?a_c1_free: (pos_l>=RS?a_c1_free:a_c1_obst));

formula a_brake_c1 = AM_car * pow(des_dyn_dis_c1 / deltaD_c1, 2);
formula des_dyn_dis_c1 = min_gap_car + max(0.0, v_c1 * T_car + (v_c1 * deltaV_c1) /
                                                    (2*pow(AM_car*BM_car,0.5) ));
formula deltaV_c1 = v_c1 - v_l;
//"max 1" to avoid division by zero
formula deltaD_c1 = max(pos_l - pos_c1 - truck_size,1);
formula muv_c1 = (v_c1 + ( a_c1*pow(time,2)) / 2) > 0 ?
         (v_c1 + (a_c1*pow(time,2)) / 2) : (-1 * (v_c1 + (a_c1*pow(time,2)) / 2));
```

Fig. 5. IDM model implementation

PRISM model comprises a set of modules which represent different components. The behavior of a module, i.e. the changes to its state that can occur, is specified by a set of *guarded commands*. These take the form:

$$[sync]guard \rightarrow rate : update;$$

where act is an (optional) action label, guard is a predicate over the variables of the model, rate is a (non-negative) real-valued expression and update is of the form:

$$(x'_1 = u_1)\&(x'_2 = u_2)\& \ldots \&(x'_k = u_k)$$

where $x_1; x_2; \ldots; x_k$ are local variables of the module and $u_1; u_2; \ldots; u_k$ are expressions over all variables.

Intuitively, a command is enabled in a global state of the PRISM model if the state satisfies the predicate guard. If a command is enabled, a transition that updates the module's variables according to update can occur with rate *rate*.

The modules Mod_vC1 and Mod_dC1 presented in Figure 6 are responsible for the transitions in the model which assign a new position and speed to vehicle $c1$, and also control the lane change of $c1$. If the vehicle is able to overtake according to the conditions presented by MOBIL model (refer to Subsection 2.2), the vehicle change to the left lane. If $c1$ is on the left lane and already overtook the leader, then $c1$ returns to the default lane. These modules are synchronized by label "m", which is placed inside the square brackets. The Mod_dC1 is also responsible for detecting a crash, which happens when $c1$ and $c2$ are in the same lane and their coordinates are overlaid or the deceleration calculated by the Torricelle equation ($v^2 = v_i^2 + 2a\Delta x$) is unfeasible to be executed in a normal situation. The modules for the other vehicles involved are similar, although simpler because they just move forwards without overtake maneuvers.

```
Modules proposed

module Mod_vC1
  v_c1 : [0..desired_speed_car];  // speed

  [m] (pos_c1 <= RS) & (v_c1 <= desired_speed_car) ->
                    (v_c1' = min(max(ceil(v_c1 + a_c1)*time,0),desired_speed_car));
endmodule

module Mod_dC1
  pos_c1 : [1..RS];          // position
  lane   : [1..2];           //lane's c1 (1 - right lane, 2 - left lane)
  carCrash : bool;

  [m] (pos_c1 <= RS) -> (pos_c1' = min( (ceil(pos_c1 + muv_c1)),RS) ) &
                    (lane' = ((lane = 2)&(pos_c1 >= (pos_l+min_gap_car+car_size)))?1:
                                        ((lane = 1)&(can_change_lane))?2:lane) &
                    (carCrash'= ((CanotDecelaration | OverlapPosition) &
                                        (lane=2) & (carCrash=false) ) ?true:false);
endmodule
```

Fig. 6. Modules implementation

5 Results

Finally, the model built using the PRISM language can be verified. The idea is to check the correctness of IDM code and analyze different situations about the modeled scenario. The experiments have been performed in an Intel(R) Xeon(R) CPU X3323 , 2.50 GHz which has 16 GB of RAM memory. The model presented has 386 243 states, 386 243 transitions and 38 400 initial states. For some properties we have varied the number of initial states through *filters*. The longest time to build the model was 2 360.838 s. The longest time to check a property was for Property 8 of Figure 11, taking 5.418 s.

In order to analyze some situations about the scenario, several interesting questions can be made. For example, the first property (Figure 7) checks the probability of a car-crash. The result was: [0.0, 1.0] for a range of values over initial states. The answer shows that there are situations without accident, however there are cases of car-crash.

The third property (Figure 7) checks the average probability of an accident taking into account all initial states. Thus, this scenario has a 98% chance of collision. The fourth property only confirms the results of these two previously mentioned properties. It is a non-probabilistic query and the result was *true* for the question "Are there situations without accidents?". The **E** (Exists) operator asks whether some path from a state satisfies a particular path formula. If the result is true, a witness will be generated. In this case, it was provided the following counter-example: (0, 0, 0, 1, 1, false, 1, 19), which represents the initial state with values for the respective variables v_c1, v_c2, v_1, pos_c1, lane, carCrash, pos_c2 and pos_1.

The second property shows another analysis, having calculated the result [0.0,1.0] considering the range of values over initial states for the question "Is it possible to finish the scenario without overtake?", in other words, the leader reaches the finish before c1. Thus, there are cases with and without overtake.

Car-crash Scenario Properties

```
(1) P=? [ F (carCrash=true) ]
What is the probability of an accident occurs?

(2) P=? [ ((pos_c1<RS & carCrash=false) U (pos_1>=RS & carCrash=false))]
What is the probability of not occurring overtakes in this scenario?

(3) filter(avg, P=? [ F carCrash=true ], "init")
What is the average probability of an accident occurs?

(4) E [ F (carCrash=false) ]
Is there, at least, one path which does not lead to the accident?
```

Fig. 7. Properties of Overtake Maneuver

As we have mentioned above, the operator **E** generates a counter-example (a path reaching the "goal" state). Using this witness, for instance in Property 4, we can analyze in detail the situation of accidents in the scenario. Since we have included rewards in our model, we are able to quantify the speed, acceleration and movement over time using the **I** (instant) operator. Some implemented rewards and properties are shown in Figure 8, the latter using the *filter* command to check specifically the counterexample available. The operator R is the responsible to get the reward values.

Movement and Lane Rewards	Movement and Lane Quantitative Properties

rewards "dLeader"
    true : pos_l;
endrewards
 	
rewards "dCar"
    true : pos_c1;
endrewards
 	
rewards "dCarOpposite"
    true : pos_c2;
endrewards
 	
rewards "laneCar"
    true : lane;
endrewards
	(5) filter(max, R{"dCar"}=? [I=T],
	        (pos_l=19)&(pos_c1=1)&(pos_c2=1)&(lane=1)&
	        (v_c1=0)&(v_c2=0)&(v_l=0)&(carCrash=false))
	
	What is the expected distance reward for the vehicle c1 on the road at time T?
	
	(6) filter(max,R{"laneCar"}=? [I=T],
	        (pos_l=19)&(pos_c1=1)&(pos_c2=1)&(lane=1)&
	        (v_c1=0)&(v_c2=0)&(v_l=0)&(carCrash=false))
	
	What is the expected lane reward for the vehicle c1 on the road at time T?
	
	(7) filter(max,RS-R{"dCarOpposite"}=? [I=T],
	        (pos_l=50)&(pos_c1=1)&(pos_c2=1)\&(lane=1)&
	        (v_c1=0)\&(v_c2=0)\&(v_l=0)&(carCrash=false))
	
	What is the expected distance reward for the vehicle c2 on the road at time T? (With different initial conditions)

Fig. 8. Movement and Lane Rewards, and Quantitative Properties

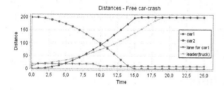

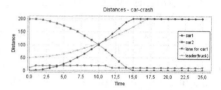

9.1 Motion in a normal overtake   9.2 Motion with accident

Fig. 9. Scenario analysis

Figure 9 shows the result of analysis, showing the position of the three vehicles over time. The red line varies between 10 and 20 and it represents the lane of the vehicle *car1* during overtaking. The first value means that *car1* is in the default lane (right lane), the value 20 means that the vehicle is traveling in the left lane to overtake. The Figure 9.1 shows the behavior of vehicles without collision. Note that *car1* overcomes the leader at the instant 7.5 and when the positions of *car1* and *car2* overlap, the first car already returned to the right lane. However, in the Figure 9.2 can be seen that the positions overlap at time 10 and *car1* is in the left lane, meaning that there was a collision.

Figure 10 shows the evolution of the acceleration and velocity of *car1* and *leader* (truck) in the scenario of overtaking without collision. Speeds rise according to acceleration until reaching the maximum limit of the road. As the acceleration and the speed limit are lower, the car can overtake easier. It is interesting to note that the acceleration modeled with IDM is affected by lane change of *car1*. Right at the instant 2, the acceleration of the *car1* rises abruptly, because in this moment, the driver concludes to be more advantageous changing to the left lane, instead of maintaining in its lane. As the *car1* is reaching the desired speed, the acceleration is decreasing, which happens linearly. The truck also reduces the acceleration linearly as the desired speed is reached. At time 8, the deceleration is slightly more accentuated due to the entrance of the *car1* on the default lane, as soon as the overtaking is completed.

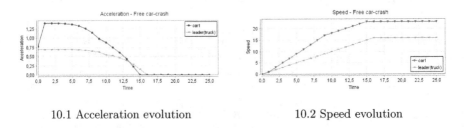

10.1 Acceleration evolution	10.2 Speed evolution

Fig. 10. Analysis in a free car-crash overtake

Analysis regarding to the time spent during overtake or going through the entire route for each vehicle can also be computed. The Figure 11 shows two examples of this type of verification. These properties use the reward "step", responsible for providing the value 1 for each change of state in the model, which is equivalent to 1 second in a real scenario. These properties use the operator **F** (reachability), which is associated with the reward "step". According to [18], the reward property "**F** prop" corresponds to the reward accumulated along a path until a satisfactory state is reached. In the case, where the probability of reaching a state satisfying prop is less than 1, the reward is equal to infinity.

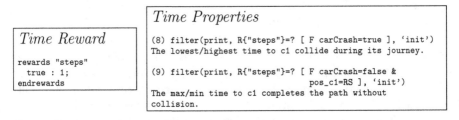

Fig. 11. Time Rewards and Properties

Property 8 calculates the overtake time, which results in a possible collision for all initial states, thus the presented result was a value range of [8.0, infinity] seconds. The infinity value represents the initial states without collision, i.e. initial states that have probability less than 1. Therefore, to find the maximum time limit for the collision it is enough to analyze the PRISM output log file which will have the travel time for all initial states and their successors, which is available due to the parameter "print" in the *filter* command.

The range of minimum and maximum time of collision is [8.0, 11.0], i.e. the shortest time of an accident is 8 seconds and the greatest time is at instant 11. Thus, they can be simulated, respectively with the following initial states

(1, 6, 1, 2, 2, false, 6, 20) and (0, 0, 1, 1, 1, false, 1, 19), for the following variable v_c1, v_c2, v_1, pos_c1, lane, carCrash, pos_c2 and pos_1.

In a similar way, the Property 9 calculates the minimum and maximum time of a successful overtake. This also takes into account all possible initial states. Thus, the range of values presented were between [13.0, Infinity] seconds. Again, for all initial states which the probability of **F** to be satisfied is less than 1, it is assigned the infinity value. Thus, analyzing the PRISM log file, we can identify the new range of values, and the infinity value is [13.0, 16.00]. Their respectively counter-examples are (4, 0, 0, 1, 1, false, 1, 40) and (0, 0, 0, 1, 1, false, 1, 19), for the same variables presented in Property 8.

6   Conclusions

It is essential to test and analyze VANETs in order to prevent loss of life. Simulations are used to check protocols and applications, however, they have to deal with two unconnected worlds – network and traffic – which must work together. In this context, there are challenges that must be addressed by the academic community. A complementary tool to simulations is model checking, a technique that automatically and exhaustively explores a model. However, researchers can use simulation to large-scale analysis and model checking to test thoroughly in a smaller proportion. Thus, they can supply solutions to known problems for simulations and model checking, such as determining exact probabilities and avoiding the state explosion, respectively.

In this article we have presented the formal modeling and analysis of mobility models using probabilistic model checking to represent an overtake situation. A microscopic vision was presented to provide a detailed analysis. This was possible using analytical formulas to represent position, speed, and acceleration. The model shows that there is a huge chance of an accident (98% in some scenarios), however there are situations without collision.

In general, during implementation we have noticed some limitations in the PRISM language, e.g., the absence of some mathematical functions, the lack of subroutine (function and procedure) and formal parameters. This fact impairs the legibility of the model and makes difficult to implement and maintain the models. However, the IDM and MOBIL models can be perfectly implemented and used in PRISM.

The implementation of motion provides important information such as instantaneous speed, acceleration and position through rewards, besides answering questions regarding the probability of events. Our model follows the framework shown in Figure 2, presenting smooth motion and human driving patterns, furthermore following speed constraints and considering obstacles. All of this is provided by IDM and the MOBIL.

The motion patterns are not considered because we are analyzing specific situations instead of a large flow of vehicles. Furthermore, the mobility modules can be easily coupled with network protocols. In addition, the modeling is easily adaptable under various situations, such as multilane highway or an intersection. For example, to implement a curve road with a higher abstraction level, it is simply necessary to change the limited speed to a value less than a straight road, thus vehicles will reduce the speed while they are crossing a curve.

Future Works: explore more mobility scenarios following the concepts and examples presented here and couple them with models that represent communication and signal propagation using a probabilistic method, such as [5], thus, making it possible to do a complete analysis of the VANET in a stochastic way.

References

1. Alves, R., et al.: Redes veiculares: Princípios, aplicações e desafios. In: Minicursos do Simpósio Brasileiro de Redes de Computadores, SBRC 2009 (May 2009)
2. Bai, F., Krishnan, H., Sadekar, V., Holland, G., Elbatt, T.: Towards characterizing and classifying communication-based automotive app. from a wireless networking perspective. In: Proc. of IEEE Workshop on Automotive Networking (2006)
3. Boban, M., Vinhoza, T.T.V.: Modeling and simulation of vehicular networks: Towards realistic and efficient models. In: Mobile Ad-Hoc Networks: Applications. Intech (2011)
4. Bouassida, M.S., Shawky, M.: A cooperative congestion control approach within vanets: formal verification and performance evaluation. EURASIP J. Wirel. Commun. Netw., 1–12 (2010)
5. Boulis, A., Fehnker, A., Fruth, M., McIver, A.: Cavi - simulation and model checking for wireless sensor networks. In: 5th International QEST 2008. QEST (2008)
6. Choffnes, D.R., Bustamante, F.E.: An integrated mobility and traffic model for vehicular wireless networks. In: Laberteaux, K.P., Hartenstein, H., Johnson, D.B., Sengupta, R. (eds.) Vehicular Ad Hoc Networks, pp. 69–78. ACM (2005)
7. Christian, A.: Reliable model checking for wsns. In: Proc. of the 8th GI/ITG KuVS Fachgesprach (2009)
8. Clarke, E., Grumberg, O., Peled, D.: Model Checking. MIT Press (1999)
9. Dirk Helbing, T., Martin, A.K.: General lane-changing model mobil for car-following models. In: Transp. Research Record: Journal of the Transp. Research Board, pp. 86–94. Transp. Research Board of the National Academies (2007)
10. Ferreira, B.: http://www.dcc.ufmg.br/~bruno.ferreira/sbmf2014/
11. Ferreira, M., Fernandes, R., Conceição, H., Viriyasitavat, W., Tonguz, O.K.: Self-organized traffic control. In: Proc. of the 7th ACM International Workshop on VehiculAr InterNETworking, VANET 2010. ACM, New York (2010)
12. Gipps, P.G.: A model for the structure of lane-changing decisions. Transportation Research Part B: Methodological **20**(5), 403–414 (1986)
13. Harri, J., Filali, F., Bonnet, C.: Mobility models for vehicular ad hoc networks: a survey and taxonomy. IEEE Communications Surveys & Tutorials **11**, December 2009
14. Hartenstein, H., Laberteaux, K., Ebrary, I.: VANET: vehicular applications and inter-networking technologies. Wiley Online Library (2010)
15. Helbing, D.: Traffic and related self-driven many-particle systems. Rev. Mod. Phys. **73**, 1067–1141 (2001)

16. Kesting, A., Treiber, M., Helbing, D.: Enhanced intelligent driver model to access the impact of driving strategies on traffic capacity. Royal Society of London Philosophical Transactions Series A **368**, 4585–4605 (2010)
17. Khosroshahy, M.: IEEE 802.11 and propagation modeling: A survey and a practical design approach (2007)
18. Kwiatkowska, M., Norman, G.: PRISM - Property Specification (2011). http://www.prismmodelchecker.org/manual/ (accessed January 28, 2014)
19. Kwiatkowska, M., Norman, G., Parker, D.: PRISM 4.0: verification of probabilistic real-time systems. In: Gopalakrishnan, G., Qadeer, S. (eds.) CAV 2011. LNCS, vol. 6806, pp. 585–591. Springer, Heidelberg (2011)
20. Lomuscio, A., Strulo, B., Walker, N.G., Wu, P.: Model checking optimisation based congestion control algorithms. Fundam. Inf. **102**(1), January 2010
21. Althoff, M., Stursberg, O., Buss, M.: Safety assessment of driving behavior in multi-lane traffic for autonomous vehicles. In: Proc. of the IEEE Intelligent Vehicles Symposium, Shaanxi, China (June 2009)
22. Mangharam, R., Weller, D.S., Stancil, R., Parikh, J.S.: Groovesim: a topography accurate simulator for geographic routing in vanet. In: Vehicular Ad Hoc Networks, pp. 59–68. ACM (2005)
23. Parker, D.: Implementation of Symbolic Model Checking for Probabilistic Systems. Ph.D. thesis, University of Birmingham (2002)
24. Treiber, M., Hennecke, A., Helbing, D.: Congested traffic states in empirical observations and microscopic simulations. Rev. E 62(62), 2000 (2000)

A Dynamic Logic for Every Season

Alexandre Madeira[1]($\boxtimes$), Renato Neves[1],
Manuel A. Martins[2], and Luís S. Barbosa[1]

[1] HASLab INESC TEC, University Minho, Braga, Portugal
{amadeira,renato.j.neves,luis.s.barbosa}@inesctec.pt
[2] CIDMA - Department Mathematics, University Aveiro, Aveiro, Portugal
martins@ua.pt

Abstract. This paper introduces a method to build dynamic logics with a graded semantics. The construction is parametrized by a structure to support both the spaces of truth and of the domain of computations. Possible instantiations of the method range from classical (assertional) dynamic logic to less common graded logics suitable to deal with programs whose transitional semantics exhibits fuzzy or weighted behaviour. This leads to the systematic derivation of program logics tailored to specific program classes.

1 Introduction

Propositions, capturing static properties of program states, and events, or actions, which are responsible for transitions from a state to another, are the key ingredients in modelling and reasoning about state-based software systems. The latter are typically combined through a Kleene algebra to express sequential, non deterministic, iterative behaviour of systems, while the former brings to the scene a logical structure.

Dynamic logic [6], a generalisation of the logic of Floyd-Hoare, is a well known and particularly powerful way of combining these two dimensions into a formal framework to reason about computational systems. Its potential stems from blending together classical logic, enriched with a modal dimension to express system's dynamics, and a (Kleene) algebra of actions to structure programs.

Over time dynamic logic grew to an entire family of logics increasingly popular in the verification of computational systems, and able to evolve and adapt to new, and complex validation challenges. One could mention its role in model validation (as in *e.g.* [10]), or the whole family of variants tailored to specific programming languages (as in *e.g.* [1,11]), or its important extensions to new computing domains, namely probabilistic [8] or continuous [13,14].

The latter is particularly relevant from an Engineering point of view: Actually, Platzer's hybrid dynamic logic, and its associated tool, KEYMAERA, combining an algebra of actions based on real numbers assignments with the standard Kleene operators and differential equations to specify continuous transitions from the "real" (physical) world, provides a powerful framework for the design and validation of cyber-physical systems with increased industrial relevance.

© Springer International Publishing Switzerland 2015
C. Braga and N. Martí-Oliet (Eds.): SBMF 2014, LNCS 8941, pp. 130–145, 2015.
DOI: 10.1007/978-3-319-15075-8_9

If cyber-physical systems gives rise to the need for ways of dealing with continuous state spaces, in a number of other cases dealing with some form of "quantitative" transitions (weighted, probabilistic, etc) is also a must. Hence the quest for dynamic logics able to capture smoothly these kind of phenomena is becoming more and more important.

This paper intends to contribute in this path. In particular, our attention is focussed on graded logics [4,16], in the broad sense of attaching partially ordered grades to logical formulas to express, in one way or another, uncertain information. In this broad sense, fuzzy [5], probabilistic [12] or weighted logics [2] may be brought into the picture.

In this context, the purpose of this work is the development of a generic method to construct graded dynamic logics. Technically, the definition of these logics is parametrized by (a specific kind of) an action lattice [7] which combines (a slight generalisation of) a Kleene algebra with a residuated lattice structure. The latter captures the graded logic dimension and fits nicely with our objectives. Moreover, the extension of Kleene algebras with residuation operators, providing weak right and left inverses to sequential composition as in [15], as well as with a lattice structure leads to a finitely-based equational variety which, as plain Kleene algebras, is closed under the formation of square matrices [9].

The relevance of this closure property lies in the fact that several problems modelled as (weighted) transition systems can be formulated as matrices over a Kleene algebra or a related structure. Following such a trend, we represent programs as matrices supporting the information about their effects when executed from each state in the state space. The interested reader is referred to [3] for a detailed discussion on the relationship between Kleene algebras, action algebras and action lattices.

The remaining of this paper is organised as follows. Section 2 recalls from [7] the definition of an action lattice and introduces a method, parametric on such a lattice, to generate graded dynamic logics. The construction put forward is illustrated with several examples. Then, in Section 3, it is shown that the resulting logic is a dynamic logic indeed, in the sense that all the rules of propositional dynamic logic restricted to positive-existential formulas still hold. Finally, Section 4 concludes and suggests points for future research.

2   The Method

This section introduces a generic method to generate *graded dynamic logics* parametric on a complete action lattice which captures both the structure of the computational domain and that of the (logical) truth space.

Let us start by recalling from [7] the following definition:

Definition 1. *An action lattice is a tuple*

$$\mathbf{A} = (A, +, ;, 0, 1, *, \leftarrow, \rightarrow, \cdot)$$

where, for A is a set, 0 and 1 are constants and $+, ;, *, \leftarrow, \rightarrow$ and $\cdot$ are binary operations in A satisfying the axioms in Figure 1, where the relation $\leq$ is the one induced by $+$ as $a \leq b$ iff $a + b = b$.

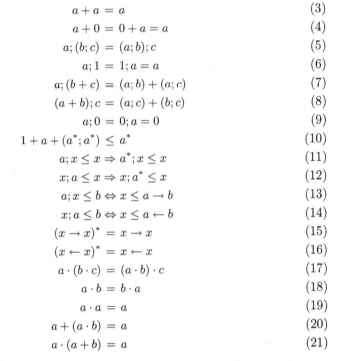

$$a + (b + c) = (a + b) + c \tag{1}$$
$$a + b = b + a \tag{2}$$
$$a + a = a \tag{3}$$
$$a + 0 = 0 + a = a \tag{4}$$
$$a; (b; c) = (a; b); c \tag{5}$$
$$a; 1 = 1; a = a \tag{6}$$
$$a; (b + c) = (a; b) + (a; c) \tag{7}$$
$$(a + b); c = (a; c) + (b; c) \tag{8}$$
$$a; 0 = 0; a = 0 \tag{9}$$
$$1 + a + (a^*; a^*) \leq a^* \tag{10}$$
$$a; x \leq x \Rightarrow a^*; x \leq x \tag{11}$$
$$x; a \leq x \Rightarrow x; a^* \leq x \tag{12}$$
$$a; x \leq b \Leftrightarrow x \leq a \rightarrow b \tag{13}$$
$$x; a \leq b \Leftrightarrow x \leq a \leftarrow b \tag{14}$$
$$(x \rightarrow x)^* = x \rightarrow x \tag{15}$$
$$(x \leftarrow x)^* = x \leftarrow x \tag{16}$$
$$a \cdot (b \cdot c) = (a \cdot b) \cdot c \tag{17}$$
$$a \cdot b = b \cdot a \tag{18}$$
$$a \cdot a = a \tag{19}$$
$$a + (a \cdot b) = a \tag{20}$$
$$a \cdot (a + b) = a \tag{21}$$

Fig. 1. Axiomatisation of action lattices (from [7])

An action lattice is said to be *complete* when there are both a supremum and an infimum, wrt $\leq$, of all subsets of A. Therefore, complete action lattices have biggest and smallest elements denoted in the sequel by $\top$ and $\bot$, respectively. Note that in any action lattice $\bot = 0$, since for any $a \in A$, $a + 0 = a$, i.e., $0 \leq a$. In this paper we resort to notation $\sum$ for the iterated version of the (join) operator $+$, and to notation $\prod$ for the iterated version of the (meet) operator $\cdot$.

The starting point for the method proposed here is thus the choice of an appropriate action lattice

$$\mathbf{A} = (A, +, ;, 0, 1, *, \leftarrow, \rightarrow, \cdot)$$

Additionally, we require $\mathbf{A}$ to satisfy the following distributive law:

$$a; (b \cdot c) = a; b \cdot a; c \tag{22}$$

As mentioned above, this structure supports both the computational paradigm (to distinguish between *e.g.* imperative, deterministic or non deterministic computations, or between plain or weighted transitions) and the truth space (to capture *e.g.* the standard Boolean reasoning or more complex truth spaces). Before proceeding let us exemplify this structure with a couple of action lattices typically found in Computer Science applications. In the examples, the logic generated by an action lattice $\mathbf{A}$ will be denoted by $\mathcal{GDL}(\mathbf{A})$.

Example 1 ($\mathcal{GDL}(2)$ — the standard propositional dynamic logic). Standard propositional dynamic logic is generated from the following structure

$$\mathbf{2} = (\{\top, \bot\}, \vee, \wedge, \bot, \top, *, \leftarrow, \rightarrow, \wedge)$$

with the standard boolean connectives:

$\vee$	$\bot$	$\top$		$\wedge$	$\bot$	$\top$		$\rightarrow$	$\bot$	$\top$		$*$	
$\bot$	$\bot$	$\top$		$\bot$	$\bot$	$\bot$		$\bot$	$\top$	$\top$		$\bot$	$\top$
$\top$	$\top$	$\top$		$\top$	$\bot$	$\top$		$\top$	$\bot$	$\top$		$\top$	$\top$

and taking $a \leftarrow b = b \rightarrow a$. It is not difficult to see that $\mathbf{2}$ is an action algebra. Moreover, the lattice is obviously complete and it satisfies the condition (22) (note that both composition and the meet operator are realized by $\wedge$).

Example 2 ($\mathcal{GDL}(3)$ — a dynamic logic to deal with unknown data). This is a three-valued logic, with an explicit representative for *unknown*, or *uncertain* information. Note that the three elements linear lattice induces an action lattice

$$\mathbf{3} = (\{\top, u, \bot\}, \vee, \wedge, \bot, \top, *, \leftarrow, , \rightarrow, \wedge)$$

where

$\vee$	$\bot$	u	$\top$		$\wedge$	$\bot$	u	$\top$		$\rightarrow$	$\bot$	u	$\top$		$*$	
$\bot$	$\bot$	u	$\top$		$\bot$	$\bot$	$\bot$	$\bot$		$\bot$	$\top$	$\top$	$\top$		$\bot$	$\top$
u	u	u	$\top$		u	$\bot$	u	u		u	u	$\top$	$\top$		u	$\top$
$\top$	$\top$	$\top$	$\top$		$\top$	$\bot$	u	$\top$		$\top$	$\bot$	u	$\top$		$\top$	$\top$

and taking $a \leftarrow b = b \rightarrow a$. It is easy to see all the conditions in Definition 1 hold. Moreover, the lattice is complete and satisfies condition (22). The reader should note that both composition and meet are realized by $\wedge$).

Example 3 ($\mathcal{GDL}(L)$ — a dynamic logic to deal with continuous levels of fuzziness).
     This is based on the well-known Łukasiewicz arithmetic lattice

$$\mathbf{L} = ([0,1], max, min, 0, 1, *, \rightarrow, \leftarrow, min)$$

where

- $x \rightarrow y = min\{1, 1 - x + y\}$,
- $x \leftarrow y = 1 - max\{0, x + y - 1\}$ and
- $*$ maps each point of $[0,1]$ to 1.

Again, this defines a complete action lattice which additionally satisfies condition (22). Note that both composition and the meet operator are now represented by function *min*.

Example 4 (GDL(FW) – a dynamic logic to deal with resource consuming systems). This example explores the so called Floyd-Warshall algebra which consists of a tuple $\mathbb{N}_{\perp\top}^{+} = (\{\perp, 0, 1, \ldots, \top\}, max, +, \perp, 0, *, \smallsmile, \smallsmile, min)$ where $+$ extends the addition on $\mathbb{N}$ by considering $\perp$ as its absorbent element and $a + \top = \top = \top + a$ for any $a \neq \perp$. The operation max (and min) are defined as the maximum (minimum) under the order $\perp \leq 0 \leq \cdots \leq \top$. The operation $\smallsmile$ is the truncated subtraction

$$a \smallsmile b = \begin{cases} b - a, & \text{if } b \geq a \text{ and } a, b \in \mathbb{N} \\ \top & \text{if } a = \top \text{ and } b \in \mathbb{N} \\ 0 & \text{otherwise} \end{cases}$$

and, for any natural $i > 0$,

$$\begin{array}{c|c} * & \\ \hline \perp & 0 \\ 0 & 0 \\ i & \top \\ \top & \top \end{array}$$

Note that the order induced by $a \leq b$ iff $max\{a, b\} = b$ corresponds to the mentioned above. The lattice is also complete and it satisfies condition (22) because $a + min\{b, c\} = min\{a + b, a + c\}$.

Illustrated the notion of an action lattice, we are now prepared to introduce the general construction of graded dynamic logics. We consider now its signatures, formulæ, semantics and satisfaction. Thus,

Signatures. Signatures of $\mathcal{GDL}(\mathbf{A})$ are pairs (Π, Prop) corresponding to the denotations of atomic computations and of propositions, respectively.

Formulæ. A core ingredient of any dynamic logic is its set of programs. Therefore, let us denote the set of atomic programs by Π. The *set of Π-programs*, denoted by $\mathrm{Prg}(\Pi)$, consists of all expressions generated by

$$\pi \ni \pi_0 \mid \pi; \pi \mid \pi + \pi \mid \pi^*$$

for $\pi_0 \in \Pi$. Given a signature (Π, Prop), we define the $\mathcal{GDL}(\mathbf{A})$-formulas for (Π, Prop), denoted by $\mathrm{Fm}^{\mathcal{GDL}(\mathbf{A})}(\Pi, \mathrm{Prop})$, by the grammar

$$\rho \ni \top \mid \perp \mid p \mid \rho \vee \rho \mid \rho \wedge \rho \mid \rho \to \rho \mid \langle \pi \rangle \rho$$

for $p \in \mathrm{Prop}$ and $\pi \in \mathrm{Prg}(\Pi)$. Note that this corresponds to the *positive existential* fragment of the propositional dynamic logic.

Semantics. The first step is to introduce the space where the computations of $\mathcal{GDL}(\mathbf{A})$ are to be interpreted. As usual, this corresponds to a Kleene algebra. Therefore, we consider the structure

$$\mathbb{M}_n(\mathbf{A}) = (M_n(\mathbf{A}), +, ;, 0, 1, *)$$

defined as follows:

1. $M_n(\mathbf{A})$ is the space of $(n \times n)$-matrices over $\mathbf{A}$
2. for any $A, B \in M_n(\mathbf{A})$, define $M = A{+}B$ by $M_{i,j} = A_{i,j} + B_{i,j}$, $i, j \leq n$.
3. for any $A, B \in M_n(\mathbf{A})$, define $M = A \,;\, B$ by taking $M_{i,j} = \sum_{k=1}^{n}(A_{i,k}; B_{k,j})$ for any $i, j \leq n$.
4. $\mathbf{1}$ and $\mathbf{0}$ are the $(n \times n)$-matrices defined by $\mathbf{1}_{i,j} = 1$ and $\mathbf{0}_{i,j} = 0$, for any $i, j \leq n$.
5. for any $M = \left[\begin{array}{c|c} A & B \\ \hline C & D \end{array} \right] \in M_n(\mathbf{A})$, where A and D are square matrices, we take

$$M^* = \left[\begin{array}{c|c} F^* & F^* \,;\, B \,;\, D^* \\ \hline C & D^* {+} D^* \,;\, C \,;\, F^* \,;\, B \,;\, D^* \end{array} \right]$$

where $F = A + B \,;\, D^* \,;\, C$. Note that this construction is recursively defined from the base case (where $n = 2$) where the operations of the base action lattice $\mathbf{A}$ are used.

Finally, we have to show that,

Theorem 1. *The structure* $\mathbb{M}_n(\mathbf{A}) = (M_n(\mathbf{A}), +, ;, \mathbf{0}, \mathbf{1}, *)$ *defined above is a Kleene algebra.*

Proof. The structure, and the respective operations, corresponds to the algebra of matrices over $(A, +, ;, 0, 1, *)$, *i.e.*, the Kleene algebra underlying action lattice $\mathbf{A}$. A canonical result establishes that Kleene algebras are closed under formation of matrices (e.g. [9]). Therefore, $\mathbb{M}_n(\mathbf{A})$ constitutes a Kleene algebra. $\square$

$\mathcal{GDL}(\mathbf{A})$-models for a set of propositions Prop and programs Π, denoted by $\mathrm{Mod}^{\mathcal{GDL}(\mathbf{A})}(\Pi, \mathrm{Prop})$, consists of tuples

$$\mathcal{A} = (W, V, (\mathcal{A}_\pi)_{\pi \in \Pi})$$

where

- W is a finite set (of states),
- $V : \mathrm{Prop} \times W \to A$ is a function,
- and $\mathcal{A}_\pi \in \mathbb{M}_n(\mathbf{A})$, with n standing for the cardinality of W.

The interpretation of programs in these models is made by matrices over the Kleene algebra of $\mathbf{A}$. Each matrix represents the effect of a program executing from any point of the model. Formally, the interpretation of a program $\pi \in \mathrm{Prg}(\Pi)$ in a model $\mathcal{A} \in \mathrm{Mod}^{\mathcal{GDL}(\mathbf{A})}(\Pi, \mathrm{Prop})$ is recursively defined, from the atomic programs $(\mathcal{A}_\pi)_{\pi \in \Pi}$, as follows:

- $\mathcal{A}_{\pi;\pi'} = \mathcal{A}_\pi \,;\, \mathcal{A}_{\pi'}$
- $\mathcal{A}_{\pi+\pi'} = \mathcal{A}_\pi + \mathcal{A}_{\pi'}$
- $\mathcal{A}_{\pi^*} = \mathcal{A}_\pi^*$

Observe that the set of states W supports the index system of the programs (adjacency) matrices. In this context, it is important to note, that, for example,

$$(M_{\pi;\pi'})_{ij} = \sum_{k=1}^{n} \{(M_\pi)_{ik}; (M_{\pi'})_{kj}\}$$

corresponds to

$$M_{\pi;\pi'}(w, w') = \sum_{w'' \in W} \{(M_\pi)(w, w''); M_{\pi'}(w'', w')\}$$

where i and j stands for the adjacency index of w and w', respectively. Actually, the latter characterisation is often used in the sequel.

Example 5 (Computations spaces)
Let us fix an action lattice $\mathbf{A} = (A, +, ;, 0, 1, *, \leftarrow, \rightarrow, \cdot)$ and a signature $(\{\pi, \pi'\}, \{p\})$. Then, consider a model $\mathcal{A} = (W, V, (\mathcal{A}_\pi)_{\pi \in \Pi})$, with $W = \{s_1, s_2\}$ and the following atomic programs

$$\mathcal{A}_\pi = \begin{bmatrix} \perp & q_{12} \\ \perp & q_{22} \end{bmatrix} \qquad \mathcal{A}_{\pi'} = \begin{bmatrix} \perp & q'_{12} \\ \perp & \perp \end{bmatrix}$$

which can be represented by the following labelled transition systems:

Let us suppose that $\mathbf{A}$ is realized by

$$\mathbf{2} = (\{\top, \perp\}, \vee, \wedge, \perp, \top, *, \leftarrow, \rightarrow, \wedge)$$

Making $q_{12} = q_{22} = q'_{1,2} = \top$ we get the standard adjacency matrices of the graph underlying the transition systems. In this case, we interpret choice $\pi + \pi'$ and composition $\pi; \pi'$ by

$$\mathcal{A}_{\pi+\pi'} = \mathcal{A}_\pi + \mathcal{A}_{\pi'} = \begin{bmatrix} \perp & \top \\ \perp & \top \end{bmatrix} + \begin{bmatrix} \perp & \top \\ \perp & \perp \end{bmatrix} = \begin{bmatrix} \perp \vee \perp & \top \vee \top \\ \perp \vee \perp & \top \vee \perp \end{bmatrix} = \begin{bmatrix} \perp & \top \\ \perp & \top \end{bmatrix}$$

The interpretation of the composition $\pi; \pi'$ is computed as follows,

$$\mathcal{A}_{\pi;\pi'} = \begin{bmatrix} \perp & \top \\ \perp & \top \end{bmatrix}; \begin{bmatrix} \perp & \top \\ \perp & \perp \end{bmatrix} = \begin{bmatrix} (\perp \wedge \perp) \vee (\top \wedge \perp) & (\perp \wedge \top) \vee (\top \wedge \perp) \\ (\perp \wedge \perp) \vee (\top \wedge \perp) & (\perp \wedge \top) \vee (\top \wedge \perp) \end{bmatrix} = \begin{bmatrix} \perp & \perp \\ \perp & \perp \end{bmatrix}$$

As expected,

$$\mathcal{A}_{\pi';\pi} = \begin{bmatrix} \perp & \top \\ \perp & \perp \end{bmatrix}$$

For the interpretation of the π closure, we have

$$\mathcal{A}_{\pi^*} = (\mathcal{A}_\pi)^* \begin{bmatrix} \bot & \top \\ \bot & \top \end{bmatrix}^* = \begin{bmatrix} f^* & f^* \wedge \top \wedge \top^* \\ \bot & \top^* \vee (\top^* \wedge \bot \wedge \top \wedge \top) \end{bmatrix}$$

where $f = \bot \vee (\top \wedge \top^* \wedge \bot) = \bot$, hence

$$\mathcal{A}_{\pi^*} = \begin{bmatrix} \top & \top \\ \bot & \top \end{bmatrix}$$

as expected.

Taking the same matrix in the case of

$$\mathbf{3} = (\{\top, u, \bot\}, \vee, \wedge, \bot, \top, *, \leftarrow, \rightarrow, \wedge)$$

and considering $q_{12} = q_{22} = \top$ and $q'_{12} = u$, let us compute composition

$$\mathcal{A}_{\pi';\pi} = \begin{bmatrix} \bot & u \\ \bot & \bot \end{bmatrix}; \begin{bmatrix} \bot & \top \\ \bot & \top \end{bmatrix} = \begin{bmatrix} (\bot \wedge \bot) \vee (u \wedge \bot) & (\bot \wedge \top) \vee (u \wedge \top) \\ (\bot \wedge \bot) \vee (\bot \wedge \bot) & (\bot \wedge \top) \vee (\bot \wedge \top) \end{bmatrix} = \begin{bmatrix} \bot & u \\ \bot & \bot \end{bmatrix}$$

As expected, the unknown factor affecting transition $s_1 \rightarrow s_2$ in $\mathcal{A}'_\pi$ is propagated to transition $s_2 \rightarrow s_2$ in $\mathcal{A}_{\pi';\pi}$.

If a continuous space is required to define the "unknown metric", one may resort to the Lukasiewicz arithmetic lattice

$$\mathbf{L} = ([0, 1], max, min, 0, 1, *, \rightarrow, \leftarrow, min)$$

Consider, for instance, $q_{12} = a$, $q_{22} = b$ and $q'_{12} = c$ for some $a, b, c \in [0, 1]$. In this case we may, for example, compute choice $\pi + \pi'$, making

$$\mathcal{A}_{\pi+\pi'} = \begin{bmatrix} 0 & a \\ 0 & b \end{bmatrix} + \begin{bmatrix} 0 & c \\ 0 & 0 \end{bmatrix} = \begin{bmatrix} max\{0, 0\} & max\{a, c\} \\ max\{0, 0\} & max\{b, 0\} \end{bmatrix} = \begin{bmatrix} 0 & max\{a, c\} \\ 0 & b \end{bmatrix}$$

The reader may check that

$$\mathcal{A}_{\pi^*} = \begin{bmatrix} 1 & a \\ 0 & 1 \end{bmatrix}$$

Note that the certainty value 1 in the diagonal of the matrix stands for the reflexive dimension of the reflexive-transitive closure $*$.

Let us now consider the action lattice

$$\mathbb{N}^+_{\bot\top} = (\{\bot, 0, 1, \ldots, \top\}, max, +, \bot, 0, *, \smile, \smile, min)$$

As stated above, the structure $\mathbb{N}^+_{\bot\top}$ is suitable to reason about resource consuming systems. The value of a transition is $\top$ when it costs an infinite amount of resources; it is $\bot$ when undefined. The composition of actions reflects the accumulation of sequential costs. For instance $\mathcal{A}_{\pi';\pi} =$

$$\begin{bmatrix} \bot & c \\ \bot & \bot \end{bmatrix}; \begin{bmatrix} \bot & a \\ \bot & b \end{bmatrix} = \begin{bmatrix} max\{\bot + \bot, c + \bot\} & max\{\bot + a, c + b\} \\ max\{\bot + \bot, \bot + \bot\} & max\{\bot + a, \bot + b\} \end{bmatrix} = \begin{bmatrix} \bot & c + b \\ \bot & \bot \end{bmatrix}$$

Moreover, the interpretation of a program $\pi + \pi'$ reflects, in each transition the most expensive choice:

$$A_{\pi'+\pi} = \begin{bmatrix} \perp & c \\ \perp & \perp \end{bmatrix} + \begin{bmatrix} \perp & a \\ \perp & b \end{bmatrix} = \begin{bmatrix} max\{\perp, \perp\} & max\{c, a\} \\ max\{\perp, \perp\} & max\{\perp, b\} \end{bmatrix} = \begin{bmatrix} \perp & max\{c, a\} \\ \perp & b \end{bmatrix}$$

Finally, observe the interpretation of the closure of π

$$A_{\pi^*} = \begin{bmatrix} \perp & a \\ \perp & b \end{bmatrix} = \begin{bmatrix} f^* & f^* + a + b^* \\ \perp & max\{b^*, b^* + \perp + \perp^* + a + b^*\} \end{bmatrix} = \begin{bmatrix} 0 & a + b^* \\ \perp & b^* \end{bmatrix}$$

where $f = max\{\perp, a + b^* + \perp\}$. Note that for any $b > 0$, the matrix assumes $\begin{bmatrix} 0 & \top \\ \perp & \top \end{bmatrix}$ which reflects the cost of an undetermined repetition of transition $s_2 \to s_2$. Naturally, when the cost of the action is 0, we have $\begin{bmatrix} 0 & a \\ \perp & 0 \end{bmatrix}$.

Satisfaction. Finally, let us define the (graded) satisfaction relation. As mentioned above, the carrier of $\mathbf{A}$ corresponds to the space of truth degrees for $\mathcal{GDL}(\mathbf{A})$. Hence, the graded satisfaction relation for a model $A \in \mathrm{Mod}^{\mathcal{GDL}(\mathbf{A})}(\Pi, \mathrm{Prop})$ consists of a function

$$\models: W \times \mathrm{Fm}^{\mathcal{GDL}(\mathbf{A})}(\Pi, \mathrm{Prop}) \to A$$

recursively defined as follows:

- $(w \models \top) = \top$
- $(w \models \perp) = \perp$
- $(w \models p) = V(p, w)$, for any $p \in \mathrm{Prop}$
- $(w \models \rho \wedge \rho') = (w \models \rho) \cdot (w \models \rho')$
- $(w \models \rho \vee \rho') = (w \models \rho) + (w \models \rho')$
- $(w \models \rho \to \rho') = (w \models \rho) \to (w \models \rho')$
- $(w \models \langle \pi \rangle \rho) = \sum_{w' \in W} \{A_\pi(w, w'); (w' \models \rho)\}$

Example 6. In order to make a case for the versatility and generality of this method, let us consider the evaluation of the very simple sentence $\langle \pi^* \rangle p$ in three of the dynamic logics constructed in the examples above. Concretely, let us evaluate $\langle \pi^* \rangle p$ in state s_1. For this we calculate

$$(s_1 \models \langle \pi^* \rangle p) = \sum_{w' \in W} \{A_{\pi^*}(s_1, w'); (w' \models p)\}$$

Starting with $\mathcal{GDL}(\mathbf{2})$, let us assume $V(p, s_1) = \perp$ and $V(p, s_2) = \top$. In this case, as expected

$$\begin{aligned}(s_1 \models \langle \pi^* \rangle p) &= \sum_{w' \in W} \{A_{\pi^*}(s_1, w'); (w' \models p)\} \\ &= (A_{\pi^*}(s_1, s_1) \wedge (s_1 \models p)) \vee (A_{\pi^*}(s_1, s_2) \wedge (s_2 \models p)) \\ &= (\top \wedge V(p, s_1)) \vee (\top \wedge V(p, s_2)) \\ &= (\top \wedge \perp) \vee (\top \wedge \top) \\ &= \top \end{aligned}$$

This means that we can achieve p from s_1 through π^*.

Considering the $\mathcal{GDL}(\text{Ł})$ and assuming $V(s_1, p) = 0$ and $V(s_2, p) = 1$, we may calculate

$$
\begin{aligned}
(s_1 \models \langle \pi^* \rangle p) &= \textstyle\sum_{w' \in W} \{\mathcal{A}_{\pi^*}(s_1, w'); (w' \models p)\} \\
&= max\{min\{\mathcal{A}_{\pi^*}(s_1, s_1), (s_1 \models p)\}, \\
&\qquad\quad min\{\mathcal{A}_{\pi^*}(s_1, s_2), (s_2 \models p)\}\} \\
&= max\{min\{1, 0\}, min\{a, 1\}\} \\
&= max\{0, a\} \\
&= a
\end{aligned}
$$

Therefore, we can assure, with a degree of certainty a, that we can achieve p from s_1 through π^*.

Interpreting now the same sentence in logic $\mathcal{GDL}(\mathbb{N}_{\perp\top}^+)$, assuming that $V(s_1, p) = \perp$ and $V(s_2, p) = 0$, we get

$$
\begin{aligned}
(s_1 \models \langle \pi^* \rangle p) &= \textstyle\sum_{w' \in W} \{\mathcal{A}_{\pi^*}(s_1, w'); (w' \models p)\} \\
&= max\{\mathcal{A}_{\pi^*}(s_1, s_1) + (s_1 \models p), \mathcal{A}_{\pi^*}(s_1, s_2) + (s_2 \models p)\} \\
&= max\{0 + \perp, a + b^* + 0\} \\
&= a + b^*
\end{aligned}
$$

Hence, we can say that p can be accessed from s_1 through π^* consuming $a + b^*$ resources unities.

3 "Dynamisations" Are Dynamic

Having introduced a generic method for generating dynamic logics, this section establishes that the resulting logics behave, in fact, as dynamic logics. In particular, all the axioms of the propositional dynamic logic involving positive-existential formulas (see [6]) remain sound in this generic construction.

In the context of graded satisfaction, the verification that a property ρ is valid corresponds to the verification that, for any state w of any model $\mathcal{A}$, $(w \models \rho) = \top$. Hence, by (13) and (14), we have that asserting $(\rho \leftrightarrow \rho') = \top$ is equivalent to prove that, for any $w \in W$, $(w \models \rho) = (w \models \rho')$; and to proof $(\rho \rightarrow \rho') = \top$ is equivalent to proof that $(w \models \rho) \leq (w \models \rho')$.

Lemma 1. *The following are valid formulas in any $\mathcal{GDL}(\mathbf{A})$:*

(1.1) $\langle \pi \rangle (\rho \vee \rho') \leftrightarrow \langle \pi \rangle (\rho) \vee \langle \pi \rangle \rho'$
(1.2) $\langle \pi \rangle (\rho \wedge \rho') \rightarrow \langle \pi \rangle (\rho) \wedge \langle \pi \rangle \rho'$

Proof. **Axiom (1.1)**

$$(w \models \langle \pi \rangle (\rho \vee \rho'))$$

$$= \quad \{ \text{ defn of } \models \}$$

$$\sum_{w' \in W} \{\mathcal{A}_\pi(w, w'); (w' \models \rho \vee \rho')\}$$

$$= \quad \{ \text{ defn. of } \models \}$$

$$\sum_{w' \in W} \{(\mathcal{A}_\pi(w, w'); ((w' \models \rho) + (w' \models \rho')))\}$$

$=$ { (7)}

$$\sum_{w' \in W} \{(\mathcal{A}_\pi(w, w'); (w' \models \rho) + (\mathcal{A}_\pi(w, w'); (w' \models \rho')))\}$$

$=$ { supremum properties}

$$\sum_{w' \in W} \{(\mathcal{A}_\pi(w, w'); (w' \models \rho))\} + \sum_{w' \in W} \{\mathcal{A}_\pi(w, w'); (w' \models \rho'))\}$$

$=$ { defn of $\models$}

$$(w \models \langle \pi \rangle \rho) + (w \models \langle \pi \rangle \rho)$$

$=$ { defn of $\models$}

$$(w \models \langle \pi \rangle \rho \vee \langle \pi \rangle \rho)$$

Therefore $\langle \pi \rangle(\rho \vee \rho') \leftrightarrow \langle \pi \rangle \rho \vee \langle \pi \rangle \rho$ is valid.

Axiom (1.2)

$$(w \models \langle \pi \rangle(\rho \wedge \rho'))$$

$=$ { defn of $\models$}

$$\sum_{w' \in W} \{\mathcal{A}_\pi(w, w'); (w' \models \rho \wedge \rho')\}$$

$=$ { defn. of $\models$}

$$\sum_{w' \in W} \{(\mathcal{A}_\pi(w, w'); ((w' \models \rho) \cdot (w' \models \rho')))\}$$

$=$ { (22)}

$$\sum_{w' \in W} \{(\mathcal{A}_\pi(w, w'); (w' \models \rho) \cdot (\mathcal{A}_\pi(w, w'); (w' \models \rho')))\}$$

$\leq$ { infimum properties}

$$\sum_{w' \in W} \{(\mathcal{A}_\pi(w, w'); (w' \models \rho))\} \cdot \sum_{w' \in W} \{\mathcal{A}_\pi(w, w'); (w' \models \rho'))\}$$

$=$ { defn of $\models$}

$$(w \models \langle \pi \rangle \rho) \cdot (w \models \langle \pi \rangle \rho')$$

$=$ { defn of $\models$}

$$(w \models \langle \pi \rangle \rho \wedge \langle \pi \rangle \rho')$$

Therefore, $\langle \pi \rangle(\rho \wedge \rho') \rightarrow \langle \pi \rangle \rho \wedge \langle \pi \rangle \rho'$ is valid.

Lemma 2. *The following are valid formulas in any* $\mathcal{GDL}(\mathbf{A})$:

(2.1) $\langle \pi + \pi' \rangle \rho \leftrightarrow \langle \pi \rangle \rho \vee \langle \pi \rangle \rho$
(2.2) $\langle \pi; \pi' \rangle \rho \leftrightarrow \langle \pi \rangle \langle \pi' \rangle \rho$
(2.3) $\langle \pi \rangle \bot \leftrightarrow \bot$

Proof. **Axiom (2.1)**

$$(w \models \langle \pi + \pi' \rangle \rho)$$

$$= \qquad \{ \text{defn of} \models \}$$

$$\sum_{w' \in W} \{ \mathcal{A}_{\pi + \pi'}(w, w'); (w' \models \rho) \}$$

$$= \qquad \{ \text{defn of programs interpretation} \}$$

$$\sum_{w' \in W} \{ (\mathcal{A}_\pi(w, w') + \mathcal{A}_{\pi'}(w, w')); (w' \models \rho) \}$$

$$= \qquad \{ (7) \}$$

$$\sum_{w' \in W} \{ (\mathcal{A}_\pi(w, w'); (w' \models \rho) + \mathcal{A}_{\pi'}(w, w'); (w' \models \rho)) \}$$

$$= \qquad \{ \text{lattice distributivity} \}$$

$$\sum_{w' \in W} \{ (\mathcal{A}_\pi(w, w'); (w' \models \rho) \} + \sum_{w' \in W} \{ \mathcal{A}_{\pi'}(w, w'); (w' \models \rho)) \}$$

$$= \qquad \{ \text{defn of} \models \}$$

$$(w \models \langle \pi \rangle \rho) + (w \models \langle \pi' \rangle \rho)$$

$$= \qquad \{ \text{defn of} \models \}$$

$$(w \models \langle \pi \rangle \rho \vee \langle \pi' \rangle \rho)$$

Therefore $\langle \pi + \pi' \rangle \rho \leftrightarrow \langle \pi \rangle \rho \vee \langle \pi' \rangle \rho$ is valid.
Axiom (2.2)

$$(w \models \langle \pi \rangle \langle \pi' \rangle \rho)$$

$$= \qquad \{ \text{defn of} \models \}$$

$$\sum_{w' \in W} \{ \mathcal{A}_\pi(w, w'); (w \models \langle \pi' \rangle \rho) \}$$

$$= \qquad \{ \text{defn of} \models \}$$

$$\sum_{w' \in W} \{ \mathcal{A}_\pi(w, w'); \sum_{w'' \in W} \{ \mathcal{A}_{\pi'}(w', w''); (w'' \models \rho) \} \}$$

$$= \qquad \{ (7) \}$$

$$\sum_{w'\in W}\left\{\sum_{w''\in W}\{\mathcal{A}_\pi(w,w');\mathcal{A}_{\pi'}(w',w'');(w''\models\rho)\}\right\}$$

$$=\quad\{\text{ commutativity}\}$$

$$\sum_{w''\in W}\left\{\sum_{w'\in W}\{\mathcal{A}_\pi(w,w');\mathcal{A}_{\pi'}(w',w'');(w''\models\rho)\}\right\}$$

$$=\quad\{\text{ since }(w''\models\rho)\text{ is independent of }w'\}$$

$$\sum_{w''\in W}\left\{\sum_{w'\in W}\{\mathcal{A}_\pi(w,w');\mathcal{A}_{\pi'}(w',w'')\};(w''\models\rho)\right\}$$

$$=\quad\{\text{ defn. of composition}\}$$

$$\sum_{w''\in W}\{\mathcal{A}_{\pi;\pi'}(w,w'');(w''\models\rho)\}$$

$$=\quad\{\text{ defn. of }\models\}$$

$$(w\models\langle\pi;\pi'\rangle\rho)$$

Therefore $\langle\pi\rangle\langle\pi'\rangle\rho\leftrightarrow\langle\pi;\pi'\rangle\rho$ is valid.

Axiom (2.3)

$$(w\models\langle\pi\rangle\bot)$$

$$=\quad\{\text{ defn. of }\models\}$$

$$\sum_{w'\in W}\{\mathcal{A}_\pi(w,w');(w\models\bot)\}$$

$$=\quad\{\text{ defn. of satisfaction}\}$$

$$\sum_{w'\in W}\{\mathcal{A}_\pi(w,w');\bot\}$$

$$=\quad\{\text{ (9) and }\bot=0\}$$

$$\sum_{w'\in W}\{\bot\}$$

$$=\quad\{\text{ (4)}\}$$

$$\bot$$

Therefore $\langle\pi\rangle 0\leftrightarrow 0$ is valid.

Lemma 3. *The following are valid formulas in any $\mathcal{GDL}(\mathbf{A})$:*

(3.1) $\langle\pi\rangle\rho\to\langle\pi^*\rangle\rho$
(3.2) $\langle\pi^*\rangle\rho\leftrightarrow\langle\pi^*;\pi^*\rangle\rho$
(3.3) $\langle\pi^*\rangle\rho\leftrightarrow\langle\pi^{**}\rangle\rho$
(3.4) $\langle\pi^*\rangle\rho\leftrightarrow\rho\vee\langle\pi\rangle\langle\pi^*\rangle\rho$

Proof. **Axiom (3.1)** In order to proof this axiom we have first to observe that for any $a, b, c \in A$, $a \leq b$ implies $a; c \leq b; c$. Supposing $a \leq b$, i.e., $a + b = b$, we have that

$$a; c + b; c =_{\{(8)\}} (a + b); c =_{\{\text{by hypothesis } a + b = b\}} b; c$$

i.e., $a; c \leq b; c$. Moreover, we have also to check that $a \leq a^*$ which comes directly from (10) by monotonicity of the supremum and transitivity. Hence (and since $\mathbb{M}_n(\mathbf{A})$ is an action lattice), we have for any $w \in W$,

$$\mathcal{A}_\pi(w, w') \leq \mathcal{A}_{\pi^*}(w, w') \text{ for any } w' \in W$$

$\Rightarrow \quad \{ a \leq b \text{ implies } a; c \leq b; c\}$

$$\mathcal{A}_\pi(w, w'); (w' \models \rho) \leq \mathcal{A}_{\pi^*}(w, w'); (w' \models \rho) \text{ for any } w' \in W$$

$\Rightarrow \quad \{ \text{monotonicity of the supremum}\}$

$$\sum_{w' \in W} \{\mathcal{A}_\pi(w, w'); (w' \models \rho)\} \leq \sum_{w' \in W} \{\mathcal{A}_{\pi^*}(w, w'); (w' \models \rho)\}$$

$\Leftrightarrow \quad \{ \text{defn of } \models\}$

$$(w \models \langle \pi \rangle \rho) \leq (w \models \langle \pi^* \rangle \rho)$$

$\Leftrightarrow \quad \{ \text{defn of } \models\}$

$$(w \models \langle \pi \rangle \rho \rightarrow \langle \pi^* \rangle \rho)$$

Therefore $\langle \pi \rangle \rho \rightarrow \langle \pi^* \rangle \rho$ is valid.

Axioms (3.2),(3.3) and (3.4) We start recalling the following well known Kleene algebra properties: $a^* = a^{**}$, $a^* = a^*; a^*$ and $1 + a; a^* = a^*$ (see [9]). Therefore, we have that

$$\mathcal{A}_{\pi^*}(w, w') = \mathcal{A}_{\pi^{**}}(w, w') \tag{23}$$

$$\mathcal{A}_{\pi^*}(w, w') = \mathcal{A}_{\pi^*; \pi^*}(w, w') \tag{24}$$

$$\mathcal{A}_{1+\pi; \pi^*}(w, w') = \mathcal{A}_{\pi^*}(w, w') \tag{25}$$

The remaining of the first two proofs follows exactly the same steps of the one for Axiom **(3.1)**. For the third case, we have that for any $w \in W$,

$$\mathcal{A}_{1+\pi; \pi^*}(w, w') = \mathcal{A}_{\pi^*}(w, w') \text{ for any } w' \in W$$

$\Leftrightarrow \quad \{ \text{program interpretation}\}$

$$\mathcal{A}_1(w, w') + \mathcal{A}_{\pi; \pi^*}(w, w') = \mathcal{A}_{\pi^*}(w, w') \text{ for any } w' \in W$$

$\Leftrightarrow \quad \{ a = b \text{ iff } a; c = b; c\}$

$$\left(\mathcal{A}_1(w, w') + \mathcal{A}_{\pi; \pi^*}(w, w')\right); (w' \models \rho) = \mathcal{A}_{\pi^*}(w, w'); (w' \models \rho)$$
$$\text{for any } w' \in W$$

$\Leftrightarrow$ { (7)}

$\mathcal{A}_1(w, w'); (w' \models \rho) + \mathcal{A}_{\pi;\pi^*}(w, w'); (w' \models \rho) = \mathcal{A}_{\pi^*}(w, w'); (w' \models \rho)$
for any $w' \in W$

$\Rightarrow$ { supremum funcionality}

$$\sum_{w' \in W} \{\mathcal{A}_1(w, w'); (w' \models \rho) + \mathcal{A}_{\pi;\pi^*}(w, w'); (w' \models \rho)\} =$$
$$\sum_{w' \in W} \{\mathcal{A}_{\pi^*}(w, w'); (w' \models \rho)\}$$

$\Leftrightarrow$ { distributivity}

$$\sum_{w' \in W} \{\mathcal{A}_1(w, w'); (w' \models \rho)\} + \sum_{w' \in W} \{\mathcal{A}_{\pi;\pi^*}(w, w'); (w' \models \rho)\} =$$
$$\sum_{w' \in W} \{\mathcal{A}_{\pi^*}(w, w'); (w' \models \rho)\}$$

$\Leftrightarrow$ { $\sum_{w' \in W} \{\mathcal{A}_1(w, w'); (w' \models \rho) = (w \models \rho)\}$ + program interpretation}

$(w \models \rho) + (w \models \langle \pi; \pi^* \rangle \rho) = (w \models \langle \pi^* \rangle \rho)$

$\Leftrightarrow$ { (2.2)}

$(w \models \rho) + (w \models \langle \pi \rangle \langle \pi^* \rangle \rho) = (w \models \langle \pi^* \rangle \rho)$

$\Leftrightarrow$ { defn of $\models$}

$(w \models \rho \vee \langle \pi \rangle \langle \pi^* \rangle \rho) = (w \models \langle \pi^* \rangle \rho)$

Therefore, $\langle \pi^* \rangle \rho \leftrightarrow \rho \vee \langle \pi \rangle \langle \pi^* \rangle \rho$ is valid.

4   Conclusions

The method introduced in this paper is able to generate several dynamic logics useful for the working Software Engineer. Some of them are documented in the literature, others freshly new. For instance, for verification of imperative programs, we may consider a logic whose states are valuations of program variables. Hence, and as usual, atomic programs become assignments of variables. In this context, a transition $w \rightarrow^{x:=a} w'$ means that the state w' differs from w just in the value of variable x, i.e., that $w'(x) = a$ and for any variable $y \neq x$, $w'(y) = w(y)$.

A very natural direction for future work is to enrich this framework with tests, i.e., programs $?cond$ interpreted as $\mathcal{A}_{?cond} = \{(w, w)|w \models cond\}$. As usual, this provides a way to express if-then-else statements in dynamic logics. Another topic deserving attention is the characterisation of program refinement in this setting, witnessed by some class of action lattice morphisms.

Acknowledgments. This work is financed by the ERDF - European Regional Development Fund through the COMPETE Programme (operational programme for competitiveness) and by National Funds through the FCT - Fundação para a Ciência e a Tecnologia (Portuguese Foundation for Science and Technology) within projects FCOMP-01-0124-FEDER-037281, PEst-OE/MAT/UI4106/2014, FCOMP-01-0124-FEDER-028923 and by project NORTE-07- 0124-FEDER-000060, co-financed by the North Portugal Regional Operational Programme (ON.2), under the National Strategic Reference Framework (NSRF), through the European Regional Development Fund (ERDF).

References

1. Beckert, B.: A dynamic logic for the formal verification of java card programs. In: Attali, I., Jensen, T. (eds.) JavaCard 2000. LNCS, vol. 2041, pp. 6–24. Springer, Heidelberg (2001)

2. Droste, M., Gastin, P.: Weighted automata and weighted logics. Theor. Comput. Sci. **380**(1–2), 69–86 (2007)

3. Furusawa, H.: The categories of kleene algebras, action algebras and action lattices are related by adjunctions. In: Berghammer, R., Möller, B., Struth, G. (eds.) RelMiCS 2003/Kleene-Algebra Ws 2003. LNCS, vol. 3051, pp. 124–136. Springer, Heidelberg (2004)

4. Goble, S.F.: Grades of modality. Logique et Analyse **13**, 323–334 (1970)

5. Gottwald, S.: A Treatise on Many-Valued Logics. Studies in Logic and Computation, vol. 9. Research Studies Press (2001)

6. Harel, D., Kozen, D., Tiuryn, J.: Dynamic Logic. MIT Press (2000)

7. Kozen, D.: On action algebras. manuscript in: Logic and Flow of Information, Amsterdam (1991)

8. Kozen, D.: A probabilistic PDL. J. Comput. Syst. Sci. **30**(2), 162–178 (1985)

9. Kozen, D.: A completeness theorem for kleene algebras and the algebra of regular events. Inf. Comput. **110**(2), 366–390 (1994)

10. Lopes, B., Benevides, M.R.F., Haeusler, E.H.: Propositional dynamic logic for petri nets. Logic Journal of the IGPL **22**(5), 721–736 (2014)

11. Mürk, O., Larsson, D., Hähnle, R.: KeY-C: a tool for verification of c programs. In: Pfenning, F. (ed.) CADE 2007. LNCS (LNAI), vol. 4603, pp. 385–390. Springer, Heidelberg (2007)

12. Nilsson, N.J.: Probabilistic logic. Artif. Intell. **28**(1), 71–87 (1986)

13. Platzer, A.: Logical Analysis of Hybrid Systems: Proving Theorems for Complex Dynamics. Springer (2010)

14. Platzer, A.: A complete axiomatization of quantified differential dynamic logic for distributed hybrid systems. Logical Methods in Computer Science 8(4) (2012)

15. Pratt, V.: Action logic and pure induction. In: van Eijck, J. (ed.) Logics in AI. LNCS, vol. 478, pp. 97–120. Springer, Heidelberg (1991)

16. van der Hoek, W.: On the semantics of graded modalities. Journal of Applied Non-Classical Logics 2(1) (1992)

Completeness and Decidability Results for Hybrid(ised) Logics

Renato Neves[1]([✉]), Manuel A. Martins[2], and Luís S. Barbosa[1]

[1] HASLab INESC TEC and University of Minho, Braga, Portugal
{renato.j.neves,luis.s.barbosa}@inesctec.pt
[2] CIDMA - Department of Mathematics, University of Aveiro, Aveiro, Portugal
martins@ua.pt

Abstract. Adding to the modal description of transition structures the ability to refer to specific states, hybrid(ised) logics provide an interesting framework for the specification of reconfigurable systems. The qualifier 'hybrid(ised)' refers to a generic method of developing, on top of whatever specification logic is used to model software configurations, the elements of an hybrid language, including nominals and modalities. In such a context, this paper shows how a calculus for a hybrid(ised) logic can be generated from a calculus of the base logic and that, moreover, it preserves soundness and completeness. A second contribution establishes that hybridising a decidable logic also gives rise to a decidable hybrid(ised) one. These results pave the way to the development of dedicated proof tools for such logics used in the design of reconfigurable systems.

Keywords: Institutions · Hybrid logic · Decidability · Completeness

1 Introduction

1.1 Motivation

The need to master ubiquitous and increasingly complex software systems, often of a safety–critical nature, has brought proof and verification to a central place in Computer Science and Software Engineering. Logics, as formal reasoning frameworks, provide tools for a rigorous specification (and analysis) of software systems, as opposed to more conventional practices in software development which are often pre-scientific and unable to prove the absence of error designs.

Ideally, the working software engineer seeks for logics that can effectively provide "yes–or–no" answers to queries regarding properties of the system (*i.e.* *decidable* logics), as well as logics with a calculus providing enough syntactic rules to derive falsehood from any false statement (*i.e.* a *complete* calculus). The engineer also looks for logics with the right expressive power to specify the system at hand, a job made difficult by the complex and heterogeneous nature of current software systems which typically require a number of different logics

© Springer International Publishing Switzerland 2015
C. Braga and N. Martí-Oliet (Eds.): SBMF 2014, LNCS 8941, pp. 146–161, 2015.
DOI: 10.1007/978-3-319-15075-8_10

to be suitably specified. For example, some form of equational logic may be used for data type specifications, while transitional behaviour my resort to a modal or temporal logic and fuzzy requirements may become in order to express contextual constraints. Actually, this justifies the quest for methodologies in which a specification framework can be tailored by combining whichever logics are found suitable to deal with the different nature of the requirements in presence. As Goguen and Meseguer put it in a landmark paper [11],

> *"The right way to combine various programming paradigms is to discover their underlying logics, combine them, and then base a language upon the combined logic."*

This line of research has been particularly active for the last twenty years. Finger and Gabbay, for example, showed in [9] how to add a temporal dimension to an arbitrary logic, and proved that decidability and completeness is preserved along this process. Baltazar [2] did similar work but with respect to adding a probabilistic dimension. Other, similar results include *e.g.* [6], [7], as well as a *hybridisation* method [14], in whose development the current authors have been involved, and constitutes the starting point of the work reported in the sequel.

1.2   Context

Essentially hybridisation turns a given logic, defined as an *institution*, into a hybrid logic, a brand of modal logics that adds to the modal description of transition structures the ability to refer to specific states (*cf.* [1,3]). This paves the way to an expressive framework, proposed in [13], for the specification of *reconfigurable* systems, *i.e.*, systems which may evolve through different execution modes, or configurations, along their lifetime. Specification proceeds in two steps:

– *globally* the system's dynamics is represented by a transition structure described in a hybrid language, whose states correspond to possible configurations;
– *locally* each state is endowed with a structure modelling the specification of the associated configuration.

The logic used locally, *i.e.* the one to be hybridised, depends on the application requirements. Typical candidates are equational, partial algebra or first-order logic (FOL), but one may equally resort to multivalued logics or even to hybrid logic itself equipping, in the last case, each state with another (local) transition system. Verification resorts to a parametrised translation to FOL (developed in [14] and [15]), but at the cost of losing decidability and adding extra complexity.

The generic character of this hybridisation process is achieved through its rendering in the context of institution theory [10]. Such a theory formalises the essence of what a logical system actually is, by encompassing syntax, semantics and satisfaction. However, its classical definition, the one in which the hybridisation method is based, does not include an abstract structure to represent a logic calculus. The problem was addressed in [8] with the introduction of $\pi-$ *institutions*, and, more recently, in [5] with the notion of an *institution with proofs*, a more general version of the previous work.

1.3   Contributions and Roadmap

This paper starts by recasting the hybridisation method in the theory of institutions with proofs, which makes possible the systematic generation of a calculus when hybridising a given logic.

Then, we prove that, under certain conditions, this method preserves decidability, and furthermore that the generated calculus is sound and complete whenever the one corresponding to the base logic is. Those are the paper's main contributions. Besides their theoretical relevance, from a pragmatic point of view they pave the way to the development of effective verification algorithms.

The paper is organised as follows. Institutions with proofs are briefly reviewed in Section 2. Then, Section 3 introduces the generation of an hybrid calculus from a base one. Section 4 establishes decidability and completeness. Finally, Section 5 concludes the paper and hints at future lines of research.

2   Background

We first recall the notion of an institution [10]. As already mentioned, it formalises the essence of a logical system, encompassing syntax, semantics and satisfaction. Put forward by J. Goguen and R. Burstall in the late seventies, its original aim was to develop as much as Computer Science as possible in a general uniform way independently of particular logical systems. This has now been achieved to an extent even greater than originally thought, with the theory of institutions becoming the most fundamental mathematical theory underlying algebraic specification methods, and also increasingly used in other areas of Computer Science. Formally,

Definition 1. *An institution is a tuple* $(Sign^I, Sen^I, Mod^I, (\models^I_\Sigma)_{\Sigma \in |Sign^I|})$, *where:*

- $Sign^I$ *is a category whose objects are signatures and arrows signature morphisms,*
- $Sen^I : Sign^I \rightarrow \mathbb{S}et$, *is a functor that, for each signature* $\Sigma \in |Sign^I|$, *returns a set of sentences over* Σ,
- $Mod^I : (Sign^I)^{op} \rightarrow \mathbb{C}at$, *is a functor that, for each signature* $\Sigma \in |Sign^I|$, *returns a category whose objects are models over* Σ,
- $\models^I_\Sigma \subseteq |Mod^I(\Sigma)| \times Sen^I(\Sigma)$, *or simply* $\models$, *if the context is clear, is a satisfaction relation such that, for each signature morphism* $\varphi : \Sigma \rightarrow \Sigma'$,

$$Mod^I(\varphi)(M') \models^I_\Sigma \rho \text{ iff } M' \models^I_{\Sigma'} Sen^I(\varphi)(\rho), \text{ for any}$$

$M' \in |Mod^I(\Sigma')|$ and $\rho \in Sen^I(\Sigma)$. Graphically,

$$
\begin{array}{ccc}
\Sigma & Mod^I(\Sigma) \xrightarrow{\;\models^I_\Sigma\;} Sen^I(\Sigma) \\[2pt]
\varphi \downarrow & Mod^I(\varphi) \uparrow \qquad\qquad \downarrow Sen^I(\varphi) \\[2pt]
\Sigma' & Mod^I(\Sigma') \xrightarrow[\models^I_{\Sigma'}]{} Sen^I(\Sigma')
\end{array}
$$

Intuitively, this property means that satisfaction is preserved under change of notation.

Definition 2. *Consider an institution I and signature $\Sigma \in |Sign^I|$. We say that a sentence $\rho \in Sen^I(\Sigma)$ is Σ–valid (or simply, valid) if for each model $M \in |Mod^I(\Sigma)|$, $M \models^I_\Sigma \rho$. Usually we prefix such sentences by $\models^I_\Sigma$ or, simply by $\models^I$ or just $\models$.*

Definition 3. *An institution I has the* negation property *if, for any signature $\Sigma \in |Sign^I|$ and sentence $\rho \in Sen^I(\Sigma)$, there is a sentence, $\neg\rho \in Sen^I(\Sigma)$, such that for any model $M \in |Mod^I(\Sigma)|$, $M \models^I_\Sigma \rho$ iff $M \not\models^I_\Sigma \neg\rho$.*

If this property holds, satisfiability of sentences may be rephrased as follows,

Definition 4. *Consider institution I with the* negation property *and a signature $\Sigma \in |Sign^I|$. For any sentence $\rho \in Sen^I(\Sigma)$,*

$$\rho \text{ is } \Sigma\text{–unsatisfiable iff } \neg\rho \text{ is } \Sigma\text{–valid.}$$

Similarly,

Definition 5. *An institution I has the* explicit satisfaction property, *if for any signature $\Sigma \in |Sign^I|$ and sentence $\rho \in Sen^I(\Sigma)$, satisfiability of ρ entails the existence of a model $M \in |Mod^I(\Sigma)|$ such that $M \models^I_\Sigma \rho$.*

Note that this last property holds in the most common logics used in specification, *e.g.*, propositional, fuzzy, equational, partial and first-order.

Definition 6. *An institution I has the* conjunction property *if, for any signature $\Sigma \in |Sign^I|$ and sentences $\rho, \rho' \in Sen^I(\Sigma)$, there is sentence $\rho \wedge \rho' \in Sen^I(\Sigma)$, such that for any model $M \in |Mod^I(\Sigma)|$, $M \models^I_\Sigma \rho \wedge \rho'$ iff $M \models^I_\Sigma \rho$ and $M \models^I_\Sigma \rho'$*

Note that with the conjunction property we are able to define a sentence $(\rho \wedge \neg\rho) \in Sen^I(\Sigma)$, denoted by $\bot$, that is not satisfied by any model of $|Mod^I(\Sigma)|$.

An institution for which both the negation and conjunction properties hold, is said to have the typical boolean connectives.

In order to better grasp this rather abstract concept of an institution let us analyse some typical examples.

Example 1. Many sorted first order logic (FOL)

- SIGNATURES. $Sign^{\text{FOL}}$ is a category whose objects are triples (S, F, P), consisting of a set of sort symbols S, a family, $F = (F_{w \to s})_{w \in S^*, s \in S}$, of function symbols indexed by their arity, and a family, $P = (P_w)_{w \in S^*}$, of relational symbols also indexed by their arity.

  A signature morphism in this category is a triple $(\varphi_{st}, \varphi_{op}, \varphi_{rl}) : (S, F, P) \to (S', F', P')$ such that if $\sigma \in F_{w \to s}$, then $\varphi_{op}(\sigma) \in F'_{\varphi_{st}(w) \to \varphi_{st}(s)}$, and if $\pi \in P_w$ then $\varphi_{rl}(\pi) \in P'_{\varphi_{st}(w)}$.

- SENTENCES. For each signature object $(S, F, P) \in |Sign^{\text{FOL}}|$, $Sen^{\text{FOL}}(S, F, P)$ is the smallest set generated by:

$$\rho \ni \neg \rho \mid \rho \wedge \rho \mid t = t \mid \pi(X) \mid \forall x : s \, . \, \rho'$$

  where t is a term of sorts with the syntactic structure $\sigma(X)$ for $\sigma \in F_{w \to s}$ and X a list of terms compatible with the arity of σ. $\pi \in P_w$ and X is a list of terms compatible with the arity of π. Finally, $\rho' \in Sen^{FOL}(S, F \uplus \{x\}_{\to s}, P)$. $Sen^I(\varphi)$, for φ a signature morphism, is a function that, given a sentence $\rho \in Sen^I(S, F, P)$, replaces the signature symbols in ρ under the mapping corresponding to φ.

- MODELS. For each signature $(S, F, P) \in |Sign^{\text{FOL}}|$, $Mod^{\text{FOL}}(S, F, P)$ is the category with only identity arrows and whose objects are models with a carrier set $|M_s|$, for each $s \in S$; a function $M_\sigma : |M_w| \to |M_s|$, for each $\sigma_{w \to s} \in F_{w \to s}$; a relation $M_\pi \subseteq |M_w|$, for each $\pi \in P_w$.

- SATISFACTION. Satisfaction of sentences by models is the usual Tarskian satisfaction.

Example 2. Equational logic (EQ)

The institution EQ is the sub-institution of FOL in which sentences are restricted to those of the type $\forall \overline{x} : \overline{s} \, . \, t = t'$

Example 3. Propositional logic (PL)

Institution PL is the sub-institution of FOL in which signatures with no empty set of sorts are discarded.

As seen above, no notion of a proof system is considered in the definition of an institution. This is a limitation if one is interested in logical systems with calculi, as is the case in this paper which aims at introducing the systematic generation of calculi for hybridised logics. To overcome this we resort to the following extended definition of an institution with proofs [5].

Definition 7. *An institution with proofs adds to the original definition a functor $Prf^I : Sign^I \to \mathbb{C}at$ such that, for each $\Sigma \in |Sign^I|$, $Prf(\Sigma)$ (called the category of Σ–proofs) has subsets of $Sen^I(\Sigma)$ (i.e., $|Prf(\Sigma)| = |\mathcal{P}(Sen^I(\Sigma))|$) as objects, and the corresponding proofs as arrows. The latter are preserved along signature morphisms. In addition, for $A, B \in |Prf^I(\Sigma)|$, if $A \subseteq B$ then there is an arrow $B \longrightarrow A$; if $A \cap B = \emptyset$ and there is $\Gamma \in |Prf^I(\Sigma)|$ such that $p : \Gamma \longrightarrow A$ and $q : \Gamma \longrightarrow B$, then there is a unique proof $\langle p, q \rangle$ making the following diagram to commute*

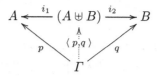

For the sake of simplicity, when a singleton set of sentences is present in a proof arrow, we may drop the curly brackets. Note that the restrictions imposed to the proof arrows oblige Prf^I to follow the basic properties of a proof system. In particular, we have

1. *Reflexivity* (if $A \in \Gamma$, then $\Gamma \vdash A$) follows from the fact that $\{A\} \subseteq \Gamma$ and therefore $\Gamma \longrightarrow A$.
2. *Monotonicity* (if $\Gamma \vdash A$ and $\Gamma \subseteq \Delta$ then $\Delta \vdash A$), follows from composition of proofs, where $\Delta \longrightarrow \Gamma$ is given by inclusion and $\Gamma \longrightarrow A$ by the assumption.
3. *Transitivity* (if $\Gamma \vdash A$ and $\{\Delta, A\} \vdash B$ then $\Gamma \cup \Delta \vdash B$), follows from the product of disjoint sets, reflexivity and monotonicity,

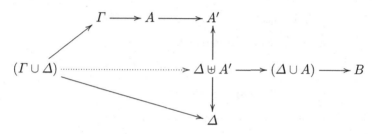

where $A' = A - (A \cap \Delta)$ ($A' \subseteq A$ and $(\Delta \cup A) \subseteq (\Delta \cup A')$).

Note that functor Prf^I distinguishes different proofs between the same pair of objects, as opposed to entailment systems[1]. In this work, however, we restrict ourselves to entailment systems in which $Prf^I(\Sigma)$ has at most one arrow for each pair of objects, *i.e.* that $Prf^I(\Sigma)$ is *thin*. Such restriction makes showing the uniqueness of $\langle p, q \rangle$ trivial.

Definition 8. *Let I be an institution with proof system Prf^I. We say that Prf^I is* sound *if, for any signature $\Sigma \in |Sign^I|$ and sentence $\rho \in Sen^I(\Sigma)$,*

$$\text{if arrow } \emptyset \longrightarrow \rho \text{ is in } Prf^I(\Sigma) \text{ then } \models^I \rho.$$

Definition 9. *Let I be an institution with proof system Prf^I. We say that Prf^I is* complete *if, for any signature $\Sigma \in |Sign^I|$ and sentence $\rho \in Sen^I(\Sigma)$,*

$$\text{if } \models^I \rho \text{ then arrow } \emptyset \longrightarrow \rho \text{ is in } Prf^I(\Sigma)$$

Hence, soundness and completeness of Prf^I entails the equivalence, for any signature $\Sigma \in |Sign^I|$ and sentence $\rho \in Sen^I(\Sigma)$,

---

[1] Typically, in an entailment system $\Gamma \vdash A$ means that Γ derives (or entails) A.

$$\models^I \rho \ \text{iff} \ \emptyset \longrightarrow \rho \text{ is in } Prf^I(\Sigma)$$

We can now show that

Theorem 1. *If an institution I has classical boolean connectives, and a sound and complete calculus Prf^I, with the* reductio ad absurdum *property, then, for any signature, $\Sigma \in |Sign^I|$, and sentence, $\rho \in Sen^I(\Sigma)$,*

$$\rho \text{ is satisfiable iff } \rho \longrightarrow \bot \text{ is not in } Prf^I(\Sigma)$$

Proof

$$\models^I \rho \ \text{iff} \ \emptyset \longrightarrow \rho \text{ is in } Prf^I(\Sigma)$$

$\Leftrightarrow$ { defn. of satisfiability }

$$\neg\rho \text{ is unsat iff } \emptyset \longrightarrow \rho \text{ is in } Prf^I(\Sigma)$$

$\Leftrightarrow$ { soundness, completeness of $Prf^I(\Sigma)$ and r.a.a}

$$\neg\rho \text{ is unsat iff } \neg\rho \longrightarrow \bot \text{ is in } Prf^I(\Sigma)$$

$\Leftrightarrow$ { defn. of negation }

$$\rho \text{ is unsat iff } \rho \longrightarrow \bot \text{ is in } Prf^I(\Sigma)$$

$\Leftrightarrow$ { de Morgan's law}

$$\rho \text{ is sat iff } \rho \longrightarrow \bot \text{ is not in } Prf^I(\Sigma)$$

Corollary 1. *In the context of theorem 1, if I has the explicit satisfaction property, then*

$$\rho \text{ is sat iff } \rho \longrightarrow \bot \text{ is not in } Prf^I(\Sigma)$$

$\Leftrightarrow$ { *explicit satisfaction property* }

$$\rho \text{ has a model iff } \rho \longrightarrow \bot \text{ is not in } Prf^I(\Sigma)$$

This last result will be essential in the sequel for proving completeness of hybridised logics.

3   Hybridisation of Logics and Their Calculi

As mentioned before, the existence of software products that are built and maintained with respect to requirements of different nature calls for techniques that favour combination of logics. Hybridisation [14] was born in this context. It aims at providing a framework to specify reconfigurable systems, whose execution modes are described by whatever logic the engineer finds suitable, whereas the transition structure is expressed in a hybrid language.

From a point of view of verification, however, the engineer is not only interested in having a hybridised logic, but also, in a very pragmatic way, in its calculus. This section addresses such issue. It starts by revisiting hybridisation and then, through the notion of institutions with proofs, it shows how to lift the calculus in the base logic to its hybridised counterpart.

3.1 Hybridisation Revisited

Definition 10. *The category $Sign^{\mathcal{H}}$ is the category $\mathbb{Set} \times \mathbb{Set}$ whose objects are pairs (Nom, Λ) with Nom denoting a set of nominal symbols and Λ, a set of modality symbols.*

Definition 11. *Provided an institution $I = (Sign^I, Sen^I, Mod^I, \models^I)$ the hybridised version $\mathcal{H}I = (Sign^{\mathcal{H}I}, Sen^{\mathcal{H}I}, Mod^{\mathcal{H}I}, \models^{\mathcal{H}I})$ is defined as follows,*

- $Sign^{\mathcal{H}\mathcal{I}} = Sign^{\mathcal{H}} \times Sign^{\mathcal{I}}$,
- *given a signature $(\Delta, \Sigma) \in |Sign^{\mathcal{H}\mathcal{I}}|$, $Sen^{\mathcal{H}\mathcal{I}}(\Delta, \Sigma)$ is the least set generated by*

$$\rho \ni \neg\rho \mid \rho \& \rho \mid i \mid @_i\rho \mid \langle\lambda\rangle\rho \mid \forall x\, \rho' \mid \psi \mid A\, \rho$$

for i a nominal, λ a modality, $\psi \in Sen^{\mathcal{I}}(\Sigma)$ and $\rho' \in Sen^{\mathcal{H}\mathcal{I}}(\Delta \uplus \{x\}, \Sigma)$ where x is a nominal. We use non standard boolean connectives $(\neg, \&)^2$ in order to distinguish them from the boolean connectives that the base logic may have.
- *given a signature $(\Delta, \Sigma) \in |Sign^{\mathcal{H}I}|$, a model $M \in |Mod^{\mathcal{H}I}(\Delta, \Sigma)|$ is a triple (W, R, m) such that,*
    - *W is a non–empty set of worlds,*
    - *R is a family of relational symbols indexed by the modality symbols, such that for each $\lambda \in \Lambda$ (where $\Delta = (-, \Lambda)$), $R_\lambda \subseteq W \times W$,*
    - *and $m : W \to |Mod^I(\Sigma)|$,*
    and for each $i \in Nom$, $(W, R, m)_i$ is interpreted as a world in W.
- *given a signature $(\Delta, \Sigma) \in |Sign^I|$, a model $M = (W, R, m)$ $\in |Mod^I(\Delta, \Sigma)|$ and a sentence $\rho \in Sen^{\mathcal{H}I}(\Delta, \Sigma)$, the satisfaction relation is defined as,*

$$M \models^{\mathcal{H}I}_{(\Delta, \Sigma)} \rho \text{ iff } M \models^w \rho, \text{ for all } w \in W$$

where,

$M \models^w \neg\rho$ *iff* $M \not\models^w \rho$

$M \models^w \rho \& \rho'$ *iff* $M \models^w \rho$ *and* $M \models^w \rho'$

$M \models^w i$ *iff* $M_i = w$

$M \models^w @_i\rho$ *iff* $M \models^{M_i} \rho$

$M \models^w \langle\lambda\rangle\rho$ *iff there is some $w' \in W$ such that $(w, w') \in R_\lambda$ and $M \models^{w'} \rho$*

$M \models^w A\rho$ *iff* $M \models^w \forall x\, @_x\rho$

$M \models^w \psi$ *iff* $m(w) \models^I_\Sigma \psi$

$M \models^w \forall x\, \rho$ *iff for all M', $M' \models \rho$*

---

[2] Implication $(\Rightarrow)$ and biimplication $(\Leftrightarrow)$ are built in the usual way.

for $(W, R, m) = M' \in |Mod^{\mathcal{H}I}(\Delta \uplus \{x\}, \Sigma)|$ a model expansion of M, with the only difference between them being the interpretation of nominal x: while it is defined in M', in M it is not.

Note that sentence ρ being satisfiable means that there is a model (W, R, m) $= M \in |Mod^{\mathcal{H}I}(\Delta, \Sigma)|$ such that $M \models^w \rho$ for some $w \in W$. Hence, hybridised logics do not have the explicit satisfaction property. One can, however, redefine the satisfaction relation in the hybridisation method to,

$$M \models^{\mathcal{H}I}_{(\Delta, \Sigma)} \rho \text{ iff } M \models^w \rho, \text{ for some } w \in W$$

which then provides to logics hybridised in this alternative way the explicit satisfaction property.

A weak hybridisation of an institution I, denoted by $\mathcal{H}'I$, is obtained as $\mathcal{H}I$, but the omission of syntax constructor $\forall x \rho$. The following decidability results are formulated with respect to weak hybridisation.

3.2   Hybridising a Calculus

We now present the hybridisation of calculi in the context of institutions with proofs. Let us assume that I has a proof system, *i.e.*, that Prf^I is well defined, and that, in particular, it is an entailment system, *i.e.*, Prf^I only defines thin categories. Then we define $Prf^{\mathcal{H}I}$ as follows:

For any $((Nom, \Lambda), \Sigma) \in |Sign^{\mathcal{H}I}|$,

1. for any $\rho \in Sen^I(\Sigma)$, if $\emptyset \longrightarrow \rho$ is in $Prf^I(\Sigma)$ then $\emptyset \longrightarrow \rho$ is in $Prf^{\mathcal{H}I}((Nom, \Lambda), \Sigma)$,
2. for any nominal $i, j \in Nom$, modality $\lambda \in \Lambda$, $\rho, \rho' \in Sen^{\mathcal{H}I}((Nom, \Lambda), \Sigma)$, proof arrows in Table 1 are in $Prf^{\mathcal{H}I}((Nom, \Lambda), \Sigma)$
3. finally, $Prf^{\mathcal{H}I}((Nom, \Lambda), \Sigma)$ has all the inclusion proof arrows and for each $A, B, \Gamma \in |Prf^{\mathcal{H}I}((Nom, \Lambda), \Sigma)|$ if $\Gamma \longrightarrow A$, $\Gamma \longrightarrow B$ then $\Gamma \longrightarrow A \cup B$.

$Prf^{\mathcal{H}I}$ is maintained thin in its construction process in order to have it as an entailment system.

4   Decidability and Completeness of Hybridised Logics

Decidability and completeness are properties that one usually looks for when defining a new logic. From a Computer Science perspective, they are essential as a basis for tool-supported proofs. Formally,

Definition 12. *Decidability of an institution I means that, for each signature $\Sigma \in |Sign^I|$ and sentence $\rho \in Sen^I(\Sigma)$, there is an effective algorithm able to decide whether ρ is valid.*

After some preliminary work, we address first this definition in the context of hybridised logics.

Table 1. Axioms and rules for $Prf^{\mathcal{H}I}$ from [3]

Axioms

(CT)	All substitution instances of classical tautologies
$(Dist)$	$\emptyset \longrightarrow @_i(\rho \Rightarrow \rho') \Leftrightarrow (@_i\rho \Rightarrow @_i\rho')$
$(\bot)$	$\emptyset \longrightarrow @_i\bot \Rightarrow \bot$
(Scope)	$\emptyset \longrightarrow @_i@_j\rho \Rightarrow @_j\rho$
(Ref)	$\emptyset \longrightarrow @_i i$
(Intro)	$\emptyset \longrightarrow (i \land \rho) \Rightarrow @_i\rho$
$(\Box E)$	$\emptyset \longrightarrow ([\lambda]\rho \land \langle\lambda\rangle i) \Rightarrow @_i\rho$
$(\forall E)$	$\emptyset \longrightarrow \forall x\, \rho \Rightarrow \rho[i/x]$

Rules

(MP)	if $\emptyset \longrightarrow \rho$ and $\rho \longrightarrow \rho'$ then $\emptyset \longrightarrow \rho'$
$(N_@)$	if $\emptyset \longrightarrow \rho$ then $\emptyset \longrightarrow @_i\rho$
$(Name)$	if i does not occur free in ρ and $\emptyset \longrightarrow @_i\rho$ then $\emptyset \longrightarrow \rho$
$(\Box I)$	if i does not occur free in ρ, ρ' and $\emptyset \longrightarrow (\rho \land \langle\lambda\rangle i) \Rightarrow @_i\rho'$ then $\emptyset \longrightarrow \rho \Rightarrow [\lambda]\rho'$
$(\forall I)$	if i does not occur free in $\forall x\, \rho', \rho$ and $\emptyset \longrightarrow \rho \Rightarrow \rho'[i/x]$ $\emptyset \longrightarrow \rho \Rightarrow \forall x\, \rho'$

4.1   Preliminaries

Recall that in the sequel we assume that the base institution I has the classical boolean connectives and the explicit satisfaction property. Furthermore, it has a calculus, Prf^I, is sound, complete and has the *reductio ad absurdum* property.

Notation 1. *Consider* $(\Delta, \Sigma) \in |Sign^{\mathcal{H}I}|$ *and* $\rho \in Sen^{\mathcal{H}I}(\Delta, \Sigma)$. *Let* $B_\rho = \{\psi_1, \ldots, \psi_n\}$ *to denote the set of all maximal sentences,* $\psi_i \in Sen^I(\Sigma)$, *occurring in* ρ. *Then, the set of base sentences,* Ω_ρ, *denotes the least set such that for each* $a \in 2^{B_\rho}$,

$$(\chi_1 \land \cdots \land \chi_n) \in \Omega_\rho \subseteq Sen^I(\Sigma)$$

where

$$\chi_i = \begin{cases} \psi_i & \text{if } \psi_i \in a \\ \neg\psi_i & \text{if } \psi_i \notin a \end{cases}$$

Whenever suitable we abbreviate $(\chi_1 \land \cdots \land \chi_n)$ *to* χ, *and refer to components of* χ *as* χ_i. *Moreover, when no confusion arises, we will also consider* χ *as the set of sentences* $\{\chi_1, \ldots, \chi_n\}$.

Lemma 1. *For any model* $M \in |Mod^I(\Sigma)|$, *M satisfies exactly one of the sentences in* Ω_ρ.

Proof. Suppose that M fails to satisfy a sentence $\chi \in \Omega_\rho$. This only happens when at least one member of χ is not satisfied by M. By definition of Ω_ρ we know that Ω_ρ has another sentence χ' which negates all the failed components in χ and therefore M must satisfy χ'.

Suppose that M satisfies a sentence $\chi \in \Omega_\rho$. Clearly, by the definition of Ω_ρ any other sentence $\chi' \in \Omega_\rho$ must negate at least one of the components of χ. Since M cannot satisfy a component and its negation, χ' cannot be satisfied by M.

Notation 2. *If Ω_ρ is not empty, Lemma 1 allows the use of notation Ω_ρ^M to denote the sentence in Ω_ρ which is satisfied by a model $M \in |Mod^I(\Sigma)|$.*

Next, in order to take advantage of the well known decidability and completeness results for hybrid propositional logic, $\mathcal{HPL}$, we define a function between $\mathcal{HI}$ and $\mathcal{HPL}$ sentences,

Definition 13. *Consider a signature $(\Delta, \Sigma) \in |Sen^{\mathcal{HI}}|$, a sentence $\rho \in Sen^{\mathcal{HI}}$ (Δ, Σ), and a PL signature Prop that, for each $\psi_i \in Sen^I(\Sigma)$, has a propositional symbol π_{ψ_i}. Then a function*
$\sigma : Sen^{\mathcal{HI}}(\Delta, \Sigma) \rightarrow Sen^{\mathcal{HPL}}(\Delta, Prop)$ *is defined to replace the base sentences that occur in ρ and B_ρ by propositions from Prop. Formally,*

$$
\begin{aligned}
\sigma(\neg\rho) &= \neg\sigma(\rho) \\
\sigma(\rho \wedge \rho') &= \sigma(\rho) \wedge \sigma(\rho') \\
\sigma(i) &= i \\
\sigma(@_i\rho) &= @_i\sigma(\rho) \\
\sigma(\langle\lambda\rangle\rho) &= \langle\lambda\rangle\sigma(\rho) \\
\sigma(\forall x\, \rho) &= \forall x\, \sigma(\rho) \\
\sigma(A\rho) &= A\, \sigma(\rho) \\
\sigma(\psi_i) &= \pi_{\psi_i}
\end{aligned}
$$

Definition 14. *For each $\chi \in \Omega_\rho$ we define function $\sigma' : \chi \rightarrow Sen^{PL}(Prop)$ such that,*
$$
\sigma'(\chi_i) = \begin{cases} \neg\pi_{\psi_i} & \text{if } \chi_i = \neg\psi_i \\ \pi_{\psi_i} & \text{if } \chi_i = \psi_i \end{cases}
$$
and denote by $\sigma'[\chi]$ the result of applying σ' to each member of χ.

Note that both σ and σ' are injective.

4.2   Decidability

Lemma 2. *Consider a signature $(\Delta, \Sigma) \in |Sign^{\mathcal{HI}}|$ and $\rho \in Sen^{\mathcal{HI}}(\Delta, \Sigma)$. For any $\chi \in \Omega_\rho$, if χ is satisfiable $\sigma'[\chi]$ is also satisfiable.*

Proof.   Unsatisfaction of $\sigma'[\chi]$ may only come from the following cases:

1. A component of $\sigma'[\chi]$ is unsatisfiable,
2. two components of $\sigma'[\chi]$ contradict each other.

A component in $\sigma'[\chi]$ is π_{ψ_i} or $\neg\pi_{\psi_i}$, hence the first case never happens. If two elements contradict each other, that is, if one is π_{ψ_i} and the other $\neg\pi_{\psi_i}$ then surely χ has elements ψ_i and $\neg\psi_i$, which renders it unsatisfiable.

Theorem 2. *Consider signature* $(\Delta, \Sigma) \in |Sign^{\mathcal{H}I}|$ *and* $\rho \in Sen^{\mathcal{H}I}(\Delta, \Sigma)$. *If* ρ *is satisfiable,* $\sigma(\rho)$ *is also satisfiable.*

Proof. If ρ is satisfiable we have a model $M = (W, R, m) \in |Mod^{\mathcal{H}I}(\Delta, \Sigma)|$ such that $M \models^w \rho$ for some $w \in W$. Through this assumption and Lemma 2, we define a model $(W, R, m') \in |Mod^{\mathcal{H}PL}(\Delta, \Sigma)|$ as follows: for any $w \in W$, $m'(w)$ is a model satisfying $\sigma'[\Omega_\rho^{m(w)}]$ (recall that Lemma 2 proves that $\sigma'[\Omega_\rho^{m(w)}]$ is satisfiable).

It remains to show that $(W, R, m') \models^w \sigma(\rho)$, for some $w \in W$. Since models (W, R, m) and (W, R, m') have the same Kripke structure and $\rho, \sigma(\rho)$ only differ in the base sentences, we just need to check that for all $\chi \in \Omega_\rho$, $m(w) \models \chi$ entails that $m'(w) \models \sigma'[\chi]$ for any $w \in W$. Actually, this is a direct consequence of condition, $m(w) \models \Omega_\rho^{m(w)}$ entails that $m'(w) \models \sigma'[\Omega_\rho^{m(w)}]$ for all $w \in W$, which is freely given by the definition of (W, R, m').

Now, we want to show the converse of Theorem 2. For this we need yet another definition to cater for the "preservation" of information with respect to satisfiability of the base sentences; information that is "lost" by $\sigma(\rho)$. Thus,

Definition 15. *Let* $Sat^{\mathcal{I}}$ *be an effective decision procedure of* $\mathcal{I}$, *and* $\bigvee$ *denote the disjunction operator, built from* $\mathbb{A}, \neg$. *Then define*

$$\eta(\rho) = \begin{cases} \bigvee\{\chi \in \Omega_\rho \mid Sat^{\mathcal{I}}(\chi) \text{ is "unsat"}\}, & \text{if } B_\rho \neq \emptyset \\ \bot, & \text{otherwise} \end{cases}$$

Corollary 2. *It is clear that satisfiability of* ρ *entails satisfiability of* $\rho \mathbb{A} A \neg \eta(\rho)$, *which in turn, by Theorem 2, entails satisfiability of* $\sigma\big(\rho \mathbb{A} A \neg \eta(\rho)\big)$.

Lemma 3. *Consider a model* $(W, R, m) \in |Mod^{\mathcal{H}PL}(\Delta, Prop)|$ *such that* $(W, R, m) \models \sigma\big(\rho \mathbb{A} A \neg \eta(\rho)\big)$. *For any* $\chi \in \Omega_\rho$, *if* $\sigma'[\chi]$ *is satisfied by a model in* $img(m)$, χ *is satisfiable.*

Proof. If χ is unsatisfiable then, by definition of η, occurs as one of the literals in $\eta(\rho)$, hence no model in $img(m)$ may satisfy it.

Theorem 3. *Consider signature* $(\Delta, \Sigma) \in |Sign^{\mathcal{H}I}|$ *and* $\rho \in Sen^{\mathcal{H}I}(\Delta, \Sigma)$. *If* $\sigma(\rho \mathbb{A} A \neg \eta(\rho))$ *is satisfiable, then* ρ *is satisfiable.*

Proof. If $\sigma(\rho \mathbb{A} A \neg \eta(\rho))$ is satisfiable we have a model $M = (W, R, m) \in |Mod^{\mathcal{H}PL}(\Delta, Prop)|$ such that $M \models^w \sigma(\rho \mathbb{A} A \neg \eta(\rho))$ for some $w \in W$. Through this assumption, and by Lemma 3, we define a model $(W, R, m') \in |Mod^{\mathcal{H}I}(\Delta, \Sigma)|$ as follows: for any $w \in W$, $m'(w)$ is a model satisfying χ where $\sigma'[\chi] = \sigma'[\Omega_\rho^{m(w)}]$

It remains to show that $(W, R, m') \models^w \rho$ for some $w \in W$. Since models (W, R, m) and (W, R, m') have the same Kripke structure satisfied by the sentences ρ, $\sigma(\rho \mathbb{A} A \neg \eta(\rho))$, we just have to show that for all $\chi \in \Omega_\rho$, $m(w) \models \sigma'[\chi]$ entails that $m'(w) \models \chi$ for any $w \in W$. Actually, this is a direct consequence of condition, $m(w) \models \sigma'[\Omega_\rho^{m(w)}]$ entails $m'(w) \models \Omega_\rho^{m(w)}$, for all $w \in W$, which is given by the definition of (W, R, m').

Corollary 3. *From Corollary 2 and Theorem 3 we have that*

$$\rho \text{ is satisfiable iff } \sigma(\rho \wedge A \neg \eta(\rho)) \text{ is satisfiable.}$$

Then, since $\mathcal{H}'PL$ was already proved to be decidable [12], we may use an effective decision procedure of $\mathcal{H}'PL$ to check for satisfiability of sentences written in $\mathcal{H}'I$. This leads to the expected result

Corollary 4. *If I is decidable then $\mathcal{H}'I$ is also decidable.*

Note that the proof of Theorem 3 paves the way for an example decision algorithm, that is, an algorithm able not only to answer "yes" or "no" to the question "Is ρ satisfiable?", but also to build a model that satisfies sentence ρ, if it exists. Technically, to construct such an algorithm one also needs to have example decision algorithms for both I and $\mathcal{H}'PL$. The latter has at least one prover that meets this requirement [12]. Then, as indicated in the proof, through a $\mathcal{H}'PL$'s decision procedure, one extracts a Kripke frame for ρ in which suitable models of I are "attached" given its example decision algorithm for I.

Finally, note that the decision algorithm for $\mathcal{H}'I$, conceptualised in Theorem 3, may be computationally hard. Indeed, in order to define $\eta(\rho)$ the decision algorithm for I must be executed 2^n times where $n = |B_\rho|$.

In addition, if we want the algorithm to give example models, the decision procedure for I must also be executed a number of times that can reach the number of worlds in the model built by the decision procedure for $\mathcal{H}'PL$.

4.3   Soundness and Completeness

In this section we focus on the entailment system for $\mathcal{H}I$, i.e., on functor $Prf^{\mathcal{H}I}$, to show that the rules in $Prf^{\mathcal{H}I}$ are both sound and complete. Note that for hybridised logics equipped with the corresponding generated proof systems $Prf^{\mathcal{H}I}$, proving soundness and completeness boils down to show the equivalence,

$$\rho \text{ is satisfiable iff } \rho \longrightarrow \bot \text{ is not in } Prf^{\mathcal{H}I}(\Delta, \Sigma)$$

Recall also that it is assumed that the base institution has the typical boolean connectives and the explicit satisfaction property, as well as that its proof system, Prf^I, is sound, complete and has the *reductio ad absurdum* property.

Theorem 4. *If Prf^I is sound, then $Prf^{\mathcal{H}I}$ is also sound.*

Proof. Consider signature $(\Delta, \Sigma) \in |Sign^{\mathcal{H}I}|$ and $\rho \in Sen^{\mathcal{H}I}(\Delta, \Sigma)$. If $Prf^{\mathcal{H}I}$ is sound then sentence ρ, being satisfiable means that there is no proof arrow $\rho \longrightarrow \bot$ in $Prf^{\mathcal{H}I}(\Delta, \Sigma)$. If such an arrow exists, however, it must come from some of the conditions imposed to $Prf^{\mathcal{H}I}(\Delta, \Sigma)$, i.e., some of these conditions must be unsound. We check each one:

1. the condition that proof arrows $\emptyset \longrightarrow \rho$ in $Prf^I(\Sigma)$ come to $Prf^{\mathcal{H}I}(\Delta, \Sigma)$ is, by assumption, sound.

2. the axioms and proof rules from Table 1 were already proved to be sound (*cf.* [3]).
3. composition, inclusion and product rules are, by definition, sound.

The proof of completeness is more complex. For this we resort to a procedure similar to the one used for proving decidability.

Theorem 5. *Consider a signature* $(\Delta, \Sigma) \in |Sign^{\mathcal{H}I}|$ *and* $\rho \in Sen^{\mathcal{H}I}(\Delta, \Sigma)$. *If there is no arrow* $\rho \longrightarrow \bot$ *in* $Prf^{\mathcal{H}I}(\Delta, \Sigma)$ *then there is also no arrow* $\sigma(\rho) \longrightarrow \bot$ *in* $Prf^{\mathcal{H}PL}(\Delta, Prop)$,

Proof. First notice that rules in Table 1 do not distinguish ρ from $\sigma(\rho)$, that is, any such rule may be applied to both sentences. Then observe that, since Table 1 contains all classical tautologies, Prf^{PL} does not bring new rules to $Prf^{\mathcal{H}PL}$ and therefore rules in $Prf^{\mathcal{H}PL}$ are also in $Prf^{\mathcal{H}I}$. Both remarks entail that if there are rules in $Prf^{\mathcal{H}PL}$ that can generate arrow $\sigma(\rho) \longrightarrow \bot$, then the same set of rules (also present in $Prf^{\mathcal{H}I}$) can surely generate it there.

Next, we show the converse of Theorem 5 holds as well. For this we define a function to play a role similar to that played by η in sub-section 4.2.

Definition 16. *Given a signature* $(\Delta, \Sigma) \in |Sign^{\mathcal{H}I}|$ *and* $\rho \in Sen^{\mathcal{H}I}(\Delta, \Sigma)$ *we define,*

$$\eta'(\rho) = \begin{cases} \bigvee \{\chi \in \Omega_\rho | \chi \longrightarrow \bot \text{ is in } Prf^I\}, & \text{if } B_\rho \neq \emptyset \\ \bot, & \text{otherwise} \end{cases}$$

Corollary 5. *Clearly if there is no arrow* $\rho \longrightarrow \bot$ *in* $Prf^{\mathcal{H}I}(\Delta, \Sigma)$ *then there is also no arrow* $(\rho \wedge A \neg \eta'(\rho)) \longrightarrow \bot$ *in* $Prf^{\mathcal{H}I}(\Delta, \Sigma)$.

Lemma 4. *Consider a model* $(W, R, m) \in |Mod^{\mathcal{H}PL}(\Delta, Prop)|$ *such that* $(W, R, m) \models \sigma(\rho \wedge A \neg \eta'(\rho))$. *For any* $\chi \in \Omega_\rho$, *if* $\sigma'[\chi]$ *is satisfied by a model member of* $img(m)$, χ *is satisfiable.*

Proof. If χ is unsatisfiable then, by definition of η' and completeness of Prf^I, occurs as one of the literals in $\eta'(\rho)$, hence no model member of $img(m)$ may satisfy it.

Theorem 6. *If* Prf^I *is complete then* $Prf^{\mathcal{H}I}$ *is also complete.*

Proof. We want to prove that given a signature $(\Delta, \Sigma) \in |Sign^{\mathcal{H}I}|$ and a sentence $\rho \in Sen^{\mathcal{H}I}(\Delta, \Sigma)$, if no arrow $\rho \longrightarrow \bot$ exists in $Prf^{\mathcal{H}I}(\Delta, \Sigma)$ then ρ is satisfiable.

Hence, let us assume that there is no arrow $\rho \longrightarrow \bot$ in $Prf^{\mathcal{H}I}(\Delta, \Sigma)$, which by Corollary 5, entails that there is no proof arrow $\sigma(\rho \wedge A \neg \eta'(\rho)) \longrightarrow \bot$ in $Prf^{\mathcal{H}PL}(\Delta, Prop)$ and therefore means that $\sigma(\rho \wedge A \neg \eta'(\rho))$ is satisfiable. In other words, we have a model $M = (W, R, m) \in |Mod^{\mathcal{H}PL}(\Delta, Prop)|$ such that $M \models^w \sigma(\rho \wedge A \neg \eta'(\rho))$ for some $w \in W$. Then, by Lemma 4, we are able to define a model $(W, R, m') \in |Mod^{\mathcal{H}I}(\Delta, \Sigma)|$, in which, for any $w \in W$, $m'(w)$ is a model for χ where $\sigma'[\chi] = \sigma'[\Omega_\rho^{m(w)}]$.

It remains to show that $(W, R, m') \models^w \rho$ for some $w \in W$. Since models (W, R, m) and (W, R, m') have the same Kripke structure satisfied by sentences ρ and $\sigma(\rho \wedge A \neg \eta'(\rho))$, it is enough to show that, for all $\chi \in \Omega_\rho$, $m(w) \models \sigma'[\chi]$ entails that $m'(w) \models \chi$ for any $w \in W$. Actually, this is a direct consequence of the fact that $m(w) \models \sigma'[\Omega_\rho^{m(w)}]$ entails $m'(w) \models \Omega_\rho^{m(w)}$, for all $w \in W$, which comes from the definition of (W, R, m').

5   Conclusions and Future Work

This paper lays the first steps towards the development of (dedicated) proof tools for hybridised logics, by providing an effective decision algorithm for the satisfiability problem. Additionally the systematic hybridisation of the calculus of a base logic was addressed, and shown to preserve both soundness and completeness.

The next step, from an engineering point of view, is, of course, to develop such a generic, dedicated prover for hybridised logics. A comparison with the strategy of using the parametrised translation to FOL will then be due.

In a similar line of research, lies the development of an alternative decision algorithm, that potentially overcomes the problem detected in the definition of η, which involves calling the decision procedure of the base logic 2^n times, for n the number of base sentences in the sentence under consideration. Such an algorithm may be based on the tableau technique (for instance, the one implemented in [12]) which opens a number of branches as the possible ways to build a model satisfying a given sentence. If the sentence is unsatisfiable then all branches must be closed. If any branch remains open then the decision procedure of the base logic is called to try to close it. Thus, the number of times the decision procedure of the base logic is called is much smaller than in the approach discussed here.

Other results in the literature abstract the combination of logics pattern by considering the "top logic" itself arbitrary. Such is the case of what is called *parametrisation* of logics in [4] by C. Caleiro, A. Sernadas and C. Sernadas. Similarly , the recent method of *importing* logics suggested by J. Rasga, A. Sernadas and C. Sernadas [16] aims at formalising this kind of asymmetric combinations resorting to a graph-theoretic approach. In both cases some decidability and completeness results are given. It should be interesting to see in which ways the hybridisation method relates to these works.

Acknowledgments. This work is funded by ERDF - European Regional Development Fund, through the COMPETE Programme, and by National Funds through FCT within project FCOMP-01-0124-FEDER-028923. M. A. Martins was also supported by the project PEst-OE/MAT/UI4106/2014.

References

1. Areces, C., ten Cate, B.: Hybrid logics. In: Blackburn, P., Wolter, F., van Benthem, J. (eds.) Handbook of Modal Logics. Elsevier (2006)
2. Baltazar, P.: Probabilization of logics: Completeness and decidability. Logica Universalis **7**(4), 403–440 (2013)
3. Braüner, T.: Proof-Theory of Propositional Hybrid Logic. Hybrid Logic and its Proof-Theory (2011)
4. Caleiro, C., Sernadas, C., Sernadas, A.: Parameterisation of logics. In: Fiadeiro, J.L. (ed.) WADT 1998. LNCS, vol. 1589, pp. 48–63. Springer, Heidelberg (1999)
5. Diaconescu, R.: Institution-independent Model Theory. Birkhäuser, Basel (2008)
6. Diaconescu, R.: Institutional semantics for many-valued logics. Fuzzy Sets Syst. **218**, 32–52 (2013)
7. Diaconescu, R., Stefaneas, P.: Ultraproducts and possible worlds semantics in institutions. Theor. Comput. Sci. **379**(1–2), 210–230 (2007)
8. Fiadeiro, J., Sernadas, A.: Structuring theories on consequence. In: Sannella, D., Tarlecki, A. (eds.) Abstract Data Types 1987. LNCS, vol. 332, pp. 44–72. Springer, Heidelberg (1988)
9. Finger, M., Gabbay, D.: Adding a temporal dimension to a logic system. Journal of Logic, Language and Information **1**(3), 203–233 (1992)
10. Goguen, J.A., Burstall, R.M.: Institutions: abstract model theory for specification and programming. J. ACM **39**, 95–146 (1992)
11. Goguen, J.A., Meseguer, J.: Models and equality for logical programming. In: Ehrig, H., Kowalski, R., Levi, G., Montanari, U. (eds.) TAPSOFT 1987 and CFLP 1987. LNCS, vol. 250, pp. 1–22. Springer, Heidelberg (1987)
12. Hoffmann, G., Areces, C.: Htab: a terminating tableaux system for hybrid logic. Electr. Notes Theor. Comput. Sci. **231**, 3–19 (2009)
13. Madeira, A., Faria, J.M., Martins, M.A., Barbosa, L.S.: Hybrid specification of reactive systems: an institutional approach. In: Barthe, G., Pardo, A., Schneider, G. (eds.) SEFM 2011. LNCS, vol. 7041, pp. 269–285. Springer, Heidelberg (2011)
14. Martins, M.A., Madeira, A., Diaconescu, R., Barbosa, L.S.: Hybridization of institutions. In: Corradini, A., Klin, B., Cîrstea, C. (eds.) CALCO 2011. LNCS, vol. 6859, pp. 283–297. Springer, Heidelberg (2011)
15. Neves, R., Madeira, A., Martins, M.A., Barbosa, L.S.: Hybridisation at work. In: Heckel, R., Milius, S. (eds.) CALCO 2013. LNCS, vol. 8089, pp. 340–345. Springer, Heidelberg (2013)
16. Rasga, J., Sernadas, A., Sernadas, C.: Importing logics: Soundness and completeness preservation. Studia Logica **101**(1), 117–155 (2013)

Parameterisation of Three-Valued Abstractions

Nils Timm$^{(\boxtimes)}$ and Stefan Gruner

Department of Computer Science, University of Pretoria, Pretoria, South Africa
{ntimm,sgruner}@cs.up.ac.za

Abstract. Three-valued abstraction is an established technique in software model checking. It proceeds by generating a state space model over the values *true, false* and *unknown*, where the latter value is used to represent the loss of information due to abstraction. Temporal logic properties can then be evaluated on such models. In case of an *unknown* result, the abstraction is iteratively refined. In this paper, we introduce *parameterised three-valued model checking*. In our new type of models, unknown parts can be either associated with the constant value *unknown* or with expressions over boolean parameters. Our parameterisation is an alternative way to state that the truth value of certain predicates or transitions is actually not known and that the checked property has to yield the same result under each possible parameter instantiation. A novel feature of our approach is that it allows for establishing logical connections between parameters: While *unknown* parts in pure three-valued models are never related to each other, our parameterisation approach enables to represent facts like 'a certain pair of transitions has unknown but complementary truth values', or 'the value of a predicate is unknown but remains constant along all states of a certain path'. We demonstrate that such facts can be automatically derived from the system to be verified and that covering these facts in an abstract model can be crucial for the success and efficiency of checking temporal logic properties. Moreover, we introduce an automatic verification framework based on counterexample-guided abstraction refinement and parameterisation.

1 Introduction

Predicate abstraction [2] is an established technique for reducing the complexity of temporal logic model checking. It proceeds by generating a state space model of the software system to be analysed. In this model, concrete states of the system are mapped to abstract states over a finite set of predicates, and admissible executions of the system are represented by sequences of transitions between states. Traditional predicate abstraction techniques are based on a boolean domain for predicates and on an over-approximation of the concrete state space. Thus, only universal properties are preserved under this form of abstraction. If checking a universal property for an abstract model yields *false*, it cannot be concluded that the original system violates this property as well. In this case, model checking additionally returns an *abstract counterexample* - a path in the model that refutes the property. In order to gain certainty about whether this counterexample is

© Springer International Publishing Switzerland 2015
C. Braga and N. Martí-Oliet (Eds.): SBMF 2014, LNCS 8941, pp. 162–178, 2015.
DOI: 10.1007/978-3-319-15075-8_11

spurious or corresponds to a real path, it has to be simulated on the original system. The simulation of counterexamples involves a partial exploration of the concrete state space, and thus, can be exceedingly costly. Spurious counterexamples are typically ruled out via *counterexample-guided abstraction refinement* (CEGAR) [4]: Further predicates over the variables of the system are iteratively added to the model until a level of abstraction is reached where the property can be either definitely proved or a real counterexample can be found. The application of CEGAR does, however, not guarantee that eventually a model can be constructed that is both precise enough for a definite outcome and small enough to be manageable with the available computational resources.

More recent approaches [3,13,18] to abstraction refinement for model checking are based on a domain for predicates with the truth values *true, false* and *unknown*. Corresponding three-valued models with the additional value *unknown* enable to explicitly model the loss of information due to abstraction. In comparison to boolean abstractions, the three-valued approach is capable of preserving universal *and* existential properties. Hence, all definite results in three-valued model checking can be directly transferred to the original system. Only an *unknown* result necessitates iterative refinement. In the latter case, an *unconfirmed counterexample* – a potential error path in the model with *unknown* transitions and predicates – is returned. Unconfirmed counterexamples directly hint at necessary refinement steps. Thus, the costly simulation of counterexamples on the original system is not required in the three-valued setting. Model checking three-valued abstractions can be conducted at the same cost as checking boolean abstractions, but it additionally comes along with the aforementioned advantages.

Continuative work in this field has shown that the precision of model checking three-valued abstractions can be increased by the concept of *generalised model checking* (GMC) [7]. While standard three-valued model checking (3MC) [3,13,18] is based on a special *three-valued* semantics that enables the direct evaluation of temporal logic formulae on three-valued models, the idea of GMC is to construct *all* boolean concretisations of a three-valued model. Then classical two-valued model checking is applied to each concretisation and it is checked whether the results are consistent, i.e. whether either all results are *true* or whether all are *false*. In case of consistency, the result can be transferred to the original system. GMC generally yields more definite results than 3MC. Hence, the application of GMC instead of 3MC can reduce the number of necessary refinement iterations in abstraction-based verification. However, the 3MC problem is PSPACE-complete, whereas the GMC problem is even EXP-complete: Number and size of concretisations can be exponential in the size of the three-valued model. Thus, GMC is rather of theoretical than of practical interest. Most existing three-valued abstraction-based verification frameworks, e.g. [8,13,14], rely on standard 3MC and try to compensate the lack of precision with additional refinement steps.

Here, we introduce *parameterised three-valued model checking* (PMC) which is a hybrid of three-valued and generalised model checking. Predicates and transitions in our parameterised three-valued models can be either associated with the values *true*, *false* or *unknown* – or with expressions over boolean parameters. Our parameterisation is an alternative way to state that the truth value of certain predicates or transitions is actually not known and that the checked property has to yield the same result under each parameter instantiation. PMC is thus conducted via evaluating a temporal logic formula under all parameter instantiations and checking whether the results are consistent. In contrast to GMC, parameterised three-valued model checking reduces to multiple instances of standard three-valued model checking, since the instantiation only affects parameters but not the explicit truth value *unknown*. Sizes of instantiations are always linear in the size of the parameterised three-valued model. Moreover, parameterisation particularly allows to establish logical connections between *unknowns* in the abstract model: While *unknown* parts in 3MC and GMC are never related to each other, our parameterisation approach enables to represent facts like 'a certain pair of transitions has unknown but complementary truth values', or 'the value of a predicate is unknown but remains constant along all states of a certain path'. We demonstrate that such facts can be automatically derived from the software system to be verified and that covering these facts in an abstract model can be crucial for the success and efficiency of checking temporal logic properties. In particular, we introduce an automatic verification framework for concurrent systems based on parameterised three-valued model checking: Starting with pure three-valued abstraction, in each iteration either classical refinement or parameterisation of *unknown* parts is applied until a definite result in verification can be obtained. The decisions for refinement or parameterisation are automatically made based on unconfirmed counterexamples. For several verification tasks our hybrid approach can significantly outperform the pure three-valued approach. Our work includes the definition of parameterisation rules for three-valued abstractions and a proven theorem which states that PMC is sound if parameterisation is applied according to the rules.

2 Background: Three-Valued Model Checking

We start with a brief introduction to three-valued state space models, here three-valued Kripke structures, and the evaluation of temporal logic properties on them. The key feature of these Kripke structures is a third truth value $\perp$ (i.e. *unknown*) for transitions and labellings, which can be used to model uncertainty.

Definition 1 (Three-Valued Kripke Structure). *A three-valued Kripke structure over a set of atomic predicates AP is a tuple $K = (S, R, L, \mathbb{F})$ where*

- *S is a finite set of states,*
- *$R : S \times S \rightarrow \{true, \perp, false\}$ is a transition function with $\forall s \in S : \exists s' \in S : R(s, s') \in \{true, \perp\}$,*

- $L : S \times AP \rightarrow \{true, \bot, false\}$ *is a labelling function that associates a truth value with each predicate in each state,*
- $\mathbb{F} \subseteq \mathcal{P}(R^{-1}(\{true, \bot\}))$ *is a set of fairness constraints where each constraint $F \in \mathbb{F}$ is a set of* non-false *transitions.*

An example for a Kripke structure K over a set $AP = \{p\}$ is depicted below.

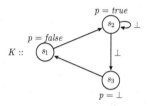

A path π of a three-valued Kripke structure K is an infinite sequence of states $s_1 s_2 s_3 \ldots$ with $R(s_i, s_{i+1}) \in \{true, \bot\}$. π_i denotes the i-th state of π, whereas π^i denotes the i-th suffix $\pi_i \pi_{i+1} \pi_{i+2} \ldots$ of π. A path π is fair if it takes infinitely often a transition from every fairness constraint $F \in \mathbb{F}$. By $\Pi(K, s)$ we denote the set of all fair paths of K starting in $s \in S$. Paths are considered for the evaluation of temporal logic properties of Kripke structures. Here we use the linear temporal logic (LTL) for specifying properties.

Definition 2. *Syntax of LTL] Let AP be a set of atomic predicates and $p \in AP$. The* syntax of LTL formulae ψ *is given by*

$$\psi ::= p \mid \neg\psi \mid \psi \vee \psi \mid \psi \wedge \psi \mid \mathbf{X}\psi \mid \mathbf{F}\psi \mid \mathbf{G}\psi \mid \psi\mathbf{U}\psi.$$

Due to the extended domain for truth values in three-valued Kripke structures, the evaluation of LTL formulae is not based on classical two-valued logic. In three-valued model checking we operate under the three-valued Kleene logic $\mathbb{K}_3$ [6] whose semantics is given by the truth tables below.

$\wedge$	$true$	$\bot$	$false$
$true$	$true$	$\bot$	$false$
$\bot$	$\bot$	$\bot$	$false$
$false$	$false$	$false$	$false$

$\vee$	$true$	$\bot$	$false$
$true$	$true$	$true$	$true$
$\bot$	$true$	$\bot$	$\bot$
$false$	$true$	$\bot$	$false$

$\neg$	
$true$	$false$
$\bot$	$\bot$
$false$	$true$

For $\mathbb{K}_3$ we have a reflexive *information ordering* $\leq_{\mathbb{K}_3}$ (in words: 'less or equal definite than') with $\bot \leq_{\mathbb{K}_3} true$, $\bot \leq_{\mathbb{K}_3} false$, and $true$, $false$ incomparable. Based on $\mathbb{K}_3$, linear temporal logic formulae can be evaluated on paths of three-valued Kripke structures according to the following definition.

Definition 3 (Three-Valued Evaluation of LTL). *Let $K = (S, R, L, \mathbb{F})$ over AP be a three-valued Kripke structure. Then the* evaluation *of an LTL formula ψ on a fair path π of K, written $[\pi \models \psi]$, is inductively defined as follows*

$$
\begin{aligned}
[\pi \models p] \quad &:= \quad L(\pi_1, p) \\
[\pi \models \neg\psi] \quad &:= \quad \neg\,[\pi \models \psi] \\
[\pi \models \psi \vee \psi'] \quad &:= \quad [\pi \models \psi] \;\vee\; [\pi \models \psi'] \\
[\pi \models \mathbf{X}\psi] \quad &:= \quad R(\pi_1, \pi_2) \wedge [\pi^2 \models \psi] \\
[\pi \models \mathbf{G}\psi] \quad &:= \quad \bigwedge_{i\in\mathbb{N}} \big(R(\pi_i, \pi_{i+1}) \wedge [\pi^i \models \psi] \big) \\
[\pi \models \mathbf{F}\psi] \quad &:= \quad \bigvee_{i\in\mathbb{N}} \Big([\pi^i \models \psi] \wedge \bigwedge_{0\leq j<i} R(\pi_i, \pi_{i+1}) \Big) \\
[\pi \models \psi \mathbf{U}\psi'] \quad &:= \quad \bigvee_{i\in\mathbb{N}} \Big([\pi^i \models \psi'] \wedge \bigwedge_{0\leq j<i} \big(R(\pi_j, \pi_{j+1}) \wedge [\pi^j \models \psi] \big) \Big)
\end{aligned}
$$

The evaluation of LTL formulae on entire three-valued Kripke structures is what we call *three-valued model checking* [3].

Definition 4 (Three-Valued LTL Model Checking). *Let $K = (S, R, L, \mathbb{F})$ over AP be a three-valued Kripke structure. Moreover, let ψ be an LTL formula over AP. The value of ψ in a state s of K, written $[K, s \models \psi]$, is defined as*

$$
[K, s \models \psi] \quad := \quad \bigwedge_{\pi\in\Pi(K,s)} [\pi \models \psi]
$$

In three-valued model checking there exist three possible outcomes: *true*, *false* and $\bot$. Three-valued model checking reduces to classical two-valued model checking if the Kripke structure K is actually two-valued, i.e. $R^{-1}(\bot) = \varnothing$ and $L^{-1}(\bot) = \varnothing$. In this case, only the outcomes *true* and *false* are possible. For our example Kripke structure $[K, s_1 \models \mathbf{G}p]$ yields *false*, whereas $[K, s_1 \models \mathbf{GF}p]$ yields *unknown*. $\mathbf{G}p$ is a temporal logic formula that characterises a typical *safety* property, while $\mathbf{GF}p$ characterises a *liveness* property. Safety and liveness are the most vital requirements in software verification. In our approach, we therefore particularly focus on these two kinds of properties.

For the sake of completeness, we also briefly review generalised model checking (for more details see [7]). Under GMC, $[K, s \models \psi]$ yields *true* iff $[K', s \models \psi]$ is *true* for all concretisations K' of K, where a concretisation is a two-valued K' such that $[K, s \models \psi] \leq_{\mathbb{K}_3} [K', s \models \psi]$ for all LTL formulae ψ. The definition of $[K, s \models \psi] = false$ is analogous. In all remaining cases $[K, s \models \psi]$ yields $\bot$.

3   Parameterised Three-Valued Model Checking

State space models constructed by three-valued abstraction techniques [8,13,14] are typically represented as (pure) three-valued Kripke structures. Here we introduce a generalisation called *parameterised three-valued Kripke structures*, and we define model checking for these structures. Later we will see that *parameterised three-valued model checking* (PMC) for three-valued abstractions can significantly enhance the precision of verification.

Definition 5 (Parameterised Three-Valued Kripke Structure). *A parameterised three-valued Kripke structure over AP and a set of boolean parameters $X = \{x_1, \ldots, x_m\}$ is a parameterised tuple $K(\overset{m}{x}) = (S, R(\overset{m}{x}), L(\overset{m}{x}), \mathbb{F}(\overset{m}{x}))$ where*

- S is a finite set of states,
- $R(\overset{m}{x}) : S \times S \rightarrow \{true, \bot, false\} \cup BE(X)$ is a transition function with $\forall\, s \in S : \exists\, s' \in S : R(\overset{m}{x})(s, s') \in \{true, \bot\} \cup BE(X)$ where $BE(X)$ denotes the set of boolean expressions over X,
- $L(\overset{m}{x}) : S \times AP \rightarrow \{true, \bot, false\} \cup BE(X)$ is a labelling function that associates a truth value or a parameter expression with each predicate in each state,
- $\mathbb{F}(\overset{m}{x}) \subseteq \mathcal{P}(R^{-1}(\overset{m}{x})(\{true, \bot\} \cup BE(X)))$ is a set of fairness constraints where each constraint $F \in \mathbb{F}(\overset{m}{x})$ is a set of non-false transitions.

Note that $(\overset{m}{x})$ is an abbreviation for the parameter tuple $(x_1, \ldots, x_m)$. An instantiation of a parameterised three-valued Kripke structure $K(\overset{m}{x})$ is a *pure* three-valued Kripke structure $K(\overset{m}{a})$ where $(\overset{m}{a}) \in \{true, false\}^m$. Hence, all parameters are substituted by *boolean* truth values. However, predicates and transitions that were not parameterised in $K(\overset{m}{x})$ may still hold the value *unknown* in $K(\overset{m}{a})$. If the current tuple of parameters or truth values is clear from the context, we will not explicitly mention it, i.e. we will just refer to R, L and $\mathbb{F}$. An example for a parameterised three-valued Kripke structure together with all its pure three-valued instantiations is shown in the figure below.

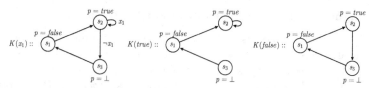

For evaluating temporal logic formulae on parameterised three-valued Kripke structures we consider all possible instantiations.

Definition 6 (Parameterised Three-Valued LTL Model Checking). *Let* $K(\overset{m}{x}) = (S, R(\overset{m}{x}), L(\overset{m}{x}), \mathbb{F}(\overset{m}{x}))$ *be a parameterised three-valued Kripke structure over* AP *and* $X = \{x_1, \ldots, x_m\}$. *Moreover, let* ψ *be an LTL formula over* AP. *The value of* ψ *in a state* s *of* $K(\overset{m}{x})$, *written* $[K(\overset{m}{x}), s \models \psi]$, *is defined as*

$$\left[K(\overset{m}{x}), s \models \psi\right] := \begin{cases} true & if \; \bigwedge_{(\overset{m}{a})\in\{t,f\}^m} \left(\left[K(\overset{m}{a}), s \models \psi\right] = true\right) \\ false & if \; \bigwedge_{(\overset{m}{a})\in\{t,f\}^m} \left(\left[K(\overset{m}{a}), s \models \psi\right] = false\right) \\ \bot & else \end{cases}$$

Thus, if checking a temporal logic property yields *true* for all instantiations, the result is transferred to the parameterised Kripke structure. The same holds for *false* results for all instantiations. In all other cases PMC returns *unknown*. For our recent example, we get $[K(x_1), s_1 \models \mathbf{GF}p] = true$ since $\mathbf{GF}p$ holds for both $K(true)$ and $K(false)$. In contrast to our example from Section 2, the two outgoing transitions of state s_2 are no longer *unknown* but parameterised. Moreover, we capture the fact that the associated transition values are *complementary*, which gives us the necessary precision for a definite result in verification.

Subsequently, we will see that such facts can be automatically derived from the control flow and program code of the modelled system in the sense that the corresponding parameterisation gives us a sound abstraction. Furthermore, we will show how parameterised three-valued model checking can be effectively integrated into an automatic abstraction refinement-based verification procedure.

4 Application to Three-Valued Abstractions

Three-valued model checking [3] is used in many abstraction-based verification frameworks for software systems [1,8,10,13]. An effective state space reduction technique for concurrent software systems is *three-valued spotlight abstraction* [12,14,15]. In previous works [16,17], we have demonstrated that verifying concurrent systems via spotlight abstraction and three-valued model checking can significantly outperform approaches based on boolean predicate abstraction [2]. In this section, we give a brief introduction to concurrent systems and spotlight abstraction (for more details see [12]). Moreover, we show how *parameterisation* can be applied to three-valued Kripke structures constructed by spotlight abstraction and how this can increase the efficiency of verification.

4.1 Spotlight Abstraction for Concurrent Systems

A concurrent system Sys consists of a number of asynchronous processes composed in parallel: $Sys = \|_{i=1}^{n} Proc_i$. It is defined over a set of variables $Var = Var_s \cup \bigcup_{i=1}^{n} Var_i$ where Var_s is a set of shared variables and $Var_1, \ldots, Var_n$ are sets of local variables associated with the processes $Proc_1, \ldots, Proc_n$, respectively. A process corresponds to a finite sequence of locations where each location is associated with an operation op on the variables in $Var_s \cup Var_i$. Operations are of the form $op = assume(e) : v_1 := e_1, \ldots, v_k := e_k$ where $e, e_1, \ldots, e_k$ are expressions over $Var_s \cup Var_i = \{v_1, \ldots, v_k\}$. Hence, an operation consists of an assume part, also called *guard*, and a list of assignments. Executing the guard blocks the execution of the assignments until the expression e evaluates to *true*. We omit the guard if e is constantly *true*. The current location of a process $Proc_i$ can be regarded as the value of an additional local counter variable pc_i over the process' locations $Loc_i = \{1_i, \ldots, L_i\}$. Locations may also be associated with compound operations, which consist of one or more sub-operations nested inside a control structure. Compound operations in our systems are, amongst others, *if-then-else* and *while-do*. An example for a concurrent system is depicted below.

$$v_1, \ldots, v_k : \textbf{integer}$$

$$Proc_1 :: \begin{bmatrix} 1: [\ \ldots &] \\ 2: \textbf{while } (v_1 > 0) \textbf{ do} \\ \quad 3: [\ \ldots &] \\ 4: progress \\ 5: [\ \ldots &] \end{bmatrix} \ \| \ Proc_2 :: \begin{bmatrix} 1: [\ \ldots &] \\ 2: v_1 := f(v_2, \ldots, v_k) \\ 3: [\ \ldots &] \end{bmatrix} \ \| \ \ldots \ \| \ Proc_n$$

Here we have a composition of n processes operating on the shared variables $v_1, \ldots, v_k$. A liveness property to verify might be whether $Proc_1$ always repeatedly reaches *progress*, which we assume is an arbitrary assertion over $Proc_1$'s variables. Subsequently, we show how this verification task can be approached by three-valued spotlight abstraction.

Spotlight abstraction involves the partition of the processes of the system into a *spotlight* and a *shade*. Predicate abstraction is applied to the spotlight, while the shade processes are abstracted away by summarising them in one approximative component. The state space of the resulting abstract system can be straightforwardly modelled as a (pure) three-valued Kripke structure. In our current verification task, the relevant process for the property of interest is $Proc_1$, which we put into the spotlight: $Spot(Proc) = \{Proc_1\}$, whereas the remaining system is for now kept in the shade: $Shade(Proc) = \{Proc_2, \ldots, Proc_n\}$. Next, a set of so-called *spotlight predicates* over the system variables is selected, here we choose $Spot(Pred) = \{progress, (v_1 > 0)\}$. By applying three-valued predicate abstraction to the spotlight processes, we obtain an abstract process $Proc_1^a$ with the same control flow as $Proc_1$ but with operations abstracted over $Spot(Pred)$. The processes in the shade are summarised to one approximative process $Proc_{Shade}$. Due to the loss of information about the shade, $Proc_{Shade}$ might set predicates over shared variables to the value $\bot$. Our abstract system now looks as follows: $Sys^a = Proc_1^a \parallel Proc_{Shade}$. The state space of Sys^a can be modelled as a pure three-valued Kripke structure over $AP = Spot(Pred) \cup \{(pc_i = j) \mid Proc_i \in Spot(Proc), j \in Loc_i\}$ where $(pc_i = j)$ refers to the program counter of $Proc_i$, and each definite model checking result obtained for this structure can be transferred to the concrete system [12]. A three-valued Kripke structure K corresponding to Sys^a is depicted in part (a) of the figure below. For simplicity, we only show the program counter predicates that are currently *true*.

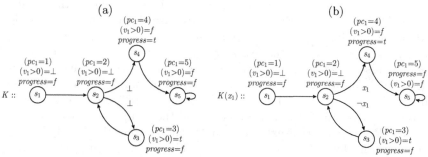

Note that the control flow of spotlight processes is always preserved under spotlight abstraction. Hence, each transition of K associated with the spotlight matches with a specific operation of the spotlight process $Proc_1$. For K and its set of atomic predicates $AP = \{progress, (v_1 > 0)\} \cup \{(pc_1 = j) \mid j \in Loc_1\}$ we can formalise our property of interest as the LTL formula **GF**$progress$ and then apply standard three-valued model checking, i.e. check $[K, s_1 \models \mathbf{GF} progress]$. The current abstraction is not precise enough for a definite result in verification. Since there exist processes in the shade that operate on the shared variable v_1, the value of the predicate $(v_1 > 0)$ in the states s_1 and s_2 is $\bot$. Thus, it is also unknown whether the body of the *while*-loop can be executed via the transition (s_2, s_3), or whether the loop can be eventually left via (s_2, s_4). The automatic abstraction refinement procedure introduced in [17] would now itera-tively shift processes from the shade to the spotlight until it can be definitively shown *which* branch of the *while*-loop can be actually taken. However, due to transitive dependencies – $Proc_2$ modifies v_1, but in turn depends on $v_2, \dots, v_k$ which may be modified by other shade processes as well – such a refinement can be exceedingly costly or can even lead to a failure of verification because of state explosion. A closer look at our simple example structure tell us that, regardless of which branch of the loop will be ever taken, *progress* will never hold repeatedly. Hence, the evaluation of **GF***progress* on K should yield *false*. However, the standard three-valued LTL semantics (compare Section 2) does not allow us to draw this conclusion. In the following we will see that automated *parameterisation* can give us the necessary precision for a definite verification result – at considerably less cost than classical abstraction refinement.

4.2   Parameterisation of Three-Valued Abstractions

As we just have seen, $[K, s_1 \models \mathbf{GF}\textit{progress}]$ yields $\bot$. Nevertheless, a $\bot$-result in 3MC always comes along with an *unconfirmed counterexample* – a potential error path in the Kripke structure with some *unknown* transitions or predicates. Four our running example the path $\pi = s_1 s_2 s_4 s_5 s_5 \dots$ is an unconfirmed coun-terexample. Such a path is typically used for *counterexample-guided abstraction refinement* (CEGAR) [4]: In our case, the $\bot$-transition (s_2, s_4) would be identified as the reason for uncertainty, and shade processes that modify the *if*-condition $(v_1 > 0)$ associated with (s_2, s_4) would be iteratively shifted to the spotlight. Now we will show that counterexamples can also be exploited for the parame-terisation of three-valued Kripke structures. We first illustrate parameterisation based on our running example and then provide the general rules for it.

Our method detects that the reason for uncertainty, the $\bot$-transition (s_2, s_4) along π, is associated with a *complementary branch* in the original system: a branch of the control flow of a single process with complementary branching conditions – here $(v_1 > 0)$ and $\neg(v_1 > 0)$. Instead of applying classical CEGAR, a fresh boolean parameter x_1 is introduced and the transition is parameterised as follows: $R(s_2, s_4) := x_1$. Next, the complementary transition (s_2, s_3) is iden-tified and parameterised by $R(s_2, s_3) := \neg x_1$. The corresponding parameterised three-valued Kripke structure $K(x_1)$ is depicted in part (b) of the figure on the previous page. Applying parameterised three-valued model checking, i.e. verify-ing $[K(x_1), s_1 \models \mathbf{GF}\textit{progress}]$ immediately returns *false*. Thus, for our running example a definite result in verification only requires the introduction of a single parameter and the consideration of the two instantiations $K(\textit{true})$ and $K(\textit{false})$ of $K(x_1)$. In contrast, a corresponding pure three-valued approach would require a large number of additional refinement steps and thus would most likely fail due to state explosion. Also the application of the computationally more expen-sive GMC would not be successful, since it cannot establish the complementary relation between (s_2, s_4) and (s_2, s_3). The following rule generalises the parame-terisation of complementary branches in three-valued Kripke structures.

Rule I (Parameterisation of Complementary Branch Transitions). *Let* $Sys = \|_{i=1}^{n} Proc_i$ *be a concurrent system and* $Spot = Spot(Proc) \cup Spot(Pred)$ *be a spotlight abstraction for Sys. Let K be a three-valued KS over* $AP = Spot(Pred) \cup \{(pc_i = j) \mid Proc_i \in Spot(Proc) \wedge j \in Loc_i\}$ *that models the abstract state space corresponding to Sys and Spot, and let s_1 be a state of K. Moreover, let ψ be a safety or liveness LTL formula and checking $[K, s_1 \models \psi]$ yields $\bot$. Let π be the unconfirmed counterexample returned by model checking which runs through a finite number of different transitions. The transitions of K can be parameterised as follows: For each transition (s, s') along π with $R(s, s') = \bot$, check if (s, s') is part of a complementary branch, i.e.: (s, s') is associated with a guard operation assume(e) of a spotlight process $Proc_i$, where e is a boolean expression – and moreover, there exists a state s'' such that (s, s'') is associated with a complementary guard operation assume$(\neg e)$ of $Proc_i$. Then introduce a fresh parameter x_j and set $R(s, s') = x_j$ and $R(s, s'') = \neg x_j$.*

This rule allows to parameterise complementary branches (e.g. *if*- or *while*-operations) in three-valued abstractions. As we have seen in our running example, this can lead to substantial savings in the number of necessary refinement steps for a definite result in verification. In fact, any verification task where the property of interest turns out to be independent from certain branches can profit from such a parameterisation in a similar manner. At the end of this section we will present a theorem which states that the application of Rule I leads to sound abstractions of concurrent systems. Beforehand, we introduce another rule that allows the parameterisation of *predicates* in three-valued abstractions.

In order to illustrate how the parameterisation of predicates works, we consider a second example, the concurrent system *Sys* depicted below. Our property of interest is now *mutual exclusion*, i.e. whether the flag variables $flag_1$ and $flag_2$ are never *true* at the same time.

$$v_1, \ldots, v_k : \textbf{integer};$$

$$flag_1, flag_2, init : \textbf{boolean where } flag_1 = false, flag_2 = false, init = false;$$

$$
Proc_1 :: \begin{bmatrix} 1: & flag_1 := f(v_1, \ldots, v_k) \\ 2: & init := true \\ 3: & flag_1 := \neg flag_2 \\ 4: & [\ldots \end{bmatrix} \parallel Proc_2 :: \begin{bmatrix} 1: & flag_2 := false \\ 2: & \textbf{await}(init) \\ 3: & flag_2 := \neg flag_1 \\ 4: & [\ldots \end{bmatrix} \parallel \ldots \parallel Proc_n
$$

Applying three-valued spotlight abstraction with classical refinement yields the following spotlight after a number of iterations: $Spot(Proc) = \{Proc_1, Proc_2\}$ and $Spot(Pred) = \{flag_1, flag_2, init\}$. Next, a corresponding pure three-valued Kripke structure K over $AP = \{flag_1, flag_2, init\} \cup \{(pc_i = j) \mid Proc_i \in Spot(Proc) \wedge j \in Loc_i\}$ is constructed, and the mutual exclusion property formalised by the safety LTL formula $\mathbf{G}\neg(flag_1 \wedge flag_2)$ is checked for K. Model checking returns *unknown*, since the assignment to $flag_1$ at location 1 of $Proc_1$ depends on the shared variables $v_1, \ldots, v_k$ which are potentially modified by a large number of processes that are currently in the shade. Thus, with classical abstraction refinement we have to expect a large number of further refinement steps necessary for a definite result in verification: Predicates over the variables $v_1, \ldots, v_k$ as well as processes modifying these variables have to be drawn into the spotlight. Nevertheless, the model checking run based on the current spotlight also returns the unconfirmed counterexample π depicted in part (a) of the figure below.

(a)							(b)					

$$\begin{array}{cccccc}
(pc_1{=}1) & (pc_1{=}2) & (pc_1{=}3) & (pc_1{=}3) & (pc_1{=}3) & (pc_1{=}3) \\
(pc_2{=}1) & (pc_2{=}1) & (pc_2{=}1) & (pc_2{=}2) & (pc_2{=}3) & (pc_2{=}4) \\
flag_1{=}f & flag_1{=}\bot & flag_1{-}\bot & flag_1{=}\bot & flag_1{=}\bot & flag_1{=}\bot \\
flag_2{=}f & flag_2{=}f & flag_2{=}f & flag_2{=}f & flag_2{=}f & flag_2{=}\bot \\
init{=}f & init{=}f & init{=}t & init{=}t & init{=}t & init{=}t
\end{array}$$

$\pi :: (s_1) \rightarrow (s_2) \rightarrow (s_3) \rightarrow (s_4) \rightarrow (s_5) \rightarrow (s_6)$

$$\begin{array}{cccccc}
(pc_1{=}1) & (pc_1{=}2) & (pc_1{=}3) & (pc_1{=}3) & (pc_1{=}3) & (pc_1{=}3) \\
(pc_2{=}1) & (pc_2{=}1) & (pc_2{=}1) & (pc_2{=}2) & (pc_2{=}3) & (pc_2{=}4) \\
flag_1{=}f & flag_1{=}x_1 & flag_1{=}x_1 & flag_1{=}x_1 & flag_1{=}x_1 & flag_1{=}x_1 \\
flag_2{=}f & flag_2{=}f & flag_2{=}f & flag_2{=}f & flag_2{=}f & flag_2{=}\neg x_1 \\
init{=}f & init{=}f & init{=}t & init{=}t & init{=}t & init{=}t
\end{array}$$

$\pi(x_1) :: (s_1) \rightarrow (s_2) \rightarrow (s_3) \rightarrow (s_4) \rightarrow (s_5) \rightarrow (s_6)$

The reason for uncertainty is the reachable state s_6 where $flag_1$ and $flag_2$ are both $\bot$. The predicate $flag_1$ is set to $\bot$ by transition (s_1, s_2), since there are not enough predicates and processes in the spotlight in order to abstract the associated operation $flag_1 := f(v_1, \ldots, v_k)$ properly. The predicate $flag_2$ is set to $\bot$ by (s_5, s_6) because the associated operation $flag_2 := \neg flag_1$ modifies this predicate in relation to the already *unknown* predicate $flag_1$. In our simple example it is easy to see that $flag_1$ and $flag_2$ must have *complementary* values in state s_6 – which would rule out the unconfirmed counterexample π. However, this fact cannot be captured by pure three-valued abstraction since it does not allow to establish connections between predicates that are associated with the value $\bot$.

Our concept of parameterisation enables us to establish such connections. For our running example we proceed as follows: We backtrack to the state s_2 where $flag_1$ was initially associated with $\bot$. Next, we introduce a fresh parameter x_1 and set $L(s_2, flag_1) := x_1$. Based on the operations associated with the succeeding transitions along π we update the labellings of the states s_3 to s_6. As a consequence, we now can capture that $flag_1$ constantly keeps the value x_1 along π, $flag_2$ keeps the value *false* until s_5, and in particular, $flag_1$ and $flag_2$ have complementary values in s_6. The resulting path $\pi(x_1)$, which is depicted in part (b) on the previous page, is no longer an unconfirmed counterexample. Thus, checking $\mathbf{G}\neg(flag_1 \wedge flag_2)$ on a corresponding parameterised Kripke structure $K(x_1)$ will immediately return that no counterexample exists, i.e. that the property is satisfied for the modelled system. Again we have seen that parameterisation – here with regard to predicates – can lead to substantial savings in the number of necessary refinement steps for a definite result in verification. The following rule generalises the parameterisation of predicates in three-valued abstractions.

Rule II (Parameterisation of Predicates along Counterexamples). *Let Sys, Spot, K, s_1 and AP be as in Rule I. Moreover, let $\psi = \mathbf{G}\neg(\bigwedge_{i=1}^{m} p_i)$ be a safety LTL formula with $\{p_1, \ldots, p_m\} \subseteq Spot(Pred)$ and model checking $[K, s_1 \models \psi]$ yields $\bot$. Let $\pi = s_1 \ldots s_k$ be the unconfirmed counterexample returned by model checking which is a path prefix that ends in a state s_k where all predicates from $\{p_1, \ldots, p_m\}$ are associated with either the value $\bot$ or true. K can be parameterised along π according to the following procedure:*

for $s := s_1$ **to** s_k **do**
  for *each* $p_i \in \{p_1, \ldots, p_m\}$ *with* $L(s_k, p_i) = \perp$ **do**
    if $L(s, p_i) = \perp$ **then**
      if $s = s_1$, *i.e. s is the initial state* **then**
        introduce a fresh parameter x_j and set $L(s, p_i) := x_j$
      else
        let s' be the direct predecessor of s along π, and let op be the operation
        associated with the transition (s', s)
        if *op is not associated with a process in Spot(Proc) or none of the*
        atomic predicates occurring in the weakest precondition[1] $wp_{op}(p_i)$ *are*
        contained in Spot(Pred) **then**
          introduce a fresh parameter x_j and set $L(s, p_i) := x_j$
        else
          set $L(s, p_i) :=$
          $wp_{op}(p_i) [p/L(s', p) \mid p \in Spot(Pred)] [p/\perp \mid p \notin Spot(Pred)]$,
          i.e. update $L(s, p_i)$ wrt. parameterisations in predecessor s'

Parameterisation of predicates is applied in a similar way for model checking liveness formulae, i.e. $[K, s_1 \models \mathbf{GF}(\bigvee_{i=1}^{m} p_i)]$ with $\{p_1, \ldots, p_m\} \subseteq Spot(Pred)$. In case of an unknown result, the model checker additionally returns an unconfirmed counterexample π of the form $(s_1 \ldots s_{l-1}) \circ (s_l \ldots s_k)^\omega$ and in all states $s_l \ldots s_k$ each predicate from $\{p_1, \ldots, p_m\}$ is associated with either the value $\perp$ or false. The finite prefix $(s_1 \ldots s_{l-1})$ of π is then parameterised in the same manner as in the case of model checking safety formulae.

The following theorem establishes the soundness, with respect to the information ordering $\leq_{\mathbb{K}_3}$ (compare Section 2), of parameterised three-valued model checking, provided that parameterisation is applied according to Rule I and II.

Theorem 1. *Let Sys and Spot be as before. Let K over AP be a two-valued KS modelling the concrete state space of Sys and let $K^\perp$ over $AP^\perp = Spot(Pred) \cup \{(pc_i = j) \mid Proc_i \in Spot(Proc) \wedge j \in Loc_i\}$ with $AP^\perp \subseteq AP$ be a pure three-valued KS modelling the abstract state space corresponding to Spot. Moreover, let s_1 and $s_1^\perp$ be states representing the initial configuration of Sys in K resp. $K^\perp$. Then for any parameterisation $K^\perp(\overset{m}{x})$ of $K^\perp$ obtained by applying the rules I and II, and for any safety or liveness LTL formula ψ^2 over $AP^\perp$ the following holds:*

$$[K^\perp(\overset{m}{x}), s_1^\perp \models \psi] \quad \leq_{\mathbb{K}_3} \quad [K, s_1 \models \psi]$$

Proof. See http://www.cs.up.ac.za/cs/ntimm/proof.pdf

Hence, every definite result in verification obtained for $[K^\perp(\overset{m}{x}), s_1^\perp \models \psi]$ can be directly transferred to the concrete system modelled by K, whereas an *unknown* result for $[K^\perp(\overset{m}{x}), s_1^\perp \models \psi]$ tells us that further abstraction refinement or parameterisation of $K^\perp(\overset{m}{x})$ is required. In the next section, we will show how we have implemented the application of the parameterisation rules within an automatic abstraction refinement procedure for the verification of concurrent systems and how verification can benefit from our parameterisation approach.

---

[1] Let $op = assume(e) : x_1 := e_1, \ldots, x_m := e_m$ then $wp_{op}(p) = e \wedge p[x_1/e_1, \ldots, x_m/e_m]$.
[2] ψ is either of the form $\mathbf{G}\neg(\bigwedge_{i=1}^{m} p_i)$ or $\mathbf{GF}(\bigvee_{i=1}^{m} p_i)$ with $\{p_1, \ldots, p_m\} \subseteq AP^\perp$.

5   Automatic Refinement and Parameterisation

We have prototypically implemented a verification framework for concurrent systems based on spotlight abstraction with counterexample-guided refinement and parameterisation. Our framework 3Spot works on top of the three-valued symbolic model checker χChek [5]. 3Spot takes a concurrent system Sys over a variable set Var and a safety or liveness temporal logic formula ψ over Sys as input. The initial spotlight $Spot$ is defined by the processes that are referenced in ψ and the atomic predicates over Var that are subformulae of ψ. Next, a parameterised three-valued Kripke structure $K^\perp(\overset{m}{x}) = (S, R, L, \mathbb{F})$ corresponding to Sys and $Spot$ is constructed with a state $s_1 \in S$ representing the initial configuration of Sys. The parameter tuple $(\overset{m}{x})$ of $K^\perp(\overset{m}{x})$ is initially empty. In order to check $[K^\perp(\overset{m}{x}), s_1 \models \psi]$, the following procedure is executed:

1. **check** $[K^\perp(\overset{m}{a}), s_1 \models \psi]$ for all valuations $(\overset{m}{a}) \in \{t, f\}^m$
   if $\forall (\overset{m}{a}) \in \{t, f\}^m : [K^\perp(\overset{m}{a}), s_1 \models \psi] = t$ **or** $\forall (\overset{m}{a}) \in \{t, f\}^m : [K^\perp(\overset{m}{a}), s_1 \models \psi] = f$ **then**
       property ψ is successfully proved resp. disproved for the concurrent system Sys; stop
   if $\forall (\overset{m}{a}) \in \{t, f\}^m : [K^\perp(\overset{m}{a}), s_1 \models \psi] \in \{\perp, t\}$ **or** $\forall (\overset{m}{a}) \in \{t, f\}^m : [K^\perp(\overset{m}{a}), s_1 \models \psi] \in \{\perp, f\}$
   then
       still some *unknown* results; further refinement or parameterisation required; go to 2.
   if $\exists (\overset{m}{a}) \in \{t, f\}^m : [K^\perp(\overset{m}{a}), s_1 \models \psi] = t$ **and** $\exists (\overset{m}{a}) \in \{t, f\}^m : [K^\perp(\overset{m}{a}), s_1 \models \psi] = f$ **then**
       current parameterisation not expedient; revoke last parameterisation; go to 2.

2. **for** each valuation $(\overset{m}{a}) \in \{t, f\}^m$ with $[K^\perp(\overset{m}{a}), s_1 \models \psi] = \perp$ **do**
       generate unconfirmed counterexample $\pi^\perp$ for $[K^\perp(\overset{m}{a}), s_1 \models \psi]$
   select unconfirmed counterexample $\pi^\perp$ with the fewest *unknown* transitions and predicates
   if Rule I is applicable along $\pi^\perp$ **then**
       apply Rule I to the corresponding branch in $K^\perp(\overset{m}{x})$
   else if Rule II is applicable along $\pi^\perp$ **then**
       apply Rule II to the corresponding path prefix in $K^\perp(\overset{m}{x})$
   else
       determine cause of indefinite result along $\pi^\perp$ and derive corresponding refinement candidate r (see our previous work [17] for an example technique for deriving refinement candidates from unconfirmed counterexamples), which can be a shade process or a predicate; add r to $Spot$
       if r is a predicate **then**
           revoke parameterisation for parameterised branches in $K^\perp(\overset{m}{x})$ where the value of r affects the branching condition
   update $K^\perp(\overset{m}{x})$ according to changes in 2. and go to 1.

Hence, the procedure terminates if for all instantiations of the current parameterised Kripke structure the same definite result in verification can be obtained. If model checking yields *true* for some instantiations and *false* for others, the last parameterisation step was not expedient: The property of interest is then obviously not independent from the most recent parameterisation. Thus, this step is revoked, which also includes that the same parameterisation will not be admissible in future iterations. In case model checking returns *unknown* for some instantiations, the abstraction has to be further parameterised or refined based on unconfirmed counterexamples obtained for these instantiations. For this purpose we always apply Rule I or II if possible, or use classical refinement (see our previous work [17]) otherwise. Adding a new predicate p to the abstraction may affect parameterised branches: An abstract state s that is the starting point of a complementary branch may be split into two new states s_a and s_b with

$L(s_a, p) = true$ and $L(s_b, p) = false$. Thus, in the general case, the parameterisation of the complementary branch starting in s has to be revoked. However, if the branch condition is independent from the value of p then the parameterisation can be kept. Alternatives to the revocation of parameterisations are: Keeping the parameterisation for only one state, either s_a or s_b. Or, introducing a fresh parameter x_j for the second branch starting in s_b. Each iteration ends with the update of the parameterised three-valued Kripke structure according to new parameterisations or additional refinements. In case a new predicate has been added to the abstraction, this update also involves the recalculation of the parameterisation of predicates (compare last step of Rule II).

So far, parameterisation resp. refinement is performed based on the unconfirmed counterexample with the fewest *unknown* transitions and predicates. The intention behind this is to minimise the expected effort to confirm or eliminate the counterexample. Moreover, the attempt to apply the parameterisation rules or classical refinement is so far always conducted in the fixed order *Rule I, Rule II, refinement*. In the future, we intend to use heuristic guidance for selecting the unconfirmed counterexample and for deciding which rule application or which refinement step is currently most promising in order to achieve a definite result in verification within a small number of iterations. Similar to our previous work on heuristics for pure refinement [17], we plan to base this heuristic approach on the structure of the underlying concurrent system, i.e. on the variable dependencies between the processes of the system.

In preliminary experiments, we applied our procedure to multiple-resource allocation systems[3] with up to 25 processes and 140 variable dependencies, and we checked safety as well as liveness properties. We compared verification under the pure three-valued approach (which has proven to be generally successful for concurrent systems in [14,15,17]) with verification under our novel approach with parameterisation. In several cases where the pure three-valued approach failed due to an out-of-memory exception, our new technique was capable of returning a definite verification result. The additional computations for parameterisation particularly paid off when the property of interest turned out to be independent from certain branches in the system, and the costs for concretising these branches via classical refinement were high. In fact, such cases are very common for systems with many *if-*, *while-*, and similar operations. We also observed verification tasks (primarily where the system only exhibited very few branches, or where the property was dependent on most of the branches) that did not profit from the application of parameterisation rules. Here verification under the new approach was slower but did not fail, since parameterisation only increases the number of checks per iteration, but not the size of the abstraction (spotlight processes and predicates). Thus, so far it is a good strategy to apply the pure three-valued approach first and in case of failure the approach with parameterisation subsequently. Nevertheless, with our intended heuristic approach, we aim at directly discovering the best possible combination of refinement and

---

[3] A detailed description of these systems can be found in [14].

parameterisation for each verification task. A more extensive experimental evaluation of such an enhanced approach is also planned as future work.

6   Related Work

Or research is situated in the field of model checking temporal logic properties on partial system models. The idea of evaluating temporal logic formulae on three-valued Kripke structures was initially proposed in [3] and is now established under the name *three-valued model checking* (3MC). Our new concept *parameterised three-valued model checking* (PMC) is an extension of 3MC. In our approach, unknown parts of the modelled system cannot only be represented by the constant $\perp$, but also by expressions over boolean parameters. The evaluation of temporal logic formulae is then performed for each possible parameter instantiation. The idea of considering possible instantiations resp. concretisations of a partial model is adopted from *generalised model checking* (GMC) [7]. In contrast to the concretisations in GMC, our instantiations only affect parameters but do not concern the constant $\perp$. Moreover, our instantiations are always of the same size as the partial model, whereas the concretisations in GMC can be exponentially larger. Neither 3MC nor GMC offer a concept for drawing connections between unknown parts. While 3MC and GMC are general concepts for the verification of partial models, our approach is application-oriented and takes advantage from the consideration of the system structure when applying the parameterisation rules within our automated verification procedure.

Another work related to ours is that of Herbstritt et al. [9] who combine three-valued logic and quantified boolean parameters for representing unspecified parts of a hardware model with different precision. Their technique is geared towards equivalence checking of circuits. In contrast to our approach, [9] do not introduce a concept for establishing connections between parameters in the model. Moreover, the decision for modelling an unspecified part via the third truth value $\perp$ or via a boolean parameter has to be done by hand and not based on automatable rules. [9] encode their hardware verification tasks as bounded model checking problems that can be efficiently solved via SAT/QBF-solvers. The definition of such encodings for our parameterised three-valued model checking is another interesting direction for future research. A similar approach to the verification of hardware circuits, but in the context of BDD-based symbolic model checking was introduced in [11]. Their method supports the verification of full CTL properties based on models with a flexible representation of unknowns. This approach necessitates the manual selection of the type of modelling unknown parts. Establishing logical relations between parameters is not possible here.

7   Conclusion

We developed a concept for modelling unknown parts of an abstract software system with different types of approximation: In our parameterised three-valued Kripke structures the loss of information about a predicate or a transition can be either represented by the constant ⊥ or by an expression over boolean parameters. A novel feature of our modelling approach is that it allows for establishing logical connections between *unknown* parameters, like equality or complementarity – and thus, to preserve more details under abstraction that can be crucial for the success and efficiency of verification. We introduced temporal logic model checking for parameterised three-valued Kripke structures and showed that this method is sound if the models are constructed with regard to parameterisation rules that we defined. These rules take the branching structure and the program code of the modelled system into account and arrange the connections between parameters in the model. We then presented an automatic verification procedure based on iterative abstraction refinement and parameterisation. For several verification tasks, particularly for verifying systems with many conditional branches, our new approach with parameterisation can significantly outperform verification based on classical modelling techniques that are not capable of characterising connections between unknown parts. We are convinced that our concept for parameterisation can be easily and effectively adapted to other types of systems and verification tasks, which we intend to investigate in our future research.

References

1. de Alfaro, L., Roy, P.: Solving games via three-valued abstraction refinement. In: Caires, L., Vasconcelos, V.T. (eds.) CONCUR 2007. LNCS, vol. 4703, pp. 74–89. Springer, Heidelberg (2007)
2. Ball, T., Majumdar, R., Millstein, T., Rajamani, S.K.: Automatic predicate abstraction of C programs. In: ACM SIGPLAN 2001, PLDI 2001, pp. 203–213. ACM, New York (2001)
3. Bruns, G., Godefroid, P.: Model checking partial state spaces with 3-valued temporal logics. In: Halbwachs, N., Peled, D. (eds.) CAV 1999. LNCS, vol. 1633, pp. 274–287. Springer, Heidelberg (1999)
4. Clarke, E., Grumberg, O., Jha, S., Lu, Y., Veith, H.: Counterexample-guided abstraction refinement. In: Emerson, E.A., Sistla, A.P. (eds.) CAV 2000. LNCS, vol. 1855, pp. 154–169. Springer, Heidelberg (2000)
5. Easterbrook, S.M., Chechik, M., Devereux, B., Gurfinkel, A., Lai, A.Y.C., Petrovykh, V., Tafliovich, A., Thompson-Walsh, C.: χChek: a model checker for multi-valued reasoning. In: ICSE 2003, pp. 804–805 (2003)
6. Fitting, M.: Kleene's three valued logics and their children. Fundamenta Informaticae 20(1–3), 113–131 (1994)
7. Godefroid, P., Piterman, N.: LTL generalized model checking revisited. In: Jones, N.D., Müller-Olm, M. (eds.) VMCAI 2009. LNCS, vol. 5403, pp. 89–104. Springer, Heidelberg (2009)
8. Grumberg, O.: 2-valued and 3-valued abstraction-refinement in model checking. In: Logics and Languages for Reliability and Security, pp. 105–128. IOS Press, Incorporated (2010)
9. Herbstritt, M., Becker, B.: On combining 01X-logic and QBF. In: Moreno Díaz, R., Pichler, F., Quesada Arencibia, A. (eds.) EUROCAST 2007. LNCS, vol. 4739, pp. 531–538. Springer, Heidelberg (2007)
10. Katoen, J.P., Klink, D., Leucker, M., Wolf, V.: Three-valued abstraction for probabilistic systems. Logic and Algebraic Programming 81(4), 356–389 (2012). http://www.sciencedirect.com/science/article/pii/S1567832612000239

11. Nopper, T., Scholl, C.: Symbolic model checking for incomplete designs with flexible modeling of unknowns. IEEE Trans. Computers **62**(6), 1234–1254 (2013)
12. Schrieb, J., Wehrheim, H., Wonisch, D.: Three-valued spotlight abstractions. In: Cavalcanti, A., Dams, D.R. (eds.) FM 2009. LNCS, vol. 5850, pp. 106–122. Springer, Heidelberg (2009)
13. Shoham, S., Grumberg, O.: 3-valued abstraction: More precision at less cost. Information and Computation **206**(11), 1313–1333 (2008)
14. Timm, N.: Three-Valued Abstraction and Heuristic-Guided Refinement for Verifying Concurrent Systems. Phd thesis, University of Paderborn (2013)
15. Timm, N.: Spotlight abstraction with shade clustering - automatic verification of parameterised systems. In: 8th International Symposium on Theoretical Aspects of Software Engineering, pp. 18–25. IEEE Computer Society (2014)
16. Timm, N., Wehrheim, H.: On symmetries and spotlights – verifying parameterised systems. In: Dong, J.S., Zhu, H. (eds.) ICFEM 2010. LNCS, vol. 6447, pp. 534–548. Springer, Heidelberg (2010)
17. Timm, N., Wehrheim, H., Czech, M.: Heuristic-guided abstraction refinement for concurrent systems. In: Aoki, T., Taguchi, K. (eds.) ICFEM 2012. LNCS, vol. 7635, pp. 348–363. Springer, Heidelberg (2012)
18. Wei, O., Gurfinkel, A., Chechik, M.: On the consistency, expressiveness, and precision of partial modeling formalisms. Information and Comp. **209**(1), 20–47 (2011)

Author Index

Ahmad, Sohaib   32
Almeida, Diego R.   48
Andrade, Wilkerson L.   48

Barbosa, Luís S.   130, 146
Bonichon, Richard   1
Braz, Fernando A.F.   113

Calegari, Daniel   64
Campos, Sérgio V.A.   113
Ciaffaglione, Alberto   80

Déharbe, David   1
Durán, Francisco   17

Fedyukovich, Grigory   96
Ferreira, Bruno   113

Gruner, Stefan   162

Hasan, Osman   32

Lecomte, Thierry   1

Machado, Patrícia D.L.   48
Madeira, Alexandre   130
Martins, Manuel A.   130, 146
Martí-Oliet, Narciso   17
Medeiros Jr., Valério   1
Moraes, Alan   48
Mossakowski, Till   64

Neves, Renato   130, 146

Sharygina, Natasha   96
Siddique, Umair   32
Szasz, Nora   64

Tahar, Sofiéne   32
Timm, Nils   162

Verdejo, Alberto   17

Printed in the United States
By Bookmasters